ALICE K. ON

The U-Do-It Pseudo-Spa Experience:

Insert the word "beauty" before all Spa-related words and activities. With this handy technique, the Ramada Inn quickly becomes your "Beauty Base," your room becomes your "Beauty Suite," and you and your Spa Partner will soon be ready to go out for a healthy "Beauty Burger."

Mandatory ingre~~~~~~~~~~~~~~~~~~~~~stard and a jar of capers from 198~~~~~~~~leftover chicken and broccoli from random and inexplicable attempts to prepare healthful dinners.

The Art of Feeling Virtuous:

Never watch a whole episode of your favorite bad sitcom. If you didn't see the whole thing, you didn't really watch it. Likewise, never order dessert. Order a fork instead. You can eat as much of your companion's dessert as you like, but if you didn't order your own dessert, you didn't really have one.

ALICE K. (not her real initial) is rumored to be the alter ego of CAROLINE KNAPP, a columnist and the Styles editor for the *Boston Phoenix*. Her column, "Out There" (which features Alice K. from time to time) has also appeared in the *Utne Reader* and *L.A. Reader*. She lives in Cambridge, Massachusetts.

Caroline Knapp

ALICE K.'S GUIDE TO LIFE

One woman's quest for survival, sanity, and the perfect new shoes

A PLUME BOOK

695

PLUME

Published by the Penguin Group
Penguin Books USA Inc., 375 Hudson Street, New York, New York 10014, U.S.A.
Penguin Books Ltd, 27 Wrights Lane, London W8 5TZ, England
Penguin Books Australia Ltd, Ringwood, Victoria, Australia
Penguin Books Canada Ltd, 10 Alcorn Avenue, Toronto, Ontario, Canada M4V 3B2
Penguin Books (N.Z.) Ltd, 182–190 Wairau Road, Auckland 10, New Zealand

Penguin Books Ltd, Registered Offices:
Harmondsworth, Middlesex, England

First published by Plume,
an imprint of Dutton Signet,
a division of Penguin Books USA Inc.

First Printing, October, 1994
3 5 7 9 10 8 6 4

Portions of this book first appeared in a slightly differen   in the Boston
Phoenix.

   REGISTERED TRADEMARK—MARCA REGISTRADA

LIBRARY OF CONGRESS CATALOGING IN PUBLICATION DATA:
Knapp, Caroline.
Alice K.'s guide to life : one woman's quest for survival, sanity, and the perfect new
shoes/Caroline Knapp.
p. cm.
ISBN 0-452-27121-5
1. American wit and humor. I. Title.
PN4874.K575A45 1994
818'.5407—dc20   94-11300
CIP

Printed in the United States of America
Set in Gill Sans, Industria, and New Baskerville
Designed by Steven N. Stathakis

IN LOVING MEMORY OF MY PARENTS

JEAN W. KNAPP
September 19, 1927–April 18, 1993

PETER H. KNAPP
June 30, 1916–April 7, 1992

ACKNOWLEDGMENTS

Warmest thanks to my friends and colleagues at the *Boston Phoenix;* to literary matchmaker extraordinaire Bill Novak; to my agent, Colleen Mohyde, of the Doe Coover Agency; and my editor, Deb Brody, at Dutton; and to each and every member of the Alice K. 24-Hour-A-Day Support Network (you know who you are). And special thanks to Dr. Y. (Okay: his real name is Dr. H.)

CONTENTS

PROLOGUE

Alice K. (not her real initial) lies in bed, writhing with anxiety.

Alice K., you see, has just been leafing through the latest issue of *Glamour* magazine and she has come across something so horrifying, so thoroughly disconcerting, it causes her hair to stand on end.

There it is, right there on the page.

A woman. A young, professional-looking woman in her thirties. A woman who looks exactly like Alice K.

And there, running straight across the woman's eyes, is one of those thick, black rectangles they use to conceal the identity.

"Oh my God," Alice K. says, *"I have turned up in a* Glamour DON'T!"

A *Glamour* DON'T. How could this be? After all, hasn't Alice K. spent the better half of her adult life attempting to fend off just such a crisis? Hasn't she read all the magazines, all the how-to books? In the crushing sea of information geared toward women just like her, hasn't she absorbed every minute detail? *She has!* She's learned it all: how to dress, how to act, how to succeed. How to win a man, how to assert, how to attain thin thighs, how to keep a man, how to cook and clean and decorate, how to dress after you've lost a man so you look like you can catch another man, how to . . . *How could this be?*

Alice K. looks down at the magazine again. She studies it from several angles. Her heart sinks. No question: it is she. Her shoulder-length, dark brown hair, kinking in the rain. Her slight frame, her nervous hands, her skinny knees. Five feet, four inches of (apparently) ill-attired Alice K., plastered over the page for all the world to see.

She looks at the adjacent photo. Next to the one of Alice K. (who's wearing leggings, an oversized black jacket, and flat black boots) is a tall, willowy, confident-looking blonde wearing leggings, an oversized black jacket, and chunky black platforms.

Under the photo of the willowy blonde, the copy reads: "DO! stay up-to-date in the wild world of contemporary footwear!"

Under the photo of Alice K., the copy reads: "DON'T! let last year's boots turn you into a fashion has-been!"

Alice K. cannot believe this.

A fashion has-been! I'm a fashion has-been!

She turns in her bed and moans softly. Perhaps this is her destiny, she thinks. Perhaps she has spent her whole adult life moving slowly and inexorably toward the *Glamour* DON'T page. Deep inside, you see, Alice K. has always suffered from the persistent sense that something is amiss, that something about her is *different*. She may appear to be like any other young woman of her era: she is professional (Alice K. is the new products editor at a glossy publication called *Green Goddess: the magazine for today's environmentally conscious woman*); she is attractive, educated, bright. But a part of Alice K. has always

2

wondered. A part of her has always looked at women's magazines, at pictures of people like the confident-looking, willowy blonde above the DO caption and thought, *That is not me. That image does not reflect life as I experience it.*

Lying there in bed, Alice K. contemplates this.

Earlier in the evening, before she realized she had become a *Glamour* DON'T, Alice K. had flunked the most recent *Cosmo* quiz: "Is Your Sex Appeal Up to Snuff?" (She blew the part about enthusiastic moaning.)

In another magazine, she'd read an article called "Yes! Yes! Yes! You Can Have a Vaginal Orgasm!" and realized that No! No! No! She Couldn't Possibly in a Million Years!

And in a third, she'd pored over a piece called "One Night Stands: How to Make Sure He'll Be Back and Drooling!" which involved a lengthy description of how to give a blow job and moan enthusiastically at the same time. The image made her gag (literally) and she'd put it away, feeling ashamed.

Not me! That is not me!

The hour grows later and Alice K. experiences a distinct pang of longing. She wishes she could stop reading books and magazines about confident-looking, willowy blondes who stride through the world with courage and élan. She wishes she could read something about women who wear flat boots instead of platform boots, and who have marginal sex appeal, and who really don't like to moan, and who *still feel okay about themselves.* She wishes she could read something—anything!— about women she could identify with.

And then suddenly, Alice K. has an idea, something so brilliant it causes her to sit bolt upright in bed.

I know, she thinks, *I'll write my own book!*

THE
GROWN-UP
YEARS

how to be a pseudo grown-up

Alice K. (not her real initial) lies in bed, worrying that she is a failure as an adult.

I ate Wheaties for dinner again, she thinks. *Two bowls of Wheaties. I am a grown woman and I sat there on my couch watching TV in my bathrobe and eating Wheaties like a six-year-old.*

Of course, Alice K. realizes that this is not an entirely bad thing. There can be something quite comforting about coming home at the end of the day and settling down in front of the TV with a bowl of breakfast cereal. But the Wheaties trouble her nonetheless.

Grown-ups, she thinks, *are not supposed to live like this. Grown-ups are supposed to come home at night and prepare healthful dinners of fish and legumes, and then they're supposed to reconcile their checkbooks, and pay some bills, and floss their teeth, and get a good night's sleep. Grown-ups are supposed to*

4

have a clear sense of themselves as responsible, self-directed, capable individuals.

Self-directed? Capable? Those are not exactly words Alice K. uses to define herself.

On the contrary, Alice K. often feels as though she is a seventeen-year-old trapped in the body of an older woman, a frightened and uncertain young thing who can pretend to be competent and mature but who secretly feels the rest of the world is getting older and wiser while she stays stuck in the same place.

I am hopeless with money, she thinks, *I can't deal with my car. I have a profound fear of unstructured time. I still take my laundry home to my mother. AND MY MOTHER LIVES IN ANOTHER STATE.*

The hour grows later and Alice K. begins to despair. She thinks about her older sister, Beth K., who's married and lives in a real house with a real husband and a real baby. She thinks about her best friend, Ruth E., who always seems to march forward into the world without fear or dread or trepidation. She thinks about all the people she knows who seem to act like real adults, who eat adult foods and accomplish adult tasks and set adult goals: marriage, mortages, mutual funds.

Is there something wrong with Alice K.? Something genetic that prevents her from feeling like a card-carrying member of adult society? On occasion, Alice K. has been known to flip through the American Psychiatric Association's *Diagnostic and Statistical Manual* searching for clues to that question, but the damn book doesn't even list breakfast cereal in the index.

Actually, though, in rare moments of clarity, Alice K. knows precisely what's wrong. Alice K. understands the source of her distress very well: it's Mary Tyler Moore's fault.

Mary Tyler Moore. She's to blame. Remember Mary in her pretty studio apartment in that nice building in Minneapolis? Remember nice Mare with the fab wardrobe and tasteful decor?

Back in her teens, an impressionable adolescent in the suburbs searching for a role model, Alice K. spent many Saturday nights watching perky Mary define modern womanhood, and her image has become burnished in Alice K.'s consciousness.

It's easy, Mary said. It's fun. Just live in a nice apartment in a safe neighborhood, have a closet full of clothes and maybe a dozen pairs of decent shoes, work in an office with colleagues who respect and admire you, have a fun best friend and a perky smile, and just to prove it's all working, spend a certain amount of time tossing your winter hat into the sky with glee.

Alice K. never exactly got the hat thing down, but she tried mightily to emulate Mary on the other fronts. She moved to the city after college. She found a pretty one-bedroom apartment, established her friendship with Ruth E., even went into journalism.

But somewhere along the line, Alice K. never made the transformation. She never woke up one morning, as deep in her heart she'd expected to, and found the right image gazing back at her in the bathroom mirror: the image of a contented, secure professional woman; the image of someone with an exciting life and a zippy, optimistic personality.

What happened? she wonders, tossing in her bed. *Where did I go wrong?*

A single word springs to mind, inevitably: men.

Men.

Alice K. has a terrible, incurable tendency to deflect her deeper anxieties about life onto men, to worry about love incessantly, to equate a truly grown-up, settled life with partnership. A real woman has a real man, right? Grown-ups have mates. Alice K. can't help this. On some level she realizes that until she can look in the mirror and see the image of a contented, secure, *partnered* woman looking back, she will never see herself as a fully formed adult.

And yet ... and yet ... Alice K. also understands something else: that behind this yearning, behind her longing for a perfect romance is a debilitating fantasy: a wish to be rescued. A belief—ingrained since girlhood and immune even to the image of perky, independent Mary Tyler Moore—that the answer to life's struggles can be boiled down to the letters L-O-V-E.

And this, Alice K. knows, is not true. *Not true!* Sometimes, she longs to shout this from the rooftops, she wants so fiercely to believe it.

You see, deep in her heart Alice K. understands that growing up involves a series of long struggles, that it's a process of shift and change and resistance and confusion that gets more complicated, not simpler, as one gets older. And although this wish for a relationship, this periodic desperation, may be real, Alice K. is wise enough to see it for what it really is: a wish to bypass the struggle, a wish for a pot of gold at the end of the psychic rainbow. A pot of gold in pants.

Alice K. often talks to Ruth E. about this. "I'm not even sure I *want* to be married," she'll say. "I'm not sure that's the answer at all."

Ruth E. will nod seriously. "Yeah, it's that thing about feeling done, isn't it?"

Ah yes, done. Done, as in a well-cooked roast. A finished product. A person who's transcended struggle and found lasting contentment and inner peace. Alice K. does not feel done. Deep within her soul, she may carry around a picture of what she'd be like at thirty-five or thirty-eight (husband, kid, house, job, doneness), but when she actually contemplates such realities, she feels fearful and confused rather than hopeful.

But I'm not sure enough about myself to get married!
But I'm not old enough to have kids!

But I'm not responsible enough to own a house!
But I'm not done yet!

The hour grows later and Alice K. begins to despair. *I am a pseudo grown-up,* she thinks. *A thirty-three-year-old fake.*

But then, somehow, she allows herself to contemplate the bigger picture. *Perhaps this is just the nature of things,* she thinks. *You expect your life to turn out one way and it turns out to be something else.*

She tries to console herself with that thought. Maybe adulthood is a fantasy, something elusive, a state of mind that ebbs and flows like any other mood. Maybe people like Beth K. and Ruth E. have moments when they feel like hapless children masquerading as grown-ups, too. And maybe the only thing Alice K. can do is to struggle along like she always has, fluctuating between periods of self-doubt and periods of conviction, moments of weakness and moments of strength. Maybe, in the end, she is just plain human.

And then, suddenly, Alice K. has an idea, something so startling it causes her to sit bolt upright in bed. Yes! She's found it! A way to struggle along in her hapless way without depriving herself of the nurturing and nourishment that every true grown-up needs!

I've got it! she thinks. *Wheaties with sliced bananas!*

how to stock your kitchen: alice k.'s. psuedo grown-up guide

Real grown-ups equip their kitchens with vegetables and fruits and a lavish array of meats and cheeses. Pseudo grown-ups, however, understand that these things tend to rot. If you, like Alice K., are a pseudo grown-up, your kitchen will look a little like this:

the refrigerator ───────────────────────

Constants
- quart of milk
- jar of extremely expensive coffee beans
- small, rock-hard cube of Parmesan cheese
- four bottles of expensive mineral water
- one jar of mayonnaise
- four jars of Dijon mustard (don't ask)
- five eggs (date of purchase uncertain)
- one jar of capers from 1987
- open box of Arm & Hammer baking soda which has been there, failing to absorb offensive odors, for at least three years

Optional
───────────────────────

- seasonal fruits (eat one piece, allow remainder to rot)
- leafy greens (prepare one salad, allow remainder to rot)
- leftover chicken-and-broccoli dish from random and inexplicable attempt to prepare healthful dinner (Leave in covered Tupperware bowl for at least two months, then uncover, shriek, and dispose of entire thing, including bowl.)
- jar of salsa
- nail polish

the cupboards ───────────────────────

Constants
- Wheaties
- sixteen assorted boxes and packages of pasta (nature's answer to breakfast cereal)
- extra virgin olive oil and imported red wine vinegar
- Flour, sugar, salt, oatmeal, rice (These are staples purchased in 1991,

when apartment was first occupied. Do not open them. In periodic cleaning frenzies, take them down from shelves and dust.)

- Cream of Wheat (Purchased one winter when idea of hot, steaming cereal seemed both appealing and feasible. Unopened.)
- Priority spices (oregano, rosemary, sage, peppercorns, etc.)
- Impulse spices (cream of tartar for random and inexplicable baking experiment; Chinese five-spice powder for random and inexplicable Chinese cooking experiment; cardamom for random and inexplicable Indian cooking experiment)
- Futile spices (Be honest; when's the last time you actually used paprika?)

Optional —————————————————————————————

- Carr's Water Crackers
- Pepperidge Farm cookies
- Campbell's Soup for One (purchased in fit of depression)

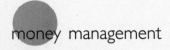 money management

Alice K. sits at her desk.

Alice K. looks at the stack of bills in front of her.

Alice K. breaks into a fine sweat.

I do not understand this, she thinks. *I do not understand how people live.*

Alice K. owes the gas company $36.96. She owes the phone company $82.90. She owes the electric company $52.39. She owes Visa and MasterCard and Tweeds and Bloomingdale's. She owes rent. She owes car insurance. Accordingly, Alice K. must make one of those agonizing moral decisions that sets her teeth on edge and causes her to tremble: does she roll up her shirt sleeves and pay the bills, or does she throw each institution a $20 minimum bone and spend the rest of the money on that pair of olive green suede shoes she's been coveting for the past two weeks?

Money. Alice K. hates money. Money to Alice K. is one of those overwhelmingly abstract entities that makes her mind boggle and her eyes glaze over.

This is Alice K.'s approach to money management:

- Make money.
- Spend money.
- When you're not making or spending money, deal with money as you would deal with the grime between your shower tiles: ignore whenever possible and hold on to the hope that someone—*someone*—will come and deal with it for you.

Alice K. is the sort of person who hits the automatic teller machine once every three days, takes out $100 a shot, and then watches in amazement as the money disappears—*vanishes!*—as if by magic.

What? How did this happen? Yesterday I had $100, today I have $11.50, and all I can remember buying is a tunafish sandwich and a pair of stockings!

Actually, it's not quite that mysterious. On the rare occasion when Alice K. is honest with herself about money, she knows exactly what happens to those five crisp $20s.

A typical day? This is what happens.

1) In the morning, Alice K. showers, glugs down a cup of coffee (made from extremely expensive coffee beans), spends fifteen unplanned minutes scouring her closet for a blouse that doesn't need to be dry-cleaned, and then realizes it's too late to make breakfast. So she races toward work, stops at the bank for her $100, and then she buys another coffee and a corn muffin (healthier than blueberry!) at the coffee shop down the street. That costs $1.37, plus 50 cents for the daily paper, and as Alice K. races into her office, she does not consider the fact that if she does this every day for a year, it comes to $488.07.

2) Lunchtime rolls around and Alice K. looks up from her desk. She is hungry. She promised herself she would make a nice sandwich to bring to work and maybe a piece of fruit, but—well, you already know the state of Alice K.'s refrigerator, plus she has a ton of work to do and she feels harassed so she decides to race out and just grab something. Alice K. doesn't go anywhere fancy—just a little café a few miles away—and she only has soup and salad and mineral water, but her share of the check comes to $10 with tip. Plus, she couldn't find a parking space and she needed to save time, so she threw her car in the lot—another $8, for a total of $18, but at least she didn't get another $15 parking ticket. So she heads back to work, again failing to acknowledge that if she does this once a week for a year, it will cost $936.

3) At about three o'clock, Alice K.'s body screams for coffee (it also screamed at ten o'clock and eleven-thirty, and it will scream again at four-thirty), so she grabs another 68-cent cup at the nearby coffee shop (total by day's end: $2.72). And yes, on some level Alice K. knows that this adds up and adds up. She knows that if she calculated the expense she would realize she spends $709.92 a year just on coffee at work, but at the time caffeine always seems key. It wakes her up, gives her a break, it keeps her going until dinner.

4) Dinner. Alice K. forgets about dinner. She works late, and on the way home she has to stop at the dry cleaner, where she shells out $12 for some blouses and a jacket (which she does at least once a month, to the tune of $144 a year). Then she stops at the drugstore for a tube of toothpaste. (Oh, and while she's at it, she also decides it would be good to have an extra pair of stockings or two in reserve so she picks up some of those, and then she sees those lightbulbs she needs, and that nail-polish remover, and—oooooh!—L'Oréal has a new kind of mousse and Alice K.'s

hair has been driving her crazy lately, so she grabs a can of that, too. Total sum: $29.17.)

Anyway, Alice K. gets home and she's hungry. She stands and contemplates. There's stuff in the freezer but it's frozen. There are Wheaties, but she's already done that twice this week and it's making her feel pathetic. And then, just as she is reaching for her bowl and spoon, the phone rings! It's Ruth E.! Or it's Beth K.! Or it's some college friend Alice K. hasn't seen in years! It doesn't matter who it is! Someone is on the phone asking Alice K. to meet for dinner!

5) Alice K. stands there with the phone in her hand and thinks. She really shouldn't go. She has already spent $63.51 on next to nothing in one day, and she promised herself she'd exercise a little restraint. She also promised herself she'd spend the night at home, just one night to sit and relax and maybe even organize her finances.

But then she thinks, well, it would be so nice just to unwind with a nice meal, it's been a rough week, it's only one little dinner. . . . And then, thinking, *Oh, shit, I'm going to have to go to the bank in the morning,* Alice K. walks out into the night and prepares to spend her remaining $36.49 on a designer pizza and two little glasses of white wine.

That's how it works. Financial bulemia.

Ruth E., who's much the same way about money, blames this on the economy, increases in the cost of living, the declining value of the dollar.

But Alice K. knows better: It all dates back to that first letter, that first evil, insidious piece of correspondence. It arrived two weeks after she graduated from college. An innocuous little letter in a business envelope.

```
Dear Alice K.,
    Because you are such a valued customer, we
have decided to raise your credit limit from
$32.95 to $7.2 billion. And don't worry your
```

```
pretty little head about the 26 percent inter-
est rate. We just want you to get out there,
have fun, and SPEND!
                    Very sincerely,
                    Your friends at MasterCard.
```

Alice K. believed her friends at MasterCard. And when they upped her credit a third and fourth and fifth time, she believed them again. Alice K. *knew* she was a valued customer. It didn't matter that she'd majored in the humanities in college and ended up with a $9000-a-year job while her other friends got sales positions with six-figure incomes. Or that she understood in a back corner of her mind the danger of that 26 percent interest rate. Alice K. had credit. Alice K. could flash that card with the best of them. And Alice K. never—*never*—let the ugly question of fiscal responsibility get in the way. No, no, *no.* You see, by the time Alice K. graduated from college, settled into her pretty studio apartment, and set out to model herself after Mary Tyler Moore, the cruel eighties had come along, boiling the whole thing down to a matter of equipment.

That's all it is! Walking out of a gourmet take-out shop with $49.95 worth of chèvre and $32 worth of sun-dried tomatoes and $79.95 worth of porcini mushrooms really does make you feel like a grown-up!

Alice K. has vivid memories of standing in the Bloomingdale's home furnishings department in 1983, $62.50 in her checking account, and thinking, *I am a grown woman and I need that $396 espresso maker. I* need *it.* Sometimes she has flashbacks about this, and they cause her to break into a fine sweat.

But that is precisely how such purchases felt at the time: like needs, as fundamental to human health and well-being as water and air. So what if she ran up $25,000 worth of credit card debt by 1987 and lived in a vague but chronic fear of the phrase "insufficient funds"? So what if the word "budget" made her twitch? As long as Alice K. could breeze into her relatively well-appointed apartment, hear the decisive *click-click* of her Ferragamo pumps on the polished wood floor, and rush about like a Busy Modern Woman (drop the grocery bag on the counter, sift through the mail, flip on the answering machine), she could feel some semblance of sophistication, some sense that she'd made the right transformation, some image of herself as having made the shift from the awkward kid in jeans and sweatshirt she'd been in college and turned into someone—*yes*—someone like Mary Tyler Moore.

Of course, what Alice K. really turned herself into was a walking financial ruin who just happened to own sixteen little black skirts, a Cuisinart, and a microwave oven. A fiscal mess. The kind of woman who'd stash her bills in the least conspicuous places she could find in order to ignore them. *Bills? What bills? That stack of envelopes jammed behind the toaster where I can't see them? Those aren't bills. They're . . . they're . . . I just put them there to catch crumbs, okay?*

Alice K. will never forget that afternoon in the late 1980s, when all her credit cards had reached their limits and she was cut off—cut off!—by MasterCard. She'd stood there in her kitchen, poised over the wastebasket, snipping the card in half and weeping. *I don't understand! They told me I was such a good customer!*

Nor will she forget those days of frenzied acquisition. The way her heart would race if she happened upon that certain suede jacket or pair of perfect pumps (*The price of my weekly paycheck? No problem!*). The extent to which her fragile self-esteem would rise or fall depending on what she was wearing, or whether her bathroom was equipped with the right skin-care products, or how cozy her apartment looked when she walked through the door at night.

Once, unable to pay her rent, Alice K. went out and spent $98 on a red suede belt and then had a huge fight with her old boyfriend, Mr. Cruel, who told her she was crazy. Alice K. looked at him at the time and actually said: "You do not understand. An insufficient number of colorful accessories can be a living hell."

And now, ripping open the Visa bill at her desk, Alice K. thinks about the sense of entitlement that lurked behind such an attitude, the idea that she genuinely *needed* a suede jacket or a new pair of shoes. She thinks about all the people in the world whose needs are so much more basic and profound and acute. She thinks about the homeless.

She runs the phrase through her head: *an insufficient number of colorful accessories can be a living hell,* and she wonders, *Is that really how I felt? Was I really so shallow and vain that I could honestly sit there and draw a parallel between colorful accessories and basic human satisfaction?*

Alice K. looks at the Visa bill and gulps. She owes $237.26. She picks up a pen and takes a deep breath. Then she thinks about those olive shoes. And she writes a check for the minimum balance.

car denial

"Alice K., when is the last time you changed the oil in this thing?"

Alice K.'s boyfriends have asked her this her whole life.

"Oil?" When this happens, she puts on an innocent face and tries to make her voice sound small and sweet. "Am I supposed to change the oil?"

The response she's looking for, of course, is manly and reassuring: *Don't worry your pretty little head about it, Alice K., I'll* take care of it. But more often, it's something along the line of, "Jesus Christ, Alice K. Why are you such a spaz about cars?"

Alice K. does not have an answer.

Alice K. hates cars.

Alice K. loathes cars.

It's not the driving she minds. Alice K. actually kind of likes getting into a car and driving down a long stretch of highway. She kind of likes pressing down on the accelerator and blasting the car radio. She understands the appeal of all that take-to-the-road, wind-in-your-hair, free-spirit stuff that's associated with driving.

In other words, Alice K. likes the *idea* of driving; it's the machinery she can't stand.

"I can't help it." This is part two of her response to men. "I am a real *girl* when it comes to cars." She means that in the most perjorative sense. Dumb. Helpless. Easily frazzled.

Fluid levels. Rotating tires. Tune-ups. Words and phrases like this make Alice K. want to flee, hide her head in the sand, lobby Congress for legislation that would guarantee every woman of driving age her own personal mechanic.

Of course, she has several theories about this problem, one of them being that since Alice K. tends to be so driven and perfectionistic in other areas of her life, her car has become the one area in which she can allow herself to surrender to slovenly, slothful impulses.

Ruth E. once told Alice K. that her apartment was so neat, you could fly an airplane over her living room and it would look like a map of the Midwest, everything lined up at perfect right angles. But her car? Crumpled memos and letters and parking tickets everywhere. Old napkins, coffee cups, and empty water bottles. Tattered books, yellowed newspapers, rotting gym clothes.

Sometimes, in a fit of reform, Alice K. will take a trash bag and stuff all the garbage and junk into it—and then leave the bag in the back seat of the car for six months until it tears or falls over and scatters the debris all over the car where it was before.

Needless to say, Alice K. applies this approach to the matter of car maintenance as well. Conveniently enough, Alice K.'s car-maintenance system is almost exactly the same as her money-management system.

- Drive the car.
- Park the car.
- Don't do anything else unless you can't get the car to start or the noises get so bad you risk arrest.

Actually, this isn't completely true. Every year or so, Alice K. will actually drive the car to the mechanic, rush in with a worried look on her face, mutter something about a tune-up, and flee.

The fear is that if she hangs around too long, the mechanic will ask her something about the car—"Do you want me to check the brakes?" or "How's the compression?"—and this will lead to a twenty-minute conversation about various knocks and miscellaneous pings and assorted ratios, and Alice K. will end up writing out a check twice the size of her monthly salary for things she doesn't understand and can't even pronounce.

Alice K. would rather go to the gynecologist than to the mechanic. It's that bad. It's less humiliating to lie there on that cold table with your feet in stirrups and your legs splayed out to there than it is to stand in a garage listening to some guy try to explain the finer points of quantum carburetor physics and pretending that you understand even a minute portion of what he's saying.

"So whatchya got here is a problem with the hydraulic connector that's linked to the fourth dimension of the wing-nut spindle factor in the right quadrant of the engine-hosing system."

To which Alice K. wants to say, *What? Hey, can we talk about emotions or beauty products or something I can grasp here?*

Of course, she never actually says that. She never actually screams, or begs the man to use a language she can understand, or even asks him to slow down so she can try to remember what he said and then ask her boyfriend if she's getting ripped off or not.

Instead, she just stands there and nods seriously and says, "Uh-huh. I see. Right. . . . So, um, how much is this going to cost?"

Then, $768.95 later, the boyfriend asks her what was wrong with the car and Alice K. struggles to find something that sounds even vaguely mechanical and ends up murmuring, "Um, something with the engine-housing system, maybe?" And then Alice K. gets a fifteen-minute lecture on the evils of her ineptitude and they have a big fight.

The romance of cars? Right.

Alice K. has had three cars. The first was a 1971 Ford Pinto, the color of slime, which spontaneously set itself on fire while parked outside her office one day in 1984. She heard fire engines and looked out the window. Then she saw this car on fire, and said, "Hey! Somebody's car is on fire!" and then she said, "Hey! *My* car is on fire!" The fireman who put it out bought the debris from Alice K. for $50 and then showed up at her apartment a few days later with a bottle of Riunite. Alice K. hid upstairs and told her roommates to tell him she'd been disfigured in a horrible accident.

The second car was a 1979 Toyota Corolla, which she managed to run so thoroughly into the ground that when she inquired about trading it in, the car dealer burst out laughing.

And next came the loathsome Hyundai. Alice K. exhibited her extraordinary consumer sophistication when purchasing the loathsome Hyundai: "It's nice. . . . Does it come in red?" Then she skillfully acquired a car loan with a 19 percent interest rate which, over a period of five years, brought the total cost of the car from $5999 up to about 8.3 million.

Today, the loathsome Hyundai is bought and paid for. It also has a broken radio, it's missing both side mirrors, the body is covered with dents and rust spots, and it's due for an inspection in a month, a reality that Alice K. will probably get around to beginning to contemplate dealing with in, oh, five or six months.

Ruth E. tells her not to worry about it. "You practice car denial," Ruth E. says. "Lots of women do."

Alice K. nods seriously. Indeed. Alice K. understands car denial very well.

Car denial is the unwavering conviction that your 1995 inspection sticker will suddenly appear, as if by an act of God, on your windshield. It is the fervid belief that if you simply stash that $40 parking ticket under the mat on the car floor, it will cease to exist. Car denial is the knowledge—yes, the *knowledge*—that dents and dings will vanish if only you don't look at them, that strange knocking sounds will stop, oil will cleanse itself, and fluids will self-replenish.

This is why Alice K. is always so utterly astonished when something bad actually happens to the loathsome Hyundai. *What? They towed it away and I owe $475 in back parking tickets,* plus *a boot fee,* plus *a towing fee,* plus *cab fare to City Hall to pay the tickets and then to the city lot to pick it up? But WHY?*

Cars may be powerful machines, but denial is a powerful tool. Alice K. considers it a gift.

Men, of course, don't understand this at all, although Alice K. has tried and tried to explain it. Perhaps she's just lazy, she says. Perhaps she's self-sabotaging, driven by some warped need to remind herself of her own irresponsibility. Or perhaps she's just human. After all, it gets tiring trying to live up to the Cult of the Modern Woman week after week. It gets tiring to feel you have to succeed on too many levels at once, burdensome to feel you have to keep proving that you can, in fact, do everything men can do.

So perhaps Alice K.'s stubborn insistence on remaining mechanically inept is a metaphor, a symbol of the very human wish that someone (in this case, someone who knows

something about cars) will come along and save her. *Help!*
*Help! I'll make my own living and I'll work hard at my job and I'll
establish my independence, but please—please!—don't make me
change the oil, too!*

Alice K. once mentioned this theory to her sister, Beth K.

Beth K. looked thoughtful for a moment, then said,
"That's one possibility. But of course, there's another possibility, too. Could be you're just a spaz."

leisurephobia

Sundays. Do you hate Sundays? Does the prospect of a full,
unplanned day with no obligations fill you with loathing and
dread? Especially if it's sunny outside?

Ah, you have leisurephobia.

And Alice K. can help.

Broadly defined, leisurephobia is a condition of anxiety
or distress felt by some members of contemporary society
when faced with many consecutive hours of unstructured
time. It is a fear of solitude and loneliness, marked by an inability to entertain oneself for prolonged periods of time
without falling into hopelessness and despair. The condition
primarily afflicts young, professional types who live alone,
undistracted by the likes of spouses or pets or small children, and it has been known to hit particularly hard in the
spring.

Alice K. used to suffer from profound leisurephobia.
Deep leisurephobia. This embarrassed her terribly. For years
she would awake on Sunday mornings with panic in her
heart. Sometimes she would stand in front of the mirror and
actually say, "Hello, my name is Alice K. and I am a
leisurephobe," as though giving the condition a name would
help. (It didn't.) Once she considered starting a support
group for leisurephobes, but then Alice K. realized that the

only day of the week such a group could realistically gather would be Sunday, and they'd all be too anxious to go out of their houses to meet.

Panic. Dread. When she thinks about her intensely leisurephobic periods now, she shakes her head in wonder.

Alice K. would get up, make coffee, and putter self-consciously in her apartment for fifteen or twenty minutes. *Here I am, puttering in my apartment. . . . Here I am, washing my coffee cup. . . . Here I am, genetically incapable of figuring out how to fill up free time and thus EXPOSING MY INADEQUACY AS A HUMAN BEING.*

For that is precisely how it felt to Alice K.: like a human failing. *What is wrong with me?* she would think, having run out of puttering steam. *The rest of the world manages to spend Sundays actually enjoying the fact that they have no tasks or obligations—why can't I? The rest of humanity spends the day outside having a glorious time—riding bikes, walking hand-in-hand in the park, falling in love—while I sit home alone. What is this?*

Alice K. realized that this was a bit of an overstatement, but it didn't help. Leisurephobia corrodes one's sense of self. It invites self-sabotage. It makes options feel like burdens, it makes activities and opportunities for human contact seem infeasible, unappealing, overwhelming.

Should I go get the paper? *Nah. Too much trouble.*

Go to a movie? *Nah.*

Clean the apartment? *I should but I'm out of Ajax.*

Write letters? *I would, but I don't have a computer at home and I seem to be at this point, given the relationship between technology and society in today's world, where I really can't write anything in longhand anymore, and I'm not even sure I have any paper at home, and . . .*

You get the idea.

Even in her more acute phases, Alice K. understood that this was a destructive state of mind. Alice K. understood that to give in to those whining inner voices would be to concede defeat to laziness and boredom. And Alice K. realized that if she didn't get up and *do* something within the first hour of rising on an unstructured day, she would fall into a profound state of inertia and risk spending the rest of the month trapped on her sofa watching cable TV.

But the knowledge didn't help. Week after week, Sunday after Sunday, Alice K. would find herself locked in her apartment, overcome with ennui and self-doubt. Was she depressed or merely lazy? Was she bored or was she a boring person? And why couldn't she haul herself up off the sofa and *do* something?

That was the worst part, the acknowledgment that there she was, a grown human being with no clear idea how to comfort or entertain herself. Alice K. would sit there and think about that. She would think about her normal, weekday life, which was full of work and plans and meetings and obligations, and she would realize the extent to which all that structure helped her distract herself from the darker things that lurk in the mind—sadness, anxiety, confusion. And then she would long for such distraction. And then she would look at her watch: *Oh, God, it's only 3:30!*

But finally, one day, Alice K. had a revelation. It was late on a Sunday afternoon, and she had been sitting on her sofa thinking. She sat and thought about how she wished she lived in a culture that taught people how to relax, and how to put a premium on things like solitude. And then she sat and thought about sitting and thinking, and about how she wished she could turn off whatever part of her brain it was that compelled her to sit around thinking about sitting and thinking. And then, in a last-ditch fit of determination, Alice K. launched herself into a flurry of activity. She scrubbed her bathroom. Cleaned the kitchen. Opened the cupboards and dusted the staples.

The activity left Alice K. exhausted, but it prevented her from sitting on her sofa and thinking about thinking, and it also made her realize something about this fear of hers, this inability to cope with unstructured time.

Deep down inside, Alice K. thought, learning to deal with this problem would involve some hard work. It would mean learning to like and take care of herself on some fundamental levels, to tease out the things that were soothing to the soul and the things that were not. It would mean learning to tolerate things like boredom, to fend off inertia on her own.

And then, suddenly, Alice K. had an idea. A perfect plan. A way to elevate her self-esteem, tend to her own needs, *and* fill her empty Sundays.

That's it! Alice K. thought. *Catalog shopping!*

an eighties flashback

Alice K. is sitting in a restaurant, about to order a beverage from the waiter, when suddenly, she has a brutal flashback. This has been happening a lot lately, and it's beginning to bother her.

The waiter asked a simple, nonchalant question: "What can I get you?" and for some inexplicable reason, Alice K. was overcome with a desire to look up and ask, "What's the Chardonnay of the month?"

Oh my God, she thinks. *What is happening to me? That question went out in 1989!*

And then it all comes back to her: the waiters who came up to you and said, "Hi, my name is Jorge, and I'll be your foodserver tonight, and soon I'll be bothering you every seven and a half minutes to see if you'd like to hear about my personal problems or maybe have some freshly ground pepper on your salad, and while I'm here, let me tell you tonight's specials." Remember that? Then came the speech, the twelve-minute dialogue about tonight's fish special being smoked salmon in a caviar-cream sauce, which is salmon that's been smoked and then served in a sauce made with caviar and cream, and tonight's pasta special being goat-cheese tortelloni in a rich roasted-red-pepper-and-sun-dried-tomato sauce, which is tortelloni stuffed with goat cheese and then tossed in a rich sauce made with roasted red peppers and sun dried tomatoes. Oh, God! It was awful! And then you'd drink six glasses of Chardonnay and the dinner would come and it would be a tiny plate of food that cost $94 and you wouldn't even eat it because you were so deep into the '80s that you'd lost your appetite to too much cocaine, and somehow all this made you feel grown-up and sophisticated at the time, but when you woke up, you had a savage hangover, and no money in your wallet, and . . .

Just then, Alice K. gave herself a mental slap and tried to shake herself back to reality. She swallowed hard and looked straight at the waiter.

"It's 1994, right?"

He nodded.

"Fine. I'll have a double cappuccino. Decaf. With two-percent milk."

too mature

"So how much do you want to know about my life?"

Mr. Cruel, Alice K.'s former boyfriend, asked her this over dinner about a year after they broke up and she almost choked on her pork chop.

How much *did* she want to know? How many details did Alice K. really need to hear about her former boyfriend's current love life? To what extent is it healthy to hunker down at the table and get the dirt: yeah, so howdjya meet? Are you in love? How's the sex? *How does she compare to me?*

Alice K. discussed this with Ruth E. the following day, over lunch.

"I think we have become too mature," Alice K. said. "Not just Mr. Cruel and me. Everybody."

Ruth E. agreed. Then she told Alice K. about a guy she knew at work. His name was Mitch and his girlfriend had recently invited an ex-lover home to her parents' for Easter, someone with a name like Antoine which was so pretentious it made Mitch want to vomit.

"Mitch wanted to scream and gnash his teeth in protest," Ruth E. said, "but instead he said, 'Sure, invite Antoine. I'm mature. I can handle it.' "

Alice K. nodded seriously. Then they talked about Beth K., who once went out with a guy who used to spend one night each week having a candlelit dinner with his ex-wife, a woman who threatened suicide when he tried to divorce her. "This is modern life," he'd say when Beth K. had a fit. "You can't just abandon the people you shared that much history with." *History shmistory,* Beth K. always wanted to say, but that would have sounded immature. So she'd nod and put up with it and then lock herself in the bathroom and cry.

Alice K. looked up from her salad. "How mature are we expected to be these days?," she asked. "Where do maturity and acceptance degenerate into self-destruction and ego loss?"

Then, out of the blue, she remembered Barry T.

She asked, "Remember Barry T.?" and they both screamed laughing.

Many dating moons ago, Alice K. went to Barry T.'s house for the first time—this was maybe a second date—and sat down at his kitchen table. Then she noticed he had a box of condoms sitting there on the table, staring her straight in the face, and Alice K. sat there for several hours trying very hard not to look at those condoms, and trying not to wonder if their presence on the table meant he was trying to tell her something, and trying to convince herself that a mature woman would have no problem with this. *Condoms on the table? So what?*

Later that evening, Barry T. gave Alice K. a speech: "I'm really attracted to you, Alice K., but I'm involved with someone else, a woman who's out of town right now, and we may move in together, but I'm not sure, and in the meantime, I'd like to go away with you for a weekend and have sex with you." This was an if-you're-mature-you-can-accept-this speech, and Alice K. remembers that the dominant feeling was an enormous pressure to act wise and accepting, even though what she really wanted to do was stand up and say: "What am I, a Buick you want to test drive?"

Ruth E. shook her head, remembering this episode, then she delivered some historical perspective.

Long, long ago—say, the '50s—Alice K. might have slapped this man in the face and run screaming.

In the '60s, she would have plunged right in, in the name of Free Love.

In the '70s or '80s, she would have launched into an excruciatingly honest dialogue about feelings and needs and what kind of "space" they were both in.

But this is the '90s. Free Love is dead. So is total honesty, which turned out to be too hideous and painful anyway. And we've been left with . . . maturity.

"Whatever happened to Barry T. anyway?" Ruth E. asked.

Alice K. couldn't remember. She remembered feeling pressure to act liberated and adult, faced with this weird proposition, and she remembered blushing and stammering the word "maybe" about eleven times and acting like she wasn't at all confused. But she didn't go away with him for the weekend, and she doesn't think she saw him again, either.

Then Alice K. remembered Bill M., a handsome, recently divorced journalist she dated for about ten hours. Alice K. slept with Bill M. the first night they went out (or almost), developed a major crush on him, and spent the next three weeks writhing with agony and trying to talk herself into a state of mature calm. "No," she'd tell herself, all rational and sane, "just because you sleep with someone, doesn't mean they're going to fall in love with you or even call you up for a second date." Then she'd call up Ruth E. and wail: "But he hasn't even called me! Do you think this means something? What does this *mean?*"

Alice K. pondered this. Once we had rules. You slept with someone, it meant you were having a romance. And if you found out you weren't, you called the guy a major schmuck and all your girlfriends rallied around you in solidarity. Now all we have to fall back on is this idea that grownups act in all kinds of bizarre and inexplicable ways and we must learn not to expect too much. It's a complex world—be mature about it.

When Bill M. finally did call, Alice K. acted calm and rational and very mature and she and Bill M. talked for about twenty minutes (about him) and then got off the phone, no future meeting planned. After that, Alice K. sat there thinking, *I am a grown-up. Not every relationship turns out the way you want it to. These things happen to modern girls, this is the nature of casual sex.* Sigh.

Then she picked up the phone and hurled it against the wall.

Sometimes, Alice K. thinks, it is not good to be so mature. Sometimes it damages your sense of self to sit there in mild, adult calm and rationalize your hurt as a simple part of life, a matter of handling disappointments with grace, of accepting life's complexity.

This, in fact, had been a problem with Mr. Cruel. Alice K. remembered that during their dinner. Once, Mr. Cruel actually sat her down and told her that his last girlfriend gave really terrific blow jobs and this was something he missed and he was only telling her this because he thought their own sex life needed a little help; he was trying to "work on the relationship." Never mind that Alice K.'s sexual self-confidence was shot for about thirteen years. This, she tried to tell herself at the time, was part of life's complexity.

But sitting there over lunch with Ruth E., Alice K. began to ponder a question: What happens to the other feelings that leap into your heart when you act so grown-up and mature? What happens to the part of you that wants to scream and pout? And what happens to the suspicion lurking deep in your soul that a lot of the behaviors you're asked to be mature about are often rude and selfish? Behaviors of men and women who can't let go of old lovers. Or who can't be honest about their ability to form attachments. Or who want things from you (blind acceptance, sex) but don't want to consider your feelings in return.

Then she remembered a conversation she'd had with Beth K. Beth K. had been sad. Her husband was mad at her because she was anxious and depressed and moping. "He wants me to act like a wife," she said, "and he thinks I'm acting like a kid." In a fit of perspective, Alice K. told her it was perfectly okay to act like a kid sometimes. That no matter how big and strong and grown-up we are, there's a part of us that always reverts to being a kid, that wants nothing more than to curl up under the covers and lie in the dark, clutching our blankets, that this was a *human* feeling, just like so many of the other human feelings we try to will away with our mature fronts: anger and confusion and jealousy and hurt and wagonloads of plain old neurosis.

Ruth E. interrupted this train of thought: "So what happened with Mr. Cruel at dinner?"

Alice K. delivered her report: she told Mr. Cruel she wanted the dirt and he gave it to her. Name, address, serial number, breast size.

Well, not really breast size, but that was beside the point. Alice K. listened with calm equanimity, asked questions, nodded with acceptance. She acted like a friend. Very mature.

Then she went home and got out her voodoo dolls.

too young

Alice K. is sitting on her sofa, a magazine on her lap and a look of horror and panic on her face.

It has happened. One of those terrible episodes. One of those moments of true horror that skewers your ego and slaps you down to size.

It happened thusly: Alice K. was sitting there, idly leafing through the magazine, when she came across a profile of a woman novelist, a young woman novelist whose book had hit the bestseller list and then been optioned for a movie by a major Hollywood studio.

She perused the profile. She thought, *how interesting.* And then she came across the novelist's picture. And then it hit her:

Oh my God. I know that woman. She was three years behind me in HIGH SCHOOL! That woman is rich and famous and doing extraordinary things and she is THREE YEARS YOUNGER THAN I AM!!

And then Alice K. suppressed the urge to vomit.

This is a horrible phenomenon, Alice K. thinks, and it explains, among other things, why she hates reading her college alumni bulletin, why she secretly seethes with resentment at many members of the Clinton administration, and why she will not read the work of Brett Easton Ellis or Douglas Coupland or pretty much any member of the twenty-something generation who managed to make it big before his or her skin even had a chance to clear up.

Too young! she thinks. *No fair! If I were king, I would man-*

date that no one be allowed to be rich or famous or to do extraordinary things if they are any younger than, say, I am.

She calls up Ruth E. and tells her what has happened. Ruth E. is most sympathetic.

"Young people should spend their time paying their emotional dues and struggling with low self-esteem," she says. "Young people should not be too confident, too poised, or too successful. We should have rules about this."

Alice K. agrees. Then she tells Ruth E. about an episode that took place a day or two earlier, when she'd found herself standing in line at the automatic teller machine behind a young woman—nineteen maybe, twenty tops—who had that obnoxious way that some young people have of oozing self-confidence in public places. The young woman bantered away at her boyfriend. She made sophisticated jokes about complicated current events. She tossed her hair, wearing an expression of utter self-assurance. Ooze, ooze.

Standing there, Alice K. had a distinct image of this young woman turning into the sort of person who becomes an ambassador at twenty-five (or writes a bestselling novel and gets it optioned for a movie by a major Hollywood studio when she's three years younger than Alice K.). She wanted to slap her.

Be a normal twenty-year-old woman, she secretly hissed. *Be insecure and riddled with self-doubt and shy and fearful of the world. In other words, be like I USED TO BE.*

After all, Alice K. is thirty-three and she still spends far too much time walking around feeling twelve, so when she sees young people waltzing about feeling self-assured and full of promise, it only serves to underscore the dichotomy between her own chronological and internal ages. It makes her feel perplexed. It makes her wonder, *At what age does one really become an adult, in the full, grown-up sense of the word?*

Alice K. knew people in college who didn't seem to have

any confusion about that question, and she hated them, too. One woman, Eliza, who looked thirty-five and didn't have a self-doubting bone in her body, announced to Alice K. early on in their freshman year that she planned to major in environmental studies, take two years off to travel in India, then move to Washington, and end up in a policy-making position at the EPA. *Huh?* Alice K. couldn't even decide what she wanted for dinner at the time. Most nights, she still can't.

Ruth E. has a theory about this: maybe the world just happens to be divided into two camps, those who struggle with growing up and those who don't. Alice K. is a card-carrying member of the former group, which means that she thinks becoming an adult is an enormously long and complex process, a life-long struggle that involves accepting your limits and those of others, understanding your own needs and foibles, gradually becoming comfortable in your own skin. This, in Alice K.'s mind, takes years and years and lots of heartache and disappointments and many, many shifts in perspective.

"I just have a hard time trusting people who seem to bypass that whole process and float off into the future with no angst," she says to Ruth E.

Ruth E. agrees, and Alice K. continues. "I don't exactly hate people who don't share the struggle," she says. "I don't hate people who instinctively know who they are and follow their own paths with grace and ease."

Ruth E. interrupts: "You just wish the little shits would do it in private, right?"

Alice K. smiles. She loves Ruth E.

an open letter to s. i. newhouse

Dear Mr. Newhouse,

As chairman of Condé Nast Publications, I know you already have a heap of magazines to worry about, but I have a proposal for a new one that I think would appeal to many of your readers.

Allow me to introduce myself. My name is Alice K., and like many members of your audience, I am a young, professional woman in my thirties. I am also a long-time reader of many of your magazines (*Glamour, Self, Vogue,* and so on), and while I think that many of these publications do a fine job of appealing to people as they would like to be (namely, self-assured, at the forefront of trends, and relatively unburdened by conflict and inner turmoil), it seems to me that very few of them appeal to people as they really are (namely, underconfident, out-of-step, and chronically burdened by conflict and inner turmoil).

I would like to help change that. I would like to add some balance to the Condé Nast editorial mix. I would like to start a new, more reality-based publication. I would like to call it *Stuck* magazine.

Herewith, my proposal.

why we need *stuck* magazine

Essentially, we need *Stuck* magazine because according to my preliminary market research, an estimated 98.5 percent of the population is, in one form or another, stuck. Stuck in their jobs. Stuck in bad relationships. Or, more universally, stuck in some set of negative and fearful perceptions about the world and/or the self that prevents them from moving forward in their lives. As Webster's Third International Dictionary defines it, to stick is "to bring to a halt, to prevent the movement or action of, to keep from proceeding."

Although many publications (including yours) address the phenomenon of being stuck in life from time to time, I feel compelled to point out that they often do so in a somewhat haphazard or problematic manner. Judging from my preliminary market research, I have found that a primary problem among many magazines is an excessive emphasis on external/cosmetic change and self-improvement. *Glamour* magazine, for example will incite women to "Find a New Job," or "Find a New Man," or "Find a New Haircut," as if the mere act of visiting an expensive *styliste* could propel one forward in life. *Self* will offer "10 Steps to a Better You," an even more insidious command in that it seems to place the blame for stucked-ness squarely on the stuck-ee (so to speak). The hidden message, if I may be so bold as to point this out, is as follows: if you are stuck, it is because you did not follow our "10 Steps to a Better You," you jackass. It is because you allowed your lack of self-esteem to prevent you from going after that job as executive vice-president of the largest conglomerate in America. Get with the program!

I don't mean to criticize you, S.I., I really don't. But this sort of message appears contrary to what my preliminary market research has discerned about basic human nature.

My preliminary market research stems from many, many years of intense psychotherapy, which has led me to the following theory, which I call the Theory of Personal Relativity, or $A = L/W^2$ (in lay terms, that translates into the following equation: Ambivalence = Love/Work^2). Simply put, the theory posits that ambivalence is at the heart of the human condition, especially when it comes to the two pursuits that Sigmund Freud (you may have heard of him) described as central to human well-being, namely, love and work. And because ambivalence is at the heart of the human condition, most people spend huge portions of their lives feeling stuck between opposing forces. This job versus that one. This romance or that one. It can be argued, in fact, that life itself consists largely of moving from one point of stucked-ness to the next, a process that's more universally known as "growing up," but that most of us know by more common terms: angst, despair, an irrational longing for potato chips.

In any event, to recognize this truth of human nature is to acknowledge the existence of a publishing vacuum. To date, no single publication speaks exclusively to the scores of men and women who do not relate to the common wisdom put forth in popular magazines. No single publication relates to those who do not *want* new haircuts, or who do not *believe* that any ten steps can create a better self, or who are *unqualified* for that job as executive vice-president of the largest conglomerate in America. In short, no single publication identifies with or gives voice to those who feel stuck.

stuck: a prototype

The cover of our prototype issue would feature
a huge reproduction of Edvard Munch's *The Scream,*
the famous woodcut that so accurately captures the
feelings engendered by years and years of feeling
stuck. In fact, *all* covers of *Stuck* magazine would
feature a huge reproduction of *The Scream.* Not
only would that hammer home what the magazine
stands for; it would also emphasize editorial
empathy with our readers, suggesting that we keep
running the same cover over and over and over
because—just like them—we are too fearful of
change, too risk-aversive—yes, *too stuck*—to do
anything different.

Inside, the magazine would consist of features
and several regular sections. The front of the
magazine would include the following:

- A monthly advice column designed to
reassure readers that their sense of being
trapped in life is entirely normal (e.g.,
Dear Tormented: Well, of course you feel
stuck in your job! You work too hard, haven't
gotten a raise in eons, your boss treats you
like garbage, and there's a recession out
there so your chances of moving on are virtually nil. Face it, pal, you're *stuck!*).
- A regular column on economics that would
recap Federal employment statistics and
provide detailed rebuttals of any economic
indicators that seem to suggest improvement,
thereby reassuring those of us who cannot
move on professionally that it's not our
fault.
- A feature called "Sticky Situation of the

Month" that would profile particularly stuck individuals, thereby making the rest of us feel a tad less stuck. (Sample: "Look at Lisa! She's thirty-five years old! She's in a nowhere job! She's been dating the same dweeb for *seven* years. *And she can't get out of any of it!*")

The middle of the magazine would include general features about what it's like to be stuck ("Stuck City: Tales from the Trenches"), how to cope with being stuck ("Still Stuck? How to Keep Your Parents Off Your Back"), and how to make the most of being stuck ("Ambivalent About Love? Try Falling in Love with *Two* Men—At Least You Won't Be Bored!). The magazine would also be full of specific tips on a variety of stuck-oriented subjects.

People who feel stuck in their jobs, for example, could pick up *Stuck* magazine and find handy tips on coping with professional lethargy and discontent. Sample subjects might include pretending you're working when you're not; the fine art of xeroxing your résumé in the office without getting caught; and writing letters on company time—a how-to guide.

People stuck with negative self-perceptions could be advised on how to meet people stuck in the same boats, how to be less hard on themselves about being stuck, and how to enjoy the hidden benefits of being stuck, specifically, the freedom from responsibility the state of stucked-ness can engender. Sample headlines: "Still Can't Get Motivated? It's Not Your Fault! Blame It on Being Stuck!" or

"Haven't Dumped That Creep Yet? Don't Worry!
You're Just Stuck!"

After all, isn't being stuck hard enough
without having to feel badly about it? Don't
the stuck among us deserve a break? Even more
important, don't they deserve a voice?

How 'bout it, S.I. What do you say?

I eagerly await your reply.

Sincerely,
Alice K.

ALICE K. IN LOVE, PART I: MEETING ELLIOT M.

Alice K. (not her real initial) lies in bed, writhing with fear, dread, and profound wardrobe anxiety.

Alice K., you see, has agreed to go out on a date. A blind date. A blind date with a man about whom she knows nothing except the most spare details: his name is Elliot M. (real pseudonym, fake initial); he's thirty-four, a "consultant" (whatever that means), and a cousin of a friend of someone Alice K. used to work with, who swears he's "cute."

What, oh what, have I done? Alice K. thinks, wishing she could pull the covers up over her head and hide until 1996. *Why did I agree to put myself through this?*

Alice K. loathes first dates. She doesn't loathe men, she doesn't loathe the concept of a relationship, but she loathes those getting-to-know-you/let's-check-each-other-out encounters, which she perceives (rightly, she believes) as charged with anxiety, self-consciousness, and the potential for unfathomable boredom.

"So . . . do you have any brothers or sisters?"

"So . . . where did you grow up?"

"So . . . um . . ." Pause. Longer pause.

"Any pets?" Excruciating silence.

Alice K. feels vaguely nauseated, imagining such conversation. It makes her wish that men and women could just give up the masquerade of dating, that they could set up quick, businesslike meetings, lay their respective cards on the table, and make immediate decisions about one another without engaging in all that covert information-gathering disguised as politeness.

"Hi," Alice K. would like to say. *"My name is Alice K. and if you have unresolved conflicts about your mother or won't go out on Monday nights because you have to stay home and watch football, I don't want to have anything to do with you, okay?"*

Wouldn't that be easier? Wouldn't it spare us all wagonloads of time and anxiety if we could offer up pre-date checklists and make sure beforehand that the prospective partner was worth the time and energy? After all, Alice K. has been through enough of these encounters to know that the checklist is at the very heart and soul of a first date. She knows that when she opens up the door to meet Elliot M. (and what kind of name is *Elliot,* anyway?), her brain will launch immediately into high criteria frenzy. She will smile and say, "Hi, Elliot, nice to meet you," but her mind will be awhirl with scrutiny.

Nice eyes. Check.

Right height. Check.

Wait a minute! Kind of chunky. Demerit.

Argh! Polyester shirt! Two demerits!

Alice K. hates this. It makes her feel superficial and shallow and horribly self-conscious, because obviously the guy is doing the exact same thing to her.

Considering this makes Alice K.'s mind leap to the next source of pre-date anxiety: what to wear. What can Alice K. wear that will say, *"Hi, I'm Alice K. and I'm sophisticated and*

*smart and just vulnerable enough not to be threatening but also con-
temporary and compelling and sexy* and *your mother would like
me,"* all at the same time? Jeans? No, too casual. A little black
dress? No, too forward. Skirt and sweater? Boring.

What will happen, of course, is that Alice K. will obsess
about the wardrobe question for several days before the date.
Then she will decide on something simple and understated,
like leggings and an oversized sweater. Then she will shower
and put on her makeup and don the leggings and sweater.
And then she will stand in front of the mirror, frown, tear off
the clothing, put on something else, frown again, tear that off,
put on something else, tear that off, continuing in this vein until the entire contents of her closet are strewn across the floor,
she's broken into a fine sweat, and she ends up forty-five minutes later wearing the exact same thing she put on in the first
place. And that doesn't even take into account the fifty-seven
minutes she'll spend hacking and fussing at her hair.

Alice K. shifts in her bed. *Why must I be so neurotic about
these things?* she thinks. *Why can't I be the kind of person who just
tosses on something and looks fine and doesn't assume that a broken
fingernail or a minor blemish will be tantamount to certain disaster?*

Why? Because that's the way Alice K. is. She realized this
as soon as Elliot M. called her on the phone to ask her out.
The moment she heard his voice, all Alice K.'s hard-won
feelings of independence and self-sufficiency and ego
strength went straight out the window and she found herself
metamorphosizing against her will into a dating chameleon,
preoccupied instantaneously with scoping out Elliot M.'s
wishes, being accommodating and agreeable, desperate to
say the right things.

"So," Elliot M. had said. "Do you like Japanese food?"

Alice K. hates Japanese food. She's a total spaz with
chopsticks and sushi makes her gag.

"Oh, sure," she said, gaily, imagining herself trying to
pick up a piece of raw eel with those two awkward sticks and
then force it into her mouth without either throwing up or

exposing herself as completely lacking in motor control. "That sounds fine."

So this is the plan: Elliot M. is going to pick up Alice K. on Friday night at 7:30, and then they will go to a movie, and then they will go to dinner, ostensibly equipped with the film to talk about, and then Alice K. will find herself groping for words because she spent the entire two hours feeling so awkward and self-conscious with this foreign presence beside her that she couldn't pay attention to the movie for a second.

The hour grows later and Alice K. tosses in her bed, the scenarios growing worse and worse:

What if he's a total geek and looks like Don Knotts and we go out and run into my ex-boyfriend who rejected me?

What if he tries to kiss me goodnight and I don't want him to?

What if I do want him to kiss me goodnight but then find out he's a disgusting, spitty kisser?

What if he spends all night talking about his mother?

Oh, no! What if he has a hairy back?

And then, suddenly, Alice K. has a truly frightening thought, something that makes her sit bolt upright in bed and fear for her very soul.

Oh my God, she thinks. *What if I* like *him?*

Twenty-four hours later:

Alice K. lies in bed, writhing with post-date anxiety.

Will he call me? What if he doesn't call? Should I call him? How soon? WHAT WOULD I SAY? Oh God, I hate this.

The date, you see, was successful. A *successful blind date.* Is that an oxymoron, or what? Alice K. can barely believe her good fortune.

I liked him, she thinks, tossing in her bed, *I actually liked him.* Elliot M. had dark brown hair and green eyes and nice forearms. He was cute in a Tom Hanks kind of way, which Alice K. found much more desirable than being cute in a Tom Selleck kind of way because women don't ogle Tom Hanks cuteness on the street the way they ogle Tom Selleck cuteness; hence, his looks were less threatening. Plus, Elliot M. seemed sweet. Nice smile. Easygoing manner. And so far he has passed three key tests: he is a registered Democrat, he had no apparent interest in Monday night football, and he didn't sneer when she dropped the word "psychotherapy." In other words, he had potential.

Of course, there was a downside to that. If Alice K. had hated Elliot M.—if he'd turned out to be a beer-guzzling, unenlightened jerk who still lived with four of his college frat buddies, or if he'd been a BMW-driving, salon-tanned, status slave who used the word "impact" as a verb, or if he'd been one of those sensitive-new-man types who hugged trees and described episodes of weeping as personal breakthroughs—then Alice K. could have written him off immediately and gotten a good night's sleep. Having liked him, though, she now finds herself lying in bed, unable to rest because she is frantically deconstructing the date.

They'd gone to the movies. Elliot M. had chosen a Steve Martin movie (post-date analysis: good choice because it implied appreciation for offbeat humor and romantic sensibility—ten points; bad choice because it meant that Alice K. had to worry about whether she was laughing too hard, not hard enough, or too obnoxiously—minus two points).

They'd gone to the Japanese restaurant for dinner (post-date analysis: bad choice because Alice K. hates Japanese food; good choice because it meant she got to admire his taste in socks when he slipped off his shoes. Cashmere. Alice K. liked a man who cared about his socks—five points).

What else? They'd talked about work (he was a computer consultant, which sounded a tad too '80s to Alice K., but he mostly did work for environmentally-progressive companies, which sounded appropriately '90s—total point value: eight). They talked about their families (Elliot M. grew up in Chicago—ten points for cosmopolitan background; he was close to his parents and two brothers—ten points for success-

ful negotiation of family ties; but he didn't have any sisters—
two points off for potential inability to fully understand
women). Throughout the evening, she also discovered that
Elliot M. exercised regularly (five points unless it indicated
obsessive/compulsive tendencies), liked good food and wine
(ditto), and used to do a lot of drugs and smoked cigarettes
but quit (indicated current concern for health but also possibility of wilder youth mitigating nerd potential—ten
points). He also used to love *LA Law* but stopped watching
when it got stupid (five points), and he read a lot of fiction,
citing Richard Ford and Larry McMurtry as current favorites
(unclear analysis: could indicate healthy identification with
male outdoorsiness; could indicate latent sexist tendencies
and inability to deal with more emotionally complex subject
matter).

Lying in bed, Alice K. tallies up the numbers. Not bad,
she thinks, although there's still a lot of outstanding information, some nagging doubts. For instance, Elliot M. drove a
Volkswagen Jetta (fine), but he had the radio tuned to a classic
hits station (not so fine; could indicate a certain thoughtless-
ness or lack of imagination about music. Hmmm.).

The hour grows later. Alice K. lies there. She liked him.
Yes, Elliot M. could be something special. But this is a diffi-
cult thought. As she contemplates his possible Mr. Rightness,
Alice K.'s post-date scrutiny begins to give way to a more
painful form of obsessiveness: self-scrutiny. What did Elliot
M. think of *her*? He said he'd call, but what did that mean?
Did it mean, "I'll call sometime next year and see if you're
still a loser," or did it mean, "I'll call you tomorrow because
I think I may want you to be the mother of my children"?
Likewise, when he dropped Alice K. off and said, "It was really good to meet you," was he saying "good to meet you" in
the polite sense or *"good* to *meet you"* in the emphatic, genuine sense? And why didn't he kiss her goodnight? Was he being gentlemanly and respectful? Did she have bad breath?
Or was he simply *not interested?*

Alice K. begins to feel fearful, pondering this, and soon she works herself into a frenzy of insecurity. He won't call. Or he will call, but ultimately he'll find her boring and inadequate and he'll leave her. He'll turn out to be perfect, *it, the one,* and he'll go off and marry someone who looks like Isabella Rossellini.

Alice K. tries to calm herself down. *What is this?* she wonders. *Why do I do this to myself?* She tells herself that Elliot M. is just a guy: she barely knows him, he could still turn out to be a lout. She reminds herself of all the times she's met guys she liked and ended up disappointed. She considers how hard she's worked to become self-sufficient, to get by in life without a man. But still. Deep inside, there is a part of Alice K. that longs for romance, and when that part of her gets touched, it turns on a switch, engaging all her most profound hopes and ideals and expectations.

And when that happens, Alice K. begins to make the wild and irrational transition from post-date mild bemusement *(Whaddayaknow, I actually like this guy)* to post-date fantasy-laden obsession *(Will we get married? have children? buy adjoining burial plots?).*

She can't help it. Against her will, Alice K. begins to imagine Elliot M. sending her flowers at work the next day. She begins to imagine their next date: a romantic dinner, sparkling conversation flowing like wine, the first kiss. She imagines the first weekend away, Elliot M. confessing his love for her in front of the fire at some cozy inn: *I've never met anyone like you, Alice K. Where have you been all my life?* She imagines the first apartment, the clear and unambivalent decision to marry, the two of them sitting around thinking of pseudonyms for their future children. And she imagines telling Elliot M. her deepest, darkest secrets, the things she never tells anyone, the things that break down boundaries and create true intimacy and lasting love. . . .

And then suddenly, Alice K. has a terrifying thought,

something that causes her hair to rise up on her scalp. She sits bolt upright in bed.

Oh my God, Alice K. thinks. *If we get married, will I have to change my initial?*

Three weeks later:

Alice K. lies in bed, wishing she were Sharon Stone.

Right this minute, you see, Alice K. is lying in bed next to Elliot M., and they have just had their first sexual encounter. This is an advancement of their relationship, an acknowledgment of their mutual interest and attraction, a tender first moment together, so of course it all throws Alice K. into an immediate and profound panic.

She stares at the ceiling. *Oh my God,* she thinks. *What if he didn't like it? What if he expected sex with me to be wonderful and perfect and instead he found it boring and unimaginative and he wakes up in one of those distant and remote moods that men get into after they sleep with you and he acts threatened and skittish like a trapped animal and he flees the apartment before he's even had coffee and I never see him again?*

Hence, of course, the wish to be Sharon Stone. If Alice K. were Sharon Stone, she would be a sexual tigress brimming with confidence and equipped with a bag full of amazing sexual tricks so erotic and tantalizing that they'd turn Elliot M. into her devoted slave for life. If Alice K. were Sharon Stone, she and Elliot M. would still be making indescribably passionate love—gazing into each other's eyes, panting—instead of just lying there like lumps, respectively snoring (him) and worrying (her). And if Alice K. were Sharon Stone, she would be feeling that she'd just won a prize, captured a man's heart, instead of feeling somehow like she'd given up something.

What is this feeling of relinquishment? she wonders. Why does sex in the early stages of a relationship always make Alice K. feel as though she's surrendered some crucial part of herself, ceded a degree of power to her partner, or crossed a critical boundary of some kind? What is it about sex that makes Alice K. so terrified of being left?

Alice K. turns (quitely) onto her side and looks at Elliot M., who's sleeping soundly (of course). She wishes she could take this feeling of vulnerability (for clearly, that's what it is) and translate it into trust, rather than wariness; she wishes sex had made her feel closer to Elliot M., rather than preoccupied and afraid. For Alice K. knows that she will wake up in the morning feeling fragile and self-conscious and burdened by the assumption that Elliot M. has found her to be a disappointment. She knows that some kind of barrier will be thrown up between them, a tentativeness toward each other, a shyness. And she doesn't know how to avoid that.

She thinks again of Sharon Stone. *Why oh why can't I be a sex goddess,* Alice K. thinks. *Why can't I be cavalier and daring and unself-conscious about sex? Why can't I see it on purely physical terms, and leave all this emotional baggage at the door?*

She felt some of those same things while she was having sex with Elliot M. Alice K. had felt as though she was watching herself from a distant part of the room, criticizing and disdainful. Against her will, images flashed through her mind—Meg Ryan's I've-come-with-the-best-of-them fake orgasm imitation in *When Harry Met Sally;* Susan Sarandon's take-charge sexuality in *Bull Durham;* Sharon Stone in *Basic Instinct.* These women approached sex like ... well, like men: with relish and abandon and a degree of selfishness that indicated a sense of their own sexual needs as valid and true; by contrast, Alice K. felt overwhelmed with a sense of all the things she lacked, all the things she *wasn't.*

Oh, Alice K. has been around long enough to know that movie sex and real-life sex have very little in common. She knows that movie sex is always fluid and steamy and beautifully choreographed whereas real-life sex involves a lot of awkward moments and unglamorous grunts and colliding body parts. Still, though, the images of sexual perfection are powerful, and they make Alice K. painfully aware of how detached she often feels from her own body, a condition that tends to persist until she develops a strong enough bond with a man to stop worrying. So, as she'd suspected she would, she just sort of lay there with Elliot M., letting him control the situation, worrying about whether she was acting interested enough to keep him from knowing how utterly self-conscious she felt.

The hour grows later and Alice K.'s mind grows crowded with other post-coital worries. Does this mean she and Elliot M. now have a *relationship,* rather than a simple romantic interest? Does it mean that from now on they'll spend all their weekends together, and if so, is that a good, positive, relieving thing, or a suffocating, complicated, negative thing? And if they do end up in a more serious relationship, will Alice K. be able to manage her fears of closeness and intimacy? To trust Elliot M.? To talk to him about the things that frighten or bother her?

Elliot M. shifts in the bed beside her and Alice K. looks at him. He is handsome in the night: tousled hair, firm jawline. Tentatively, she reaches out her hand and rests it on his shoulder. It feels solid and manly and after a moment or two, Alice K. very gently extends her reach across Elliot M.'s chest and snuggles a little closer.

He turns in the bed then, and puts his arms around Alice K., giving a little sigh of satisfaction. And as she lies there, sheltered in Elliot M.'s embrace, Alice K. slowly begins to relax.

Sort of.

Two months later:

Alice K. lies in bed, writhing with emotional claustrophobia.

Alice K., you see, is in bed with Elliot M., and she is entering a familiar and difficult phase of the relationship, one she calls the "Oh my God, what am I doing with this man" phase.

Alice K. hates this. She first noted the onset of this stage about two weeks earlier, when she and Elliot M. were eating

Alice H.'s Wish List, Part 1

Over the course of her adult life, Alice K. has designed a
special wish list consisting of tools that would help the ordinary angst-ridden woman of today cope more effectively
with modern life. After all, as Alice K. sees it, we have tools for every other
facet of life—to help us fix our cars and keep our homes clean and prepare
our meals. And if we are to traverse the rocky roads of romance with any degree of success, we should have equivalent tools for our personal lives, equipment that will allow us to efficiently build, repair, and maintain relationships.
Here, then, is an example:

The Sleeping Sex Polygraph Hit

This tool would be designed to help men and women cope with two basic
truths—one, that human beings are too shy and inhibited to talk about sex;
and two, that even the best sexual relationships tire after a while, a fact that
leads to disillusionment, frustration, and usually, rage.

Like regular polygraphs, the sex polygraph would record bodily reflexes; the
key difference is that you could hook it up to your mate *in his or her sleep*,
thereby eliminating the half-truths and awkwardness that traditionally accompany wide-awake discussions of sex.

Say, for example, that you are plagued with feelings of insecurity, worried that
your partner is bored with you in bed, and unsure what to do about it. Without
the sleeping sex polygraph, these feelings would seethe below the surface for
months and months where, unaddressed and undiscussed, they would set the
stage for a self-fulfilling prophecy: the longer you fret, the more inhibited you feel
and—presto!—the more dull and lifeless your sex life becomes.

With the sleeping sex polygraph, all that would change. While your partner
is fast asleep, you would strap the small instrument onto his or her wrist. Then
you would sit back, ask many detailed, graphic, personal questions and watch
the data on the polygraph, which would provide you with all the answers you
need to know.

Sample Q&As: "Are you bored with me?" (high reading indicates positive
response); "Is it the way I kiss?" (low reading, negative response); "Is it the lack
of variety?" (high reading, another "Yes"); "Would you like me to greet you at
the door dressed in Saran Wrap?" (low reading, bad idea); and so on, until
you've answered all your questions.

Easy, yes? No fuss, no muss, and best of all, no humiliation.

dinner together at her apartment. They'd spent all day together, as well as the previous night, and all of a sudden, Alice K. was struck with a profound longing for solitude, distance, and personal space.

Of course, she didn't exactly recognize that emotion at the time; instead, what hit Alice K. was the awareness that all of a sudden, she could not stand the sound of Elliot M. chewing his food. In fact, she could not bear it. They were eating chicken, and Elliot M. was gnawing at a drumstick, making hideous little slurping noises. She sat there and watched him. He was hunched over his plate, elbows on the table, going after that drumstick like a starved man. He had a little smear of chicken grease on his chin and a tiny piece of chicken skin caught in the corner of his mouth. And all of a sudden, Alice K. wanted to get up from the table and run away and never see Elliot M. again.

What is this? Alice K. wonders. *Why is it that as soon as I begin to get close to a man, he starts to grate on my nerves and drive me totally nuts?* For that, Alice K. knows, is precisely what has begun to happen with Elliot M. He was getting too close, too soon. He had looked too *familiar* at her kitchen table that night, hunched over his chicken, too much as though he felt he belonged there, and that made Alice K. go into a mild panic.

She turns in her bed and looks at Elliot M., who is sleeping soundly beside her. *I don't want to blow this,* Alice K. thinks, *but I can feel myself pulling away.* This makes Alice K. sad. After all, for the first six weeks of their relationship, Alice K. had been virtually giddy. She found herself smiling at odd times during the day, and doodling Elliot M.'s name on her blotter at work, and dreaming about him at night. She looked forward to getting together with him, and she felt those little stabs of excitement when she discovered things about him that she liked or admired: the first time she went to Elliot M.'s apartment, for example, she immediately scanned the bookshelves in his living room and discovered that he had excellent taste in books—a huge mystery collection, all of Paul Auster's novels, a lot of Anne Tyler. *Ah,* she thought, *more evidence that he's right, that he* fits.

But now, Alice K. can feel herself becoming testy and petulant. She can feel herself begin to eye Elliot M. more critically, and to feel little stabs of discomfort when they're together. The other day, for example, Alice K. and Elliot M. were in the video store looking for a movie to rent, and Elliot M. picked up *Cannonball Run* and said, "Have you ever seen this? I love this movie."

Alice K. was mortified. *Cannonball Run? I'm going out with a man who likes Burt Reynolds movies?*

She knows this is ridiculous, this instinct to toss Elliot M.'s entire character down the drain on the basis of one poor movie selection. But Alice K. can't seem to stop herself. Part of the problem, she realizes, lying there in her bed, is that Elliot M. is simply too nice. Too available. Too interested in a real relationship. Too interested in *Alice K.* And this makes Alice K. feel edgy and confused.

Why must I be like this? she wonders. *Why must I be one of those women who only fall in love with men who refuse to fall in love back?* The famous Groucho Marx line springs to mind— the one about not wanting to join a club that would have him as a member—and Alice K. begins to despair.

After all, Alice K. has been involved with more unavailable, disinterested, commitment-phobic, unappreciative men than she can count, and she knows by now how awful *that* can feel: that's been the story of Alice K.'s romantic life, tale after tale of obsessive/unrequited/I-love-you-more-than-you-love-me relationships with men who are distant and elusive and remote, who make Alice K. do all the work and all the pining, and who leave her feeling rejected and inadequate and crying in her apartment.

So what is it about being with a genuinely nice guy, in a relationship with a future, that makes her so uncomfortable? Alice K. thinks back to an episode that took place a few weeks ago, when she and Elliot M. were sitting in a restaurant. He had looked up at Alice K. with an expression of incredible tenderness and said, "How did I end up with you? I feel like I've won the lottery." At the time, Alice K.'s heart swelled—he looked so sweet, saying that—but now she looks back at that moment and finds it terrifying: *End up with me?* The phrase sounded so ... permanent. In a way, Elliot M.'s affection for Alice K. made her doubt him, made her call into question his worth somehow. She was used to feeling inferior in relationships, inadequate, equipped with just a shade less power than her partner, and having Elliot M. seem so captivated by her triggered in Alice K. a disconcerting set of feelings: if she wasn't the inferior one in the relationship, maybe *he* was.

The hour grows later, and Alice K. lies in the dark, tossing in her bed. *Oh my God,* she thinks, *what if Elliot M. begins to depend on me, and need me? What if he decides he wants to share the rest of his life with me?* She carries the thought further: *What if Alice K. actually tries to make this relationship work? What if she gives up this crazy need to be involved with unattainable men* (which, Alice K. knows, is really a way of not being involved at all) *and takes the big leap, intimacy-wise?*

She contemplates this. Her sister, Beth K., who is married and who believes that establishing and maintaining intimacy is very hard work, would encourage her to take the plunge. She would also point out some facts to Alice K.: becoming involved with a man like Elliot M. would mean acting like a real human being in a relationship. It would mean doing all that horrible work like allowing herself to show Elliot M. her less pleasant sides, and allowing herself to be vulnerable with him, and negotiating all those issues like how much distance and space to give each other, and learning how to tolerate those moments when she can't stand the sound of him chewing.

And with that thought, Alice K. is suddenly gripped with profound panic and dread. The hair on the back of her neck rises. She sits bolt upright in bed.

Oh my God, she thinks, *I would have to act like an* adult.

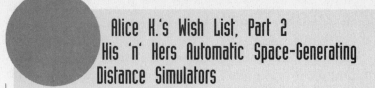

Alice K.'s Wish List, Part 2
His 'n' Hers Automatic Space-Generating Distance Simulators

At last, a simple solution to those pesky need-for-personal-space conflicts.

You know the situation: you've had a bad day. You want nothing more than to sit in the living room, stare at the wall, and withdraw. Your partner, on the other hand, wants nothing more than to go out to dinner, hold hands and "connect." Without the right tools, chances are you'll arrive at some sort of ugly, unspoken compromise that will leave you both feeling cheated and depressed. (You'll make dinner together, but you won't utter more than a grunt; your partner will begin sulking because you're being inattentive; you'll get ticked off because your mate won't give you a break, and—well, you know.)

But enter the His 'n' Hers Automatic Space-Generating Distance Simulator and you get an entirely different scenario: you come home from work after a bad day, feeling like you need to unwind alone. But instead of ignoring your partner, you take a special seat in your Space-Generating Distance Simulator (it resembles a simple armchair but comes equipped with a set of electrodes and a computer). Next, you attach the electrodes to your head, and enter into the computer the amount of distance you feel you need—an hour, a night out, a weekend, and so on. Then press a button and—voila!—the electrodes kick into gear and your brain is infused with the *experience* of distance. Within minutes, you will feel as though you've been far, far away, all by yourself, for whatever period of time you've deemed necessary. No need to leave home. No need to reject that loving partner. Your handy His 'n' Hers Automatic Space-Generating Distance Simulator will make you feel calm, refreshed, and ready to confront the challenges of an intimate relationship.

See? Isn't romance fun?

3

HOW
TO BE
A GIRL

alice k's u-do-it pseudo-spa experience

The U-Do-It Pseudo-Spa experience begins when you face
two simple facts.

1) You are tired, burned out, depressed, and in need of a serious pampering experience.
2) You are flat broke.

Yes, Alice K. understands. These are the cruel and frugal nineties, and for girls in need of a serious pampering experience, those extravagant, eighties-style spas are a thing of the past. No more packing up your Reeboks for a $750 weekend of gentle massage and cleansing facials and brisk morning jaunts through the woods. No more nine-hundred-calorie-per-day Spa meals served up by specially trained Spa dieticians. No more low-impact Spa aerobics classes led by eager, Jane Fonda look-alike Spa aerobics instructors. Wake up and smell the recession.

Once you have accepted that reality, however, all is not lost. Here, for burned-out girls on a budget, is your answer: Alice K.'s U-Do-It Pseudo-Spa experience. This is how U-Do-It.

- Phone a supportive friend, who will henceforth be known as your "Spa Partner."
- Have Spa Partner spend several hours on the phone tracking down an extremely cheap motel in a distant land. Said motel should be at least an hour away, so as to impart a sense of sufficient distance from your life; it should also come equipped with several spa accoutrements—namely, pool and sauna.
- Wait for Spa Partner to phone you back, and then respond with the following phrases.
    1. "What? The Ramada Inn? In Mystic, Connecticut? In February?"
    2. "It's only $39?"
    3. "Let's go!"
- Meet Spa Partner at designated location on Friday night. Inspect room carefully and notice small table with mirror outside bathroom. Unpack cosmetics and toiletries on said table. This will henceforth be known as your "Beauty Bar" and will be of central importance to the Psuedo-Spa experience.
- Discover the first and most important key to a successful U-Do-It Pseudo-Spa experience: it works best if you insert the word "Beauty" before all Spa-related words and activities. With this handy technique, the Ramada Inn quickly becomes your "Beauty Base," your room becomes your "Beauty Suite," etc.
- You and your Spa Partner are now ready to go out for a healthy Beauty Burger. Wash said food item down with a cold Beauty Beer, then retire to Beauty Suite, lie down, and discover the second most important key to a successful U-Do-It Pseudo-Spa experience: conceptualizing. Lie very still. Conceptualize a long, gentle massage. Now conceptualize a scalp rub. A pedicure. Rise, feeling refreshed. Watch some television. Giggle intermittently with Spa Partner.

- Engage in first of two ten-hour Beauty Rests. Rise, leave Beauty Base, enjoy a leisurely Beauty Lunch, then prepare for your third most important Pseudo-Spa activity: the pre-pampering drugstore run.
- Find a large drugstore. Enter. Fill a large basket with $52.79 worth of Beauty Products, including some or all of the following: Clairol Deep Conditioning Beauty Pack Treatment for hair; Clay Facial Masque for smoothing and cleansing skin; L'Oréal Pléntitude Floral Tonic for toning skin; deep-red nail polish (try Revlon's Indian Spice) for painting toenails; huge quantities of foam rollers for curling hair; various hair clips and gels and sprays; all manner of cosmetic puffs and squares; assorted skin creams and moisturizers; and several women's magazines (any kind will do, but *Cosmo* is mandatory).
- Pay for said items and giggle incessantly as you realize they cost almost twice as much as your room.
- Return to Beauty Base, stopping en route to purchase $2.55 worth of Beauty Fudge.
- Inspect Spa accoutrements at Beauty Base. Notice that pool is filled with screaming children and looks unappealing. Decide you're "not in the mood" for a sauna. Retire to Beauty Suite and spend some time conceptualizing an exercise experience.
- Leaf through *Cosmo*. Take the *Cosmo* quiz (this month: "How Much of a Princess Are You?"). Read extensive article called "How to Bag a Rich Man." Giggle. Then feel exhausted and settle down for a Beauty Nap. Sleep deeply.
- Awaken, ready for further Pseudo-Spa activities. Take an extremely long, hot shower, pausing on occasion to conceptualize a Jacuzzi experience.
- Apply gobs of Clairol Deep Conditioning Beauty Pack Treatment to wet scalp in an effort to "Restore Life and Lustre to Damaged Hair."
- While goo sits in hair, apply Clay Facial Masque. Clay Facial Masque resembles a thick, white, wet cement. Note that you resemble a Beauty Mime.
- Clip and polish fingernails. Clip toenails, and realize with glee that one of the great things about staying in a $39 room at the Ramada Inn is that you can clip your toenails onto the carpet without feeling

compelled to clean it up. Polish toenails the rich, deep shade of Indian Spice. Admire handiwork.

- Wash off Clay Masque and admire your smooth, poreless skin. Wash goo out of hair. Dry hair and admire its shiny glow. Ask Spa Partner to teach you the intricate art of liquid eyeliner application. Apply other makeup (your choice) in leisurely manner. Feel extremely clean. Get dressed and prepare for Spa Dinner Outing.

- Find large, suburban steak house, the kind where they serve big, stiff drinks and the salads come in buckets. Order a Beauty Scotch while friendly wait staff prepares table. Once seated, order the following: one trip to Beauty Salad Bar; one Large Beauty Sirloin; one Beauty Baked Potato with Beauty Sour Cream (which you will dutifully refer to as the cream for "Nature's Inner Facial").

- Complete Spa Dinner and retire to hotel lounge for a special Beauty Cognac.

- Retire to Beauty Suite (or, depending on your tolerance for alcohol thus far, stagger there) and prepare for second ten-hour Beauty Sleep. Awaken feeling refreshed and rested. Then, for the final leg of your Spa experience, find a nearby Howard Johnson's Motor Lodge.

- Indulge in fabulous All-You-Can-Eat Beauty Buffet. Eat eggs, sausage, bacon, muffins, apple pancakes, and a fried donut substance. Drink coffee. Wonder if perhaps you have transformed the Pseudo-Spa experience into the Anti-Spa experience. Obliterate that thought by returning to All-You-Can-Eat Beauty Buffet and helping yourself to some healthy fruits.

- Check out of Beauty Base. Take a long Beauty Drive, perhaps stopping for a Beauty Stroll. Finish off the last of the Beauty Fudge.

- Bid your Spa Partner goodbye and turn toward home, thinking all the while about how lucky you were not to spend the weekend at one of those places where they make you eat rice cakes. Sigh happily as you drive. Ah, the nineties.

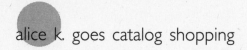 alice k. goes catalog shopping

Alice K. lies in bed, worrying about her wardrobe.

And about her wardrobe budget.

And about leggings and tights and cotton sweaters, and about the subtle difference between "midnight" and "raven," and about how it is that, once again, she spent a Sunday afternoon leafing through the fall catalogs and somehow managed to spend something in the order of $734.95.

Oh my God, Alice K. thinks. *How has this happened?*

She rolls over in the bed and tries to re-create this frenzy of consumption, tries to understand it. There she was, sitting on her sofa on a quiet Sunday afternoon, paging through the J. Crew catalog. And there they were, all those clean-scrubbed, casual, sun-kissed models in their khaki pants and rumpled linen shirts and one-hundred-percent cotton crew-neck sweaters, every one of them looking like they'd just graduated from Yale and stepped off the polo field or the beach, and, well, something in Alice K. just snapped.

It must have been subconscious, Alice K. thinks, but all of a sudden she happened upon a lovely, tailored pair of flannel pants with a matching jacket and vest. And she looked at the picture of the tall, reedy model wearing these clothes, her head thrown back and a blissful smile upon her lips. And the model just looked so . . . so together and composed and upper-middle-class that Alice K. simply couldn't stop herself from feeling that if she, too, owned that jacket and vest and pants that she, too, would look together and composed and upper-middle-class.

So she ordered the outfit in heather.

And then, thinking about how nice it would be to, you

know, be able to mix and match, she ordered it again. In taupe.

And then she turned another page and saw another model with gorgeous skin and lovely tousled hair wearing a pale silk blouse (available in cream, rosebud, vodka, and gin-and-tonic) and, well, maybe it was reading all those colors but Alice K. has to admit it: she just got drunk—*drunk*—with the sense of possibilities. She sat on her sofa and imagined: she could wear the rosebud blouse with the heather pants, and the cream blouse with the taupe vest, and the taupe pants with the vodka blouse *and* the heather vest, and . . . well, suffice it to say that Alice K. ordered all four, even though she's not quite sure whether the addition of a gin-and-tonic blouse will do anything for her personal life, let alone her wardrobe.

Oh dear, Alice K. thinks, tossing in her bed. *Why do I do this? Why, why, why?*

Alice K., after all, has been here before, trapped in the land of catalog excess. She lies in bed, thinking about the seven pairs of leggings she ordered from Tweeds at one time, and about the nine cotton sweaters from Smythe & Co., and about the eleven pairs of underwear from Victoria's Secret that arrived for her at work one day, sending Alice K. into a fit of public humiliation because some ignorant, low-level assistant inadvertently gave it to her boss who opened it and then spent the next forty-five minutes roaring with laughter at the thought of Alice K. (who's a 34 triple A) wearing a plunging, padded, lace, magenta push-up bra with tiny bow accents.

Alice K. cringes at the memory.

But this, she thinks, is the nature of catalog shopping. It's almost impossible to avoid. Alice K. has a theory that catalog companies have invented all those bizarre and multiple names for colors in order to confuse customers and force them into a mind-boggling train of thought that makes it practically impossible to settle on just one. That happened to

Alice K. during the leggings episode. She sat there looking at the leggings page and thinking, *Well, I'll get them in jade and mahogany . . . but wait, maybe they'd look better in moss than in jade . . . but what's the difference between moss, jade, deep forest, and envy? And for that matter, what's the difference between mahogany, deep mahogany, double-deep mahogony, and double-deep-mahogony-chocolate chunk?* So, of course she did what most women in that situation would do and bought them all.

The rationalization, of course, is that when they arrive in their nice box, you can open them up, try them on, decide which one or two you prefer, and send the rest back. But that involves actually putting them back in the box, taking them all the way over to the Post Office, and spending your hard-earned money to send them back to Columbus, Ohio, or Roanoke, Virginia, or wherever they came from. And more often than not, Alice K. puts it off and puts it off, and then figures it's too late to take them back, and besides, there's something about spending money through a catalog that makes you feel like you're not really spending money at all. You just check off all those little boxes on the order form, and write down your credit card number, and, well, it feels like spending play money.

The other problem is that clothes in catalogs always look like such reasonable purchases. Never mind that Alice K.'s closet is filled with bad catalog buys—party dresses from Victoria's Secret that look good on the page but are actually pretty cheesy when you take them out of the box, and stuff from Tweeds-wannabe catalogs that's cheaper but sags and bags in the wrong places and never quite looks right. Never mind all that. When all is said and done, the stuff looks seductive.

Why just today, Alice K. was leafing through the new Tweeds catalog, and she saw that lovely scoop-neck tee (available in mountain, moonlight, and paprika), and that silk V-neck sweater (russet, moon dance, patina, adriatic, and bittersweet), and that little cotton-Lycra tube skirt (charcoal, pumpernickel, and oatmeal), and, well, everything just looked so wearable, and so matchable, and the skirt only cost $29.99, and the sweater only cost $49, and the tees were a mere $19 each, and it couldn't cost *that* much to get a couple of shirts and a few lousy little skirts. So she ticked off about 22 items and before she realized it—*ooooops!*—she'd spent $734.95.

Alice K. rolls over in her bed and wonders what she's going to say when the UPS man arrives. Plead insanity? Tell him there's no Alice K. here and send him away? Simply take all the packages straight to the PO without opening them and send them back?

And then, suddenly, Alice K. has a brainstorm. *Ha!* she thinks, *at last! A way to shop through the catalogs and never, ever worry about blowing her budget! A way to remain clad in pumpernickel and paprika from now until the end of time!*

Alice K. sits up in bed and smiles. Why didn't she think of this before?

The answer: credit card fraud.

the purse

"Why do you need that huge thing? It's the size of a watermelon. What do you carry in there?"

This took place on their third date: Alice K. and Elliot M. were walking to a restaurant, and Elliot M. was referring to Alice K.'s purse.

Alice K. shook her head. Men always asked questions like that. Men lead wallet-size lives. They can stuff everything they need into a single pocket. They are men, and they just don't get it.

"You just don't get it, Elliot M.," she said. "If you menstruated, you would understand, but you don't, so you can't."

Of course this comment was lost on Elliot M., so Alice K. had to spend fifteen minutes explaining her Theory of Purse Size Based on Menstruation. To wit: the average woman usually carries an average of forty-two tampons with her at all times, arming herself against disaster. Many of these tampons have been there for months, and they lie, bent and wrinkled in their wrappers, in errant corners of the purse. But women carry them nonetheless because the Theory of Purse Size Based on Menstruation is closely tied to the Theory of Relativity Based on Tampons, a most delicate science which says that the more there are, the better chance that one of them will actually be in working order when you need it.

"Accordingly," Alice K. concluded, "we are loathe to throw out a tampon, and we need a large bag in order to cart them all around."

She paused for a moment, then added, "Also, you don't have breasts." Again, Elliot M. was confused, so Alice K. was forced to describe her Breast Size = Purse Size Theory of Relativity. "If you had breasts," she told Elliot M., "you would understand how it feels to march down the street with your arms swinging at your side, leaving your breasts exposed to every leering, jeering truck driver in sight." A large bag is the answer: clutched at the side or swung across the chest, a large bag gives a woman a certain feeling of physical safety. She can shield herself with it. Or, if necessary, use it as a handy weapon.

Elliot M. still didn't understand. "Okay. So the bag has to be big and it has to hold a lot of tampons. But why is there so much other stuff in there?"

Alice K. sighed. "Don't you know anything? Have you never heard of Office Face?"

And then she thought, *Well, of course he hasn't.* This was another fact: men don't get Office Face, because their faces look the same all the time, no matter what they've been doing. Women, on the other hand, get it all the time, and it makes them very unhappy. The Office Face is blotched and pale and shiny in all the wrong places. It has little flecks of mascara here and there, and smudged eyeliner, and dry, cracked lips. So when a woman sees the Office Face staring back at her in the mirror at the end of the workday, she naturally reaches for her purse, which contains at least eight (but probably more) of the following items: astringent, moisturizer, powder, blush, foundation, lipstick, lip pencil, eyeliner, eye shadow (one to five colors), mascara, hair spray, cosmetic brush, hair brush, and lip brush.

"That's a lot of stuff," said Alice K. "You need a big bag to carry it all."

Of course, Alice K. did not tell Elliot M. the whole story. After all, there is lots more in those big bags. Wallet. Checkbook. Keys. A few pens. Chapstick. Hand cream. A novel in case she's stuck waiting somewhere. Breath mints. Aspirin. Sunglasses. Stamps.

And more. Lists. Scraps of paper with phone numbers on them. And the more telling items. At that very moment, for example, Alice K. had three outstanding parking tickets in her bag, an overdue bill from her therapist, Dr. Y., and a recall notice from Hyundai from 1992 about some part that had been recalled.

These are the items she could not—and would not—explain to Elliot M. It would make her feel sheepish and ashamed. Elliot M., you see, would have paid the parking tickets, paid the therapy bill, and driven the Hyundai straight over to the dealer without further delay.

But Alice K.? No. When Alice K. came home from work and found that recall notice from Hyundai in the mail, her train of thought went something like this: *oh shit, I'm going to have to call the car dealership, and then I'm going have to bring the car in, and that means I'm going to have to find the* time *to bring the car in, I* hate *dealing with cars, I wish someone would deal with the car for me, I* hate *having to be responsible, I HATE THIS,* and so on.

And she promptly stuffed the notice into her purse

where, stashed beneath the debris, she could neither ignore it totally (which would be too irresponsible) nor deal with it directly (which would be too grown-up).

See? The purse is a very convenient tool.

Besides, Alice K. has tried to get by without. Once, after an extended period of haranguing from Mr. Cruel about the size of her purse, Alice K. spotted a small bag in a downtown leather store, a compact little thing about the size of a man's shoe. She told herself, *I am confident and grown-up and mature and I don't* need *to carry around seven tubes of lipstick and three combs and forty-two tampons; I can* do *this.*

So she bought the bag and put her bare essentials into it. Wallet, checkbook, keys. One lipstick. One comb. A single lonely tampon.

The bag bulged unhappily at her hip. Walking down the street, she felt naked, exposed, unprotected.

She was miserable.

A man would never understand.

the compliment

The male human was merely trying to be congenial to Alice K. "You look nice today," he said, lightly.

Then a look of panic came over his face and he began to qualify. "Um, I mean, you look nice *every* day. It's not that you don't usually look nice . . . I just meant that today you look . . . I mean . . ."

Alice K. felt sorry for him. Poor man. Clearly a battered complimenter. A victim of female compliment assault.

Yes, this is true and Alice K. knows it. Once upon a time, a man would compliment a woman and she would smile demurely, blush perhaps, and say a modest, "Thank you." Today, there's no such thing as a compliment. A compliment is merely an insult in disguise.

I look nice today? Does that mean I usually look like hell? What does that mean, *"You look nice today"?*

Later, Alice K. reported this observation to Ruth E., and Ruth E. nodded enthusiastically.

"This is especially true when we cut our hair," she said. "Some guy comes up and says, 'Oh, you cut your hair,' and you go into major F.I.D."

Alice K. nodded. Ah, yes. F.I.D.: Furious Inner Dialogue. Man notes haircut. Woman smiles politely. F.I.D. ensues.

"What did that mean, 'Oh, you cut your hair.' Of course, I cut my hair, isn't that clear? Yes, it's clear, so obviously it must be a bad haircut. A really bad haircut. Right? If it was a good haircut, he would have said, 'Hey, your hair looks great!' But he didn't say that. Being a modern man, he felt compelled to acknowledge the new haircut, but he couldn't bring himself to lie and say it looked good, so obviously I look like hell and I'll never be able to show my face in public again."

The F.I.D. lasts about ten seconds and by the time it's over, the woman in question is filled with self-loathing, despair, and hatred for the man who got her started.

Alice K. has a theory about this phenomenon: women are trained to mistrust compliments, to read into them all kinds of hidden meanings.

One reason for this is that once upon a time, all grown women were evil little girls. Evil, vengeful, hateful little girls who used to stand around the girls' bathroom in school and lie to each other about how they looked. Sample dialogue:

Girl A, standing in front of mirror, inspecting pimple on her nose the size of a Volkswagen: "Ohmygod, look at this zit!"

Girl B: "It's nothing! Honest! I wouldn't have even noticed it if you hadn't pointed it out."

Girl A: "Really? You mean it?"

Girl B: "Honest, I swear."

Girl A does not believe Girl B for a minute, but has no choice but to pretend she does, lest she be forced to remain in the bathroom for two weeks until the zit goes away. Girl B, meanwhile, feels a secret stab of glee in her evil soul at her friend's misfortune. *Nya-nya!* she thinks, *Alice K. has a zit on her nose the size of a Volkswagen, so I'm prettier than she is.*

Alice K., you see, knows another fact about evil young girls: they are also hideously competitive, and this makes any sort of compliment highly suspect. *Maybe she wants me to look bad,* the recipient of a compliment may think. *Maybe she wants me to buy this mucus-colored dress with the leg-o'-mutton sleeves because that way she'll look better at the dance.*

Most women will not admit this, Alice K. believes, but it's true. We learn from an early age not to trust each other, especially when it comes to matters of appearance.

Alice K. has two other theories about compliments: the style thing and the man thing. The style thing is a phenomenon that usually takes place when a woman is in her early to mid-twenties and has not yet developed a true sense of what she looks like. At this point, she is experimenting with all kinds of bizarre and horrible attire—skirts that are too short or too long, colors that look hellish—and she knows in her soul that she hasn't yet hit upon the right look. A man who compliments her at this stage is just asking for trouble. "I look awful in these combat boots, don't I?" the woman will wail, standing before the mirror. Agree with her and she will burst into tears and accuse you of being shallow and unsupportive; disagree and she will accuse you of lying, which you probably are. Either way, you lose.

The man thing is more complicated, but it has to do with how weird it can be to be a woman, especially around the matter of being attractive (or not) to the opposite sex. Even now, at a point in life where she is more self-assured about how she looks, Alice K. understands how complex a compliment can be, how many questions can leap to mind when the pleasantries come from a man.

If you're in a setting where you don't want your looks to be important—like work—a compliment can seem threatening or inappropriate; it can make you worry that men are only being nice to you because they think you look good.

If you're in a major depression, haven't washed your hair for a week, and genuinely feel unattractive, you simply don't trust compliments from a man: he must have some huge character flaw, you think, or he's legally blind, or he's trying to trick you into believing something that's not true.

And if you have mixed feelings about your appearance, some flaw of self-esteem or crisis of confidence—well, a compliment can feel downright unsettling, unleashing a train of conflicted thought that could drive even the sanest women to drink.

Mr. Cruel was the first man to buy Alice K. lingerie, for example, and she spent weeks assuming that this meant not that he liked her body but that he hated her underwear. And if he hated her underwear, she thought, well, he must have hated the way she dressed, and if he hated the way she dressed, well, he must have hated the way she was, and if he hated the way she was, well, he must have wanted to change her, and if that was true, well, then she should have felt resentful instead of merely insecure, and . . .

Weird logic, yes, but hey: that's what it's like to be female sometimes.

Ah, but Alice K. has found a solution, and she struggles mightily to train the men she knows in its execution. There are three simple rules and Alice K. has even written them down:

- Try to limit compliments to jewelry and shoes, which tend to be less laden with complexity than, say, underwear.
- Don't ever phrase a compliment as a question. To ask, "Is that a new blouse?" and leave it at that is to invite a major F.I.D. on the part of the complimentee. A simple, "That's a really nice blouse" is much safer.
- And when it comes to hair, there's only one sure trick. Simply adopt your most genuine look of sincerity and practice saying aloud this

simple phrase: "You look just like Michelle Pfeiffer. You look just like Michelle Pfeiffer. You look just like Michelle Pfeiffer."

It's a bald-faced lie, but what the hell. Alice K. buys it.

alice k.'s male sensitivity assessment quiz

Alice K. has designed the following quiz to help women determine whether or not the men in their lives are sufficiently sensitive to the female experience to be deemed suitable long-term partners.

This is a critical assessment. As many women know, relationships with men who lack sensitivity to the female experience always fail in the long run. Without that paramount quality, a man cannot be supportive when we have bouts of PMS, or screaming fights with our mothers, or terrific fits of insecurity about our looks. Without that quality, he is incapable of giving a woman what she really needs: sympathy for hair trauma and menstrual distress; support through diets and trips to the gynecologist; lots of unqualified adoration; and the occasional well-chosen piece of lingerie.

Let us begin.

1. Identify the following and note where they may be found (i.e., on the female body, in the female closet, in the female medicine cabinet, etc. Hint: these do not have male counterparts):

T zone
bikini area
purse spray
combination skin
tap pants
clincher comb
dress shield

2. Describe and explain the following:
    yeast infection
    Pap smear
    discharge
    rampant hormonal shift
    underwire ache

3. Compare and contrast the following:
    tweezing and plucking
    lipstick, lip gloss, and lip pencil
    panty hose and panty liners
    sculpting gel and contraceptive gel
    "light days" and "heavy days"

4. Explain the significance of the following in women's lives:
    cranberry juice
    Jeff Bridges
    little black dress
    little black pumps
    straight seams
    good gynecologist

5. Explain the connection between the following:
    elbows and lemons
    hair spray and panty hose
    masking tape and hems
    bananas and PMS
    failed relationships and suicidal depression

6. Would a woman rather have:
    shoulder pads or maxi-pads
    an IUD or a D&C
    a camisole or a filet of sole
    a bad relationship or no relationship at all

7. Match the products in column A with the functions they provide women in column B.

Column A	Column B
exfoliating sponge	evens facial skin tone
toner	softens eyeliner
top coat	tightens pores and refreshes skin
hydrating fluid	removes leg hair
Q-tips	removes dead skin
cover stick	protects nail polish
foundation	hides facial blemishes
depilatory	moisturizes skin

8. Which of the following statements will cause a woman the most distress?
- "Here's the speculum.... You'll just feel a little pinch...."
- "Your last period was eight weeks ago?"
- "Why did we break up? She wanted to get married and I didn't."
- "Hey, honey—aren't those pants getting a little tight on you?"

9. Identify the following words or phrases and rank them according to the amount of anxiety they provoke.

a) edema
endometriosis
episiotomy
electrolysis
b) varicose veins
vaginal itch
venereal warts
Vaseline
c) cystitis
cellulite
celibacy
season basketball tickets

10. In the following lists, identify the word or phrase that does not belong.
a) crying jag

uncontrollable outburst of rage
bloating
cramps
euphoria
b) distorted body image
binging and purging
cottage cheese and carrot sticks
long-term psychotherapy
self-acceptance
c) cervix
clitoris
Fallopian tube
vulva
Velveeta

11. If your girlfriend is traumatized by an extremely bad haircut, the correct response is
    a) "Your hair looks *great!*"
    b) "Your hair looks *great!*"
    c) "Your hair looks *great!*"
    d) "Your hair looks *great!*"

12. The reason this quiz has no answers is
    a) Alice K. assumes that you care enough about the female experience to know all this stuff.
    b) Alice K. now realizes women's lives are even more complex than she initially thought and she isn't sure of some of the answers herself (purse spray?).
    c) Alice K. believes that it's important to keep a few secrets in order to help women maintain their aura of mystery.
    d) Alice K. believes deep in her heart of hearts that when it comes to explaining women to men, there are no answers.

good shopping

Alice K. lies in bed, contemplating the importance of the occasional really good shop.

Not as in "a really good clothing shop" or "a really good shoe shop." No, she means it in the experiential sense; she means a really good shop the way men talk about a "really good lay" (a phrase which Alice K. finds revolting, by the way) or "a really good game" (considerably less offensive). She means the adrenaline rush, the promise of elevated self-esteem that comes when you try on something that automatically makes you look ten pounds thinner or ten degrees more sophisticated than you did before. She means the indulgence in vanity, the fantasies of forthcoming nods of approval (*Great sweater, Alice K. You look terrific.*). But above all, she means the emotional ties that come with good shopping: the shared experience with other women, the bonding.

That day, you see, Alice K. had gone shopping with her sister, Beth K. Beth K. had had a fight with her boss, and her infant daughter had been up three nights running with a cold, and Beth K. was feeling beleaguered and sad. "Let's go buy you something," Alice K. had said on the phone. "A new coat. Some new shoes."

Beth K., who doesn't believe in the healing power of new shoes quite as fervidly as Alice K., was reluctant at first, but Alice K. pressed and pressed, and finally they met downtown and spent the afternoon shopping. They drifted from store to store. They spent about an hour in one of those little lotion/potion shops that sells bath oils and scented powders, and they stood around opening little glass bottles and vials, sniffing things. They lingered for a long time in a store that sold nothing but accessories: they tried on hats and scarves, Alice K. bought a belt, Beth K., a new bag. In another, they looked at silk nightgowns and fancy underthings. In another, stockings and shoes.

By the end of the afternoon, neither had acquired much of anything—some earrings for Beth K., a camisole for Alice K.—but when they finally parted for the day, when Beth K. gave Alice K. a quick, hard hug and said, *"Thanks, that was great,"* Alice K. understood that something rather important had taken place between them, something that had to do with sharing and indulging, with connecting in a way that's at once intimate and stress-free.

Intimate and stress-free. Lying in bed, Alice K. contemplates that juxtaposition. At heart, you see, Alice K. finds it quite difficult to be truly close to other people, women as well as men. She's an incurable introvert, the sort of person who finds it terribly hard to get out of her own head for any length of time, to escape her own thoughts. That's part of the reason she's drawn to Ruth E., who's extroverted and talkative and practical and direct. She doesn't find Ruth E.'s presence burdensome because Ruth E. is so expert at moving things along, moving the conversation, moving the ideas, moving Alice K. from place to place in both the physical and emotional sense. But Ruth E. is the exception: more often than not, Alice K. finds it draining to be with other people for more than short periods of time. She longs for closeness and yet when it's at hand, she longs for escape, for privacy and retreat.

Which is why shopping can be such a wonderful solution. At one point that afternoon, Alice K. had drifted off toward a cosmetics counter while Beth K. looked at stockings across the way. For a few minutes, she'd sort of lost herself, standing there testing lipstick colors against the skin on her hand. Then, almost at the same moment, she and Beth K. had looked up, searching for each other across the store. Their eyes had met and Beth K. had grinned hugely, an expression of true delight in her eyes. It was as though Beth K. had said, *You're my sister. You're my sister and your presence in my life cheers me more than I can say.*

In that moment, Alice K. had felt a pang of tenderness

for Beth K. so strong she'd almost wanted to cry. It was so simple—just shopping together, just meandering around a department store—but also so real. No conversation necessary, no long dialogues about their lives, nothing overt required. There, just pawing through stockings and lipstick, they'd momentarily combined the best of both worlds, the best of solitude and closeness, the way only sisters and best friends can.

how to ask a stupid question

About two months into her relationship with Elliot M., Alice K. turned and asked him, in a rather whining, pained voice, "Do you think I'm pretty?"

He looked at her for a second like she had two heads, and in a flash, Alice K. understood: uh-oh, she had trapped him. Trapped him in the land of Stupid Questions.

Isn't that how it always happens? Say you're a guy. You've been seeing a woman for about eight weeks. Everything is going along smoothly, you're attracted to each other, you both feel comfortable, everything's fine, and then—wham!—out of the blue, she looks at you with that pained expression, her voice rises several octaves, and she hits you with one of those . . . those *questions*.

"Do you think I'm fat?" (Whine.)

"Do these pants look okay on me?" (Whimper.)

"Do you like my hair? Do you think I should cut it? *Are you sure?*" (Whine, whine, whimper, whimper.)

You gag. You choke. You have an intense feeling of déjà vu and it's an apt one, indeed: for you have been here before, and you'll be here again—trapped, just like Elliot M.

There is no right answer in the land of Stupid Questions. Alice K. knows that and so do you.

Late that night, lying in bed, Alice K. contemplated the stupid-question phenomenon. Where do they come from? Why do women act like this?

She considered. She and Elliot M. had been seeing each other for two months, so they'd entered that phase where he no longer felt compelled to woo her with his initial vigor. Early on, he'd lavished her with dinners, noticed her jewelry, complimented her on her shoes. And initially, because she had been taught that men lack kindness and soul and the ability to sustain long-term romances, Alice K. had kept her distance. Slowly, though, she began to warm to Elliot M.'s attention and let down her guard. For three or four weeks (the period before they slept together and really screwed things up), Alice K. and Elliot M. were actually on the same wavelength, relationshipwise, and—amazingly, and quite possibly for the only time ever in their entire union—they both seemed to want the same degree of closeness and intimacy.

And then something shifted. Maybe Elliot M. began to let down *his* guard. Or maybe he began to choke in the face of said closeness and intimacy. Or both. In any event, he seemed to ease up on the lavishing and the complimenting of shoes, and Alice K. began to worry. They'd sat at home that night watching a rented movie. *A movie?* she thought. *What does this mean? Why is Elliot M. no longer gazing at me across a candlelit table? Has he even noticed my new shoes?*

Other questions followed. *Was Elliot M. still attracted to her? Was there someone else? And now, just as she'd begun to think of the relationship as a Relationship, complete with implications of permanency and commitment and companionship on weekend nights, was he losing interest?*

Of course, she couldn't ask *those* questions because they would make her feel more vulnerable than she already felt. So she tried to scope out clues in a simpler way. *"Um, honey? Do you think I'm pretty?"*

Voilà—stupid question.

Alice K. shifted in the bed and thought some more.

Lurking behind such questions, she understood, were wag-onloads of insecurity and a host of problems with direct communication and self-esteem. *We ask these questions in order to test men,* she thought. Early on, a woman needs to know that if she masks her sexual insecurity in a vague (*i.e.,* stupid) question about a guy's ex-girlfriend (*i.e.,* "So, um, what did X look like?"), he won't pop back with a loutish response (*i.e.,* "God, she was good in bed"). Later, she needs to spot-check his level of long-term supportiveness: can he put up with a woman's tendency to get up in the morning at least twice a week, look in the mirror, and beg him for confirmation that she does not look exactly like Totie Fields? Can he stand the fact that nothing he says will really be good enough? And most important, can he help her through those moments?

The next day, Alice K. discussed this phenomenon with Ruth E., and they decided that women's stupid questions actually serve a noble purpose.

"It's protective," Ruth E. said. "It keeps you from having to talk about the big stuff."

"You mean like life and disappointment and vulnerability?"

"Exactly."

Alice K. looked at Ruth E. "But I hate asking them," she said. "They make me feel so . . . so stupid."

"That's because they *are* stupid," Ruth E. said. "They disguise real issues with shoe issues. With hair and thigh issues. Asking them makes you feel foolish and weak."

"So why do we keep asking them?"

"Because we're women."

Alice K. asked her what she meant, and Ruth E. went into one of her famous dialogues about the difference between the way men and women experience the world. Men live *in* their bodies, Ruth E. pointed out; women live outside of them. Women grow up thinking of their bodies as things that are viewed and touched by other people, as things that are compared, relentlessly, with the bodies of other women. Accordingly, even the most independent-thinking and self-possessed woman has fits of fear and insecurity, moments when her mind leaps out from inside her head and scrutinizes her body—and her boyfriend's former girlfriend's body, and the bodies of women in magazines and catalogs, and those of women everywhere around her—from the outside. At those moments, she is judging herself with extreme severity. She is quite sure that she doesn't measure up to the ideal du jour (thin thighs and small breasts; thin thighs and large breasts; toned thighs and muscular breasts; whatever it happens to be this week). And she is assuming two things: that men are judging her just as harshly, and that they find her lacking too.

The result? She needs a bit more confirmation than men do. She needs men to be nice.

Ruth E. concluded her dialogue and Alice K. nodded soberly. And that night, walking toward a restaurant with Elliot M., she looked at him and said, "Elliot . . . do you think these shoes make my feet look fat?" But she didn't mean it. Honest.

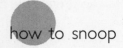

how to snoop

Here's another thing that happened in the first two months of Alice K.'s relationship: she snooped. She was at Elliot M.'s apartment, and he ran out to get a bottle of wine for dinner, and she snooped. She snooped through a stack of mail on his kitchen counter. She snooped through the pocket of a coat that was thrown across a chair. She snooped through an address book.

Why? Easy. She was looking for clues, trying to glean information about Elliot M.: where he'd been, or who he'd seen, or what he might be hiding.

Guess what else? All women snoop. Or, at least, all women want to from time to time. Big girls and little girls. Secure girls and frightened ones. Married, single, happy, sad—you name it. Sooner or later, no matter how averse to the practice she may be in theory, every woman in America is struck with a fit of curiosity or suspicion and left powerless to fight the urge. She must snoop. She simply must.

Ruth E. reminded Alice K. of this some time ago, over dinner. She'd been seeing some guy from her office, she'd been feeling vaguely suspicious about him, and she'd ended up confronting him about a former relationship with a woman named Eva B.

Alice K. asked, "How did you know about this Eva woman in the first place?"

Ruth E. said, "He wasn't around, so I looked through his calendar and there it was. Eva B., lunch. Eva B., dinner."

Alice K. and Ruth E. exchanged a knowing look. Ah, yes: the calendar snoop.

Ruth E.'s discovery, of course, was unusual. Nine times out of ten, women find little of import on their small scavenger hunts: gas-station receipts, maybe. Or matchbooks or old handkerchiefs (which can get pretty disgusting, if you ask Alice K.). But by the same token, Alice K. suspects that finding something is really beside the point. Probe the hearts and souls of most woman snoops and you will discover that this is really not about spying or curiosity at all; it's about insecurity, self-destruction, and control.

Here are Alice K.'s three stages of snooping.

1) Snooping 101. This is the initial, low-level stage, like the one she did at Elliot M's. You're at his house. You're in the bathroom brushing your teeth. You roam a little bit and cast a curious eye on the surface of things. You look on top of the dresser. The desk. Perhaps you peek into his refriger-

ator to see if the contents suggest an ability to cook; perhaps not. At this point, you're really only looking for small hints, clues about his behavior or personality. How tidy is he? How discreet? If he has a box of Trojans sitting on his night table, you'll be a little put off. If his closets are neat and brimming with attractive shirts, you'll like him.

This sort of snooping usually takes place at the beginning of a romance. Alice K. calls it the "getting-to-know-you snoop."

2) Snooping 201. You graduate to this phase at the point in a relationship when you've begun to develop tensions and insecurities. Now, you snoop below the surface. You go into desk drawers and pants pockets when he's not at home. You look for bigger clues about his life and history. Is there someone else? Who was there before you? What was she like? And how do you stack up?

3) Advanced Snooping. Here, you move from drawers to documents. You read old letters and credit-card bills (He blew $90 at that new Italian place without you? *What?*). You open mail. You actually wait for him to leave the house so you can flip through the Rolodex in search of unfamiliar female names. At this point, an element of desperation has entered the process. You want information. You want the upper hand.

And that, as Alice K. understands it, is the key. The upper hand. Information is power, and women want to control the flow of facts. That is why we're so ruthless about snooping, so devious and underhanded. If a woman can happily answer the questions she's afraid to ask (Do you really love me? How much? More than you loved her?), she'll feel safe, secure, in control. On the other hand, if she finds documentation of roses sent to someone else, if she finds a level of passion in an old letter that's never been expressed to her, at least she'll be braced for the hurt.

Of course, all of this makes a girl feel lousy. She feels stupid for having been reduced to a snoop. She realizes she's acting out of insecurity. She understands that it's valid and reasonable and none of her business for a man to have loved other people before her.

Worst of all, if a woman does happen to stumble on some critical information, she's in a terrible bind. Snoop-gathered facts are completely useless unless you're willing to admit that you've been engaged in this immature and privacy-invading behavior. That's why snooping is so self-destructive. Alice K. will never forget the time that Mr. Cruel was away for a weekend and she spent two whole days pawing through a box of letters he'd kept from old girlfriends. One was from a woman she'd never heard of, someone named Tiffany. An-other wrote a long, descriptive letter about some "hot week-end" they'd spent together in the country. Alice K. spent the next six months preoccupied with these pieces of informa-tion. *He went out with a woman who used the word 'hot'? Tiffany? Who the hell was Tiffany?* It made her feel awful and of course she couldn't say a word.

Beth K. says she's been "snoop free" for three years, since she got married. "I won't do it anymore," she says. "It's like quitting smoking or something. You know it's bad and you just have to force yourself not to do it."

But Alice K. thinks that this is a rare decision. She and Ruth E. talked about it recently, and Ruth E. described snooping as a reality of womanhood and female insecurity, a biological urge, not unlike the drive to have babies. "I've done it before and I'll do it again," Ruth E. said. "It's terri-ble, there's no justification for it. But I'll do it."

Alice K. nodded soberly.

"Girls are so bad," Ruth E. said. Then she paused and added, "It's a good thing we're cute."

pseudo-spa ii: the all-shoe weekend

Alice K.'s U-Do-It All-Shoe Weekend, an advanced version of the U-Do-It Pseudo-Spa Experience, begins when you face two more simple facts:

1. You are a woman, so you are prone to feelings of depression and existential despair.
2. One of the only things that truly cheers you when you feel depressed and existentially despairing is the experience of buying new shoes.

That's how Alice K. happened upon the U-Do-It All-Shoe weekend. She was feeling hopeless and sad. Lethargic and bloated and premenstrual. Then she had a thought: "If these were the '80s, I'd have to start a diet and head to the gym. But no! The '80s are long gone! To hell with 800-calorie-a-day diets! To hell with cottage cheese and aerobics class! What I really need is some new shoes!"

And lo, the Alice K. Pseudo-Spa U-Do-It All-Shoe Weekend was born.

Here's how U-Do-It.

- Phone a supportive friend, who, as in the U-Do-It Pseudo-Spa Experience, will be known as your "Spa Partner."
- With the aid of Spa Partner, locate an area that's in close proximity to many shoe outlets. New York is fine if you have vast amounts of disposable income, but this being the recessionary '90s, it's wiser to pick somewhere more sensible, such as one of those Dream Malls which contain, among others, a 9 West outlet, a Saks Fifth Avenue outlet, a Nordstrom's outlet, and a Bloomingdale's outlet. (Hint: there's a great one in Philadelphia.)
- When you and Spa Partner determine destination, squeal with glee. (Example: "Ooooooh!")
- Pack up your Alice K. U-Do-It All-Shoe Weekend wardrobe. This should consist of at least one (1) particularly shoe-friendly shopping

outfit which *(a)* clearly exposes the foot and ankle area, thereby facilitating the unobstructed viewing of shoes, and *(b)* requires no elaborate maneuvers to get in or out of, thereby facilitating the fast and efficient trying on of shoes. You may also bring one pair of really bad or worn-out shoes in order to reinforce your compelling need for new ones.

- Spend a vast sum of money getting to your destination. Fly! Go first class on the train! Rationalize that your travel expenses are roughly equal to the cost of a single pair of shoes in your home town, whereas you will be able to buy at least three (3) pairs for that price at the Saks outlet alone. Therefore, you are saving scads of money just by going there (or something like that).

- Arrive at Pseudo-Spa destination. Travel to expensive hotel (follow instructions for rationalization above). Drink wine, discuss shoe needs. Commiserate on inherent difficulty of finding neutral-colored pumps that don't look "old-ladyish." Nod seriously when Spa Partner says, "Yes, neutral is really tough."

- Retire early for Alice K. Pre-All-Shoe-Weekend beauty rest. Sleep for eleven hours.

- Awake. Drink approximately fourteen cups of coffee in order to rev up adrenal glands and prepare yourself for day's activities.

- Drive to mega mall, park, enter. Head first to Saks outlet and execute preliminary warm-ups by browsing through designer clothing department. Try on assorted designer garments and decide you really don't need a black velvet Donna Karan minidress, even though it's only $95, marked down from $179.99. Feel proud of your restraint.

- Now go to shoe department. Abandon restraint. Note table after table after table of shoe boxes, all neatly laid out by size and containing nearly unimaginable shoe bargains. Via Spiga pumps for $39.95, marked down from $165. Ferragamo shoes for $50, marked down from nearly $200. Saks brand name, $29.95, marked down from $120. Feel your blood pressure escalate and your adrenaline begin to pump.

- Go into high shoe frenzy. Stand in front of mirror with Spa Partner, an olive pump on one foot, a red suede pump on another, and three more boxes of shoes in your arms. Observe onset of serious shoe binge symptoms (jaw drops, eyes take on wild and rabid expression) and realize it is quite possible that you will buy all five pairs.

- Try on pair of high-heeled, dusty blue suede pumps with exceptionally elegant line. Realize you will probably never have occasion to actually wear them, but try to rationalize the purchase anyway. Ask Spa Partner, "But what if I end up buying a really elegant dusty blue cocktail dress sometime ... won't I *need* these?" Debate purchase for at least twenty minutes.

- Finally weed Saks purchases down to three pairs of shoes (olive pumps, red suede pumps, olive suede flats; total cost: $164.60). Feel proud of yourself for passing up not only dusty blue heels but also a really cool pair of violet suede pumps.

- Stand in mall corridor. Take deep breaths. Calm down. Then go to Macy's outlet.

- Approach Macy's shoe department. Observe rack upon rack of shoes of every conceivable color and shape. Flats and sling-backs and shoe boots and pumps. Shoes with straps and buttons and ties. Gasp, then plunge in with vigor.

- Try on twenty-six pairs of shoes within about twenty minutes. Express disbelief at prices: $140 black heels marked down to $20. Black-and-purple leather flats marked down to $16. *Sixteen!* Red suede flats for $6.59! Feel yourself beginning to lose control and notice that your head is reeling. Run amok. Grab shoes off rack, exchanging frenzied dialogue with Spa Partner:
"Look! Peach flats!"
"Oooooh! But look at those rose-colored suede ones!"
"Oooooh!"
"And over there! Moss sling-backs!"
"Oooooh!"

- Take brief break and observe other women in high shoe frenzy. Nod and smile as nearby young, pregnant woman with armload of shoe boxes slips on a pair of brown leather pumps and says, "Ohmygod, this is *so much fun!*" Realize that shoe shopping is for women what spectator sports are for men: an activity that truly engages and thrills, a common experience that binds our gender. Feel twinge of pride at being female.

- Stand with many boxes of shoes and insist to Spa Partner that you cannot buy seven pairs of shoes in one day, then permit Spa Partner (without much difficulty) to convince you otherwise. Have her point to pair of black velvet flats which, if purchased, will constitute seventh purchase of day, and listen as she says, "You *have* to buy them! How can you not?" Agree, then convince her to buy black suede shoe boots even though she just bought a pair of black leather shoe boots last month and hasn't even worn them yet ("Yeah, but these are *suede!*").

- Purchase four (4) pairs of shoes. When salesclerk looks at your out-of-state driver's license and asks how long you've been in town, tell her, "Oh, about twelve hours." When she raises eyebrows and says, "Twelve hours and you're already shopping?" smile sheepishly and reach for your very large shopping bag. Realize that you have had a wild change of perspective: you have spent $82.96—the likely cost of a single pair at home—and the thought of buying seven pairs of shoes in a day now seems perfectly reasonable.

- Investigate shoe departments at 9 West and Bloomingdale's, but observe that you have become jaded. Point to pair of red suede flats (remember—yours only cost $6.95) and say, "Thirty-five bucks for these? Hah!"

- Wend your way back to car. Express amazement when Spa Partner informs you that four hours have elapsed—it feels like about thirty minutes. Drive back to hotel, line new shoes up on carpet, and admire. Look at Spa Partner's purple suede flats and say, "Great shoes!" Try on brown suede Via Spiga's and listen as Spa Partner says, "Great shoes!" Continue this exercise for approximately forty-five minutes.

- Sit down with Spa Partner and try to assess the amount of time you have both spent thinking and talking about shoes within the past eighteen hours. Decide it's about six, possibly more.

- Dress for dinner. Wear new shoes. Go off to restaurant, discuss other topics during dinner (men, work), and feel your heart begin to sink at the thought of life's essential meaninglessness. Then think of new shoes and brighten. Return discussion to footwear. Talk with Spa Partner about how a great pair of shoes can change your whole outlook on life. Talk about how it feels to look down and see your feet encased in some lovely new color and shape. How your very stride can acquire a certain confidence just by dint of a fabulous shoe.

- Return to the hotel, admire shoes once more, and retire for second beauty rest. Awake eleven hours later and contemplate going out for a pedicure. Decide that would be "too ironic." Then pack shoes in a huge bag, and prepare to head home, safe in the knowledge that no matter what else happens to you in life, at least you'll have one hell of a well-turned ankle.

an open letter to the miss america commission

Once, when Alice K. was feeling depressed, full of existential despair, and unable to arrange a U-Do-It All-Shoe Weekend, she sat at her desk and typed the following letter to the Miss America Commission.

Dear Commission Members,

Hello. My name is Alice K. and I am writing because I have a few ideas that might make your annual pageant a little more successful.

I understand that in the last year or so, you have been attempting to redirect the pageant yourselves in an effort to make the contestants appear more "real" to the average American woman. I admire that impulse, but it seems to me that most of your ideas fall a bit short. So now the contestants have to do their own hair and makeup. Hmmmm. So now they can wear pants instead of gowns. Ho-hum.

It seems to me that far more radical changes are in order. If you truly want to make the average American woman relate to your contestants, you need to focus on women whose lives genuinely resemble our own.

Luckily, I have some ideas.

Imagine, if you will, the following:

First, live, from the fabulous Trump Plaza in fabulous Atlantic City . . .

The 1994 Miss Vague Competition

Yes! Meet fifty-two stellar examples of complete confusion, total lack of direction, and essential uncertainty about the meaning of life! From across the nation (and Guam!), the Miss Vague Competition draws women in the throes of career crises, women who cannot decide whether or not to bear children, and women whose sense of self is so uncertain and ill-formed that they can barely decide what they want for breakfast, let alone what they want out of life. Some sample contestants: there's the reigning Miss Vague of West Virginia, who's been going out with the same guy for eleven years and still doesn't know if she wants to marry him. There's the reigning Miss Vague of Oklahoma, who dropped out of nursing school because she couldn't stand the sight of blood, then opened a nail salon in Oklahoma City because she didn't know what else to do, and is now totally disenchanted with her life and completely unsure about what to do next. And there's the reigning Miss Vague of Rhode Island, who spends much of her time roaming the streets of downtown Providence muttering, "Huh?" Which one of these lovely young women will become the next Miss Vague champion: Stay tuned!

Next? Live from the fabulous Desert Sands Hotel in beautiful Las Vegas . . .

The 1994 Miss Anxious Competition

These lovely American beauties have competed in regional pageants across the nation, where they've scored points for high blood pressure, vastly overcommitted work schedules, and accumulation of unused vacation days. In order to determine overall levels of stress, our distinguished panel of judges will be paying close attention this year to the girls' heart rates, coffee- and cigarette-consumption levels, and general sleep-and-sweat patterns. A special Miss Fatigue award will also be granted to the girl who scores highest on the Individual Filofax Competition, which measures the appointment book's overall heft and density. And as an extra treat for our viewing audience, our contestants will also take part in a fabulous Parade of Paranoias, in which each local Miss Anxious is allotted two minutes to recount the particular fears, obsessions, and ruminations that keep her awake long into the night. What an event!

Next? Live, from the perfectly ordinary Motel 6 on the nondescript fringes of Dubuque, Iowa . . .

The 1994 Miss Mediocre Pageant

Here, you'll meet fifty-two absolutely unremarkable women from all corners of our fine nation. Women with little or no talent or ambition! Women with really boring jobs! Women with blotchy skin, bad teeth, and overworked hair! Minimum requirements for entry include a C average through high school, a lack of hobbies, pets, or other outside interests, and a basic aversion to change, personal growth, and accomplishment. You'll meet Miss Mediocre of Minnesota, who lives in a bland two-bedroom apartment outside the Twin Cities, works as a clerk in a 7-Eleven, and hasn't gone out on a date in seven years. You'll meet Miss Mediocre of Arizona, who lives in a trailer park in Sun City and hasn't read a book since she graduated from high school. And you'll meet the winner of the Regional Mediocrity Championships in New England, Miss Mediocre of Connecticut, who stunned last year's judges in the special interview segment by failing to come up with even one remotely interesting thing to say about her life. Finally, a competition for women you can relate to.

This, of course, is just the beginning. If real-life pageants for real-life women begin to catch on, we could establish a slew of ancillary competitions. We could have the *Miss Slightly Overweight Pageant,* where contestants would be judged on poor dietary habits, upper arm jiggle, and inappropriateness of appearance in leggings. We could have the *Miss Mildly Depressed Pageant,* where girls from all over the nation would basically sit around and complain. We could have the *Miss Untidy* competition, where girls would match skills on car clutter, home dust accumulation, and laundry procrastination techniques. We could even have the *Miss Not-Very-Good-In-The-Kitchen Pageant,* where contestants would be rated on blandness of spicing techniques, inability to cut up a chicken, and basic lack of culinary imagination.

Can't you imagine it? It'll be great. No matter how basic, boring, or unaccomplished, women everywhere will be able to excel at something. And from coast to coast, you'll be able to turn on your TV and hear the dulcet tones of Bert Parks singing, "There she is, Miss Not-Very-Good-In-The-Kitchen . . ."

In sum, Commission members, I think these are fine ideas and I hope you will consider them. Please don't hesitate to get back to me if I may be of any further assistance. Thank you for your time.

Sincerely,
Alice K.

the indignities of being female

Beth K. and Alice K. are sitting in a restaurant and Beth K. is recounting an exceptionally painful tale, a story that, to Alice K., speaks to the unique anguish of being a woman.

"It was awful," she says, a slight quiver in her voice. "I was standing there, waiting for a cab, and I got one of those holes in the big toe of my stocking—you know how that happens? The nylon gets stretched all tight around your toe and it's like a knife. It starts cutting off the circulation to your entire foot."

Beth K. shivers. "I swear," she says. "It's worse than labor."

Alice K. nods soberly. Ah, yes. The indignities of being female.

Not that there aren't plenty of non-gender-specific sources of indignity out there for all of us—any man, woman, or child who's ever been to the dentist, for instance, can testify to the sense of humiliation and loss of control one feels when one is strapped to a chair, head yanked back, mouth jammed full of metal instruments, and then asked to respond to a series of questions ("So, how's work?" "Ine." "And the family?" "Ood." And so on.). Likewise, men have to endure a variety of undignified, unpleasant conditions unique to their gender (the phrase "premature ejaculation" springs to mind).

But women's lives are peppered with such small realities, aspects of life that don't necessarily impair our ability to function but that are nonetheless painful, embarrassing, and decidedly undignified. Instruments, pieces of apparel, and tools of daily life that no male would ever design for himself. Procedures that would send a chill through the soul of even the most hardened he-man. And small moments that remind us, time and again, of how downright uncomfortable it can be to live in a world that was shaped largely by men—by people, in other words, who have never had to wrestle their way into a pair of nylons, teeter across a brick sidewalk in high heels, or look up from a cold table at a strange man wielding a speculum.

Indeed. Once, after a particularly brutal trip to the gynecologist (don't ask), Alice K. and Ruth E. sat down and compiled a woman's guide to the indignities of being female.

stockings

Stockings top the list, and this is not surprising. As anyone who's mastered the simultaneously delicate and gymnastic art of hoisting a long, thin nylon tube up above her thighs knows, stockings are a major source of indignity in and of themselves. Consider this short list of hosiery ills:

- Stockings that rip above the knee, causing a piece of flesh from your thigh to burst through the nylon, where it becomes trapped, vise-like, causing a searing pain to shoot through your leg every time you try to move, cross, or bend it.
- Stockings that refuse to obey the laws of gravity and, instead, insist on slipping downward, downward, downward through the day, thereby bagging at the knees and ankles and creating an exceedingly uncom-fortable case of "crotch sag," a syndrome whose only remedy is a mad dash to the ladies' room and an unsightly series of hiking and stretching exercises not unlike deep knee bends.
- Being in between stocking sizes, so that you have to endure either the phenomenon of slippage (see above) or an even more discomfitting state, being trapped in too-small stockings that won't go up all the way, leaving a two-inch gap between the crotch of the stocking and the crotch of the wearer. This is incredibly uncomfortable, even more so because the waistband of the too-small stockings also hits you at the hips, where it digs into your skin like a knife.

female shoes, clothing mishaps ——————————————————————

High heels come in second on the appearance/apparel list, with special emphasis on:

- Smushed-toe syndrome, which occurs when you actually have to wear the four-inch heels that looked so fab in the shoe store for more than about two minutes.
- Frightened-colt syndrome, which occurs every time you have to walk in heels with a tall man who's in a hurry. (This is a particular indignity if it takes place on a brick or cobblestone street.)
- Uncooperative clothing, i.e., moments when your clothes suddenly turn on you. When you look down at a meeting, say, and realize that your blouse has sagged open, allowing full view of your bra. Or that your skirt has hiked itself up too high, exposing either too much slip or too much leg. Or those many, many moments when your apparel

seems to have a mind of its own. The skirt that spontaneously turns, leaving the rear zipper over by your hip. The slip that spontaneously hikes its way up your thighs, forcing you to reach up and grab it surreptitiously. Or the bra (shudder) that spontaneously pops.

menstruation _____

A woman's menstrual cycle is the physiological counterpart of her stockings, an inherent and constant source of indignity. Premenstrual anything (bloat, break-outs, cramps, syndrome) are high on the list; so are an astonishing number of things that have to do with tampons:

- The tampon you can't get unwrapped (and if you do not adhere to Alice K.'s Theory of Purse Size Based on Menstruation, this will be the only one in your possession).
- The tampon you accidentally drop in the public toilet (ditto: this will be your only one).
- The tampon with the broken string.
- The leaking tampon (enough said).
- The slightly dislodged tampon, which causes a severe discomfort not unlike hole-in-toe-of-stocking syndrome.

sex, contraception, and female health _____

Again, many, many candidates. The top contenders:

- The diaphragm that won't go in.
- The contraceptive sponge that won't come out.
- The cervical cap that won't go in or come out.
- The diaphragm that spontaneously flings itself out of your purse while you are in a public place (e.g., on the bus).
- The full pelvic exam.

- The phrase, "Just put your feet in the stirrups and scoot down ... a little further ... a little further ... just a little further."
- And last, but certainly not least, that central reality that truly separates the men from the women in heterosexual society: post-coital oozing.

why women should be called girls

Fact 1: Alice K. is a feminist.

Fact 2: Alice K. has no trouble referring to herself as a "girl."

Do you have a problem with that? Are you threatened or offended by the term? If so, Alice K. thinks you should stop reading right now, go take a long, hot bath, maybe paint your toenails, spend some time leafing through a trashy women's magazine, and try to remember what's nice about feeling female.

Get it?

It's not that Alice K. disagrees entirely with criticism of the term. At times, she thinks using it is wholly inappropriate and demeaning—she would never, for example, refer to equal rights as a "girls' issue." But she also believes that when it's used in the proper context, with the proper tone, the word "girl" can be very useful, providing women with some critical life-simplifying tools.

For instance:

1. It provides women with a handy way to protect their privacy. If you're trying to avoid a dialogue with a man, for example, you simply wave your hand and say, "Oh, don't worry about it—this is a *girl* thing." Even the most bravely feministic man will automatically assume you're talking about some hideous oozing cyst or vaginal discharge and will be only too willing to change the subject.

2. It also provides a handy way to preserve independence. If you need a night alone, or a night out with a close friend, you simply say, "This dinner is just girls—you wouldn't be interested." This tactic is similar to the privacy-protector above: no matter how serious your plans, the man will instantly imagine a horde of women cackling about shoes, contraception, and other women, and he will have no desire to intrude or interfere with your solitude.

3. It offers women, most of whom are secretly burdened by a poorly understood perfectionist gene that causes them to be ceaselessly hard on themselves, a critical way to excuse the inevitable moment of imperfection (*e.g.,* the random bout of weakness or immaturity, the occasional shopping binge, or the premenstrual moment of explosive rage). "Oooops!" you say. "Sorry! Just acting like a girl." The man you say this to may roll his eyes or take on an expression of disgust; no matter—the point is, you'll have given yourself permission to do something you rarely do: let yourself off the hook.

Alice K. also believes that the use of the word "girl" can have important social and personal implications. Really. Alice K. has become so tired of the word "woman." It is so serious, so weighty. You can't utter a phrase like "women's issues" or "women's health" or "women's rights" without being flooded with a host of grave realities: abortion and equal pay and rape and battering and sexism and breast cancer and what have you. And although Alice K. believes in her soul that the word *woman* needs to be serious and weighty, that it ought to have as much heft and weight as the word *man,* she also believes there's a downside. When you spend that much energy attempting to define yourself as a Woman—a powerful, deserving, equal being who can do everything a man can—you can lose sight of what it's like to be a girl—a powerful, deserving, equal being who's *also* capable of being vulnerable and playful, who's drawn toward what are known (for good or ill) as "feminine" things like intimacy or feelings or the occasional new suede jacket.

So when someone bridles at the word "girl," a part of Alice K. always wonders if he or she is implying that those aspects of women's lives or natures are somehow embarrassing, or unimportant, or cause for shame. And to not enjoy an occasional indulgence in the term is, in her mind, to lose sight of some of the things that are nice about the difference between the genders. There is something very comforting about reverting to the status of "girl." It helps give Alice K. permission to sit around giggling with Ruth E. To stand around in the ladies' room at work gabbing about men and hair-care products. To let go of the desperate seriousness with which she pursues the business of being a big, strong, grown-up Woman.

Ruth E. puts it most succinctly: "A girl," she says, "is a woman with a sense of humor."

ALICE K. IN LOVE, PART II: MEETING MR. DANGER

One month later:

Alice K. (not her real initial) lies in bed, filled with tension, anxiety, and guilt.

Alice K., you see, has met Mr. Danger.

Of course, Mr. Danger is not his real name. His real name is Jack S., but Alice K. knew him as Mr. Danger as soon as she laid eyes upon him. She met him at a party she'd attended with Elliot M., running into him in the kitchen while Elliot M. was in another room.

Mr. Danger was tall and dark and rangy-looking. Mr. Danger wore faded blue jeans and black cowboy boots and a white t-shirt. Mr. Danger had a strong jaw and intense eyes and thick, dark hair, a strand of which curled seductively across his forehead. A friend of Elliot M.'s introduced them, and Mr. Danger smiled coyly and said hello, and Alice K. nearly dropped her beer.

Oh my God, she thought, recognizing his type immediately. *This is one of those handsome, elusive, heart breaking men who turns smart, capable women into obsessive, competitive, crying fools, and if I had an ounce of common sense, I'd walk out of this kitchen right now and never even look him in the eye.*

At which point, of course, Alice K.'s common sense made a beeline for the front door and she found herself gazing up into Mr. Danger's eyes and longing to engage him in a conversation.

She lies in bed, contemplating what happened next. They talked for half an hour. Mr. Danger turned out to be an artist (danger!) who played the drums in a local band called The Ice Picks of Love (danger! danger!) and who appeared to lead a rather wild and footloose life: painting by day, practicing with the band by night, traveling to exotic places on vacations, staying up for forty-eight hours at a stretch on wild weekends in New York *(danger! danger!)*.

Warning bells went off in Alice K.'s head repeatedly. He used the word "party" as a verb more than once. Bad sign. He talked vaguely about his future, indicating that he wasn't really sure if he wanted to be a painter or a musician or maybe, you know, move to Vermont someday and do, like, you know, carpentry or something. Very bad sign.

But Alice K. couldn't help herself. The good side of her brain kept whispering little messages: *Stay away! He's unsettled! He's the kind of man who makes women crazy! He's nothing like Elliot M., who's stable and kind and interested in a genuine long-term relationship.* But as soon as she thought these things, the bad side of her brain would butt in and whisper the single phrase: *God, he's cute.*

What is wrong with me? Alice K. wonders, tossing in her bed. *Why do I find men like this attractive? Why does a man like this make me look at Elliot M. and think . . . blah?*

For that's exactly what happened next. Elliot M. walked into the kitchen, came up to Alice K., and put his arm around her, and Alice K. had this horrible moment of wishing that the kitchen floor would open right then and there and swallow him up. Next to Mr. Danger, he looked so . . . so average. So normal. In a flash, Alice K. imagined introducing him—*This is my boyfriend, Elliot M. He's a computer consultant*—but she simply couldn't get herself to say that. Somehow it felt to Alice K. that admitting her liaison with a nice, sweet computer consultant like Elliot M. would expose something to Mr. Danger about her own life or personality, reveal her as much more boring and plain and unadventuresome than the women he no doubt found attractive. So she shied away from Elliot M. just a little and introduced him to Mr. Danger simply as "my friend."

Soon after that, Elliot M. disappeared into the bathroom, and Mr. Danger leaned toward Alice K. and said, "So, The Ice Picks of Love are playing at the Cove for a couple of weeks. . . . Want me to put you on the guest list?" And against all her better judgment, Alice K. heard herself say, as gaily and casually as she could, "Sure, I'd love to." Mr. Danger said "Great," and then he said something about going out for a drink afterward, and then he winked at her, and then he said he had to leave. As he walked out of the kitchen, he brushed past her and gave her arm a little squeeze, and Alice K. felt herself literally swoon.

Later that night, of course, Alice K. found Elliot M. grating on her nerves. She found herself scrutinizing his wardrobe (khaki pants, sneakers) and his hair (thinning a little) and thinking, *shit, kinda . . . well, just not all that sexy.*

She found herself noticing how cautiously he drove the car, and wishing he'd rev the engine just a bit, or go speeding around a corner. And she found herself wanting to test him, wanting to ask if he'd ever even heard of The Ice Picks of Love, and realizing all the while that what she really wanted to do was to trap him into admitting that he simply wasn't as cool a man as Mr. Danger.

But what does that even mean? Alice K. wonders, lying awake and staring at the ceiling. *What is 'cool'?* When they got home, Elliot M. went right to bed and she stayed up in the living room, pretending to read, because at the moment she couldn't stand the idea of getting into bed with him and having him want to touch her and knowing she'd be feeling tense and withdrawn and conflicted. But now she looks at Elliot M., who's sleeping soundly beside her. He does look sweet, she thinks. Those long eyelashes. Those sturdy shoulders.

Alice K. feels a stab of guilt. She forces herself to think about some of the things that attract her to Elliot M.: his gentle manner, his intelligence and insight, the way he really *listens* to her when she talks about things that matter. She acknowledges that her attraction to Mr. Danger has to do with her fear of being close to Elliot M., of being in a relationship with a real possibility of intimacy. And she thinks, *Okay, I will be mature here. I will not run away from Elliot M. I will forget about Mr. Danger and I will not go hear The Ice Picks of Love.*

She turns on her side and watches Elliot M. as he sleeps. And then, all of a sudden, something happens, something that makes Alice K. want to leap out of the bed and dash for the phone and call up Mr. Danger and beg him to take her away.

Yes, there's no mistaking it. Lying there asleep, Elliot M. has drooled on the pillow.

A few days later:

Alice K. lies in bed, contemplating the fine line between boredom and lust.

Alice K., you see, has spent the better part of the past week feeling quietly fed up with Elliot M., and secretly lusting after Mr. Danger, and this new obsession troubles her and keeps her awake long into the night.

Is she lusting after Mr. Danger because she's feeling bored with Elliot M.? Is she feeling bored with Elliot M. because she's lusting after Mr. Danger? Is there any real difference?

Alice K. fights the urge to pull the covers up over her

head and lie there moaning. *What is this?* she wonders. *Why am I investing a man I barely know with so much power simply because he looks good in cowboy boots?*

For that is precisely what Alice K. has done in the days since she met Mr. Danger. She has surrendered her hopes and dreams and fantasies to the very idea of him. She has allowed him to become the potential solution to everything that's wrong in her life, to everything that's missing or unanswered in her relationship with Elliot M. Never mind that she's only spent about thirty minutes actually talking to Mr. Danger. Never mind that, on a purely objective level, he doesn't seem like a guy who's looking to settle down with one woman any time soon. All that fades when she thinks about Mr. Danger.

This is what's happened between them in her fantasies since they met: she has shown up at the bar where he plays; they have made serious, heavy-duty eye contact throughout the band's set; they have sat together at a darkened table at the end of the night; she has poured her heart out to him; he has gazed into her eyes and told her he's never met anyone like her; they have left the bar and kissed passionately under the stars; they . . . well, you get the idea.

One part of Alice K.'s mind knows this is an absurd set of fantasies and another part can't stop them. One part of Alice K. realizes that her sudden infatuation with a near stranger is directly tied to her ambivalence about closeness in relationships, and another part says, *So what?* One part of Alice K. understands that she ought to deal with her conflicted feelings about intimacy and dependence, and another part says, *Oh, fuck the self-analysis: I just want to feel excited.*

Alice K. contemplates that thought. It's not true that Elliot M. bores her, really. They actually have a lot in common, and over the past few months, they've had many, many pleasant times together: they cook dinners together, they go to the movies together, they share their favorite books with each other, they even had a lovely romantic weekend at an inn in the country, complete with candlelit dinners and long walks in the woods. But Alice K. has come to that weird point in the relationship, where the novelty of the union has worn off, the feelings of courtship have wound down into feelings of stability, and the prospect of being in a secure relationship has degenerated into a profound fear of being trapped.

Hence the attraction to Mr. Danger, who represents the thrill of fantasy, the allure of pursuit. This understanding upsets Alice K., and she begins to despair in the night. *Why can't I just be happy with reality?* she wonders. *Why can't I appreciate what's right here in front of me? And why does a stable relationship make me feel so ill-at-ease?*

Of course, Alice K. has been asking herself these questions for some time now. Over the course of the past month, as she and Elliot M. have spent more time together, she's often felt as though she's watching the two of them together from a distance, measuring his suitability as a partner. She'll watch him do the dishes after dinner and think, *Yes! A good man! He'd be a good husband!* And then she'll catch him picking his nose behind his newspaper at the breakfast table and that earlier feeling will crash. *Argh! He picks his nose! Get him out of my life!*

But it's not just the occasional episode of nose picking. Lying there in bed, Alice K. thinks back to an incident several nights ago, when she walked into the bathroom and watched Elliot M. flossing his teeth. Elliot M. is a dedicated flosser, the kind of guy who simply won't go to bed until he's picked and brushed and rubber-tipped and flossed his teeth to a furious degree of cleanliness. Standing there in the bathroom, watching him in mid-ritual, Alice K. found herself struggling with the impulse to scream. *He is so damn . . . responsible,* she thought. Elliot M. flosses his teeth, and he pays his bills on time, and he reconciles his checking account every month, and he changes the oil in his car on a regular basis, and Alice K. can't help it: watching Elliot M. responsibly executing all these little duties and tasks is beginning to give her a paralyzing feeling of dread, an overwhelming sense of the banality of everyday existence.

This is what life with Elliot M. would be like, she thought, standing there watching him in the mirror. *Flossing and doing errands and paying bills and acting like grown-ups.* And with that thought, Alice K. began to long for something different: she longed for her single days, when she could idealize romance, instead of struggling to tolerate its less passionate moments; she longed for the fantasy of idyllic love, rather than the ordinariness of real love; she longed for . . . Mr. Danger.

And so began the Ritualistic Polling of Select Girlfriends. Following the flossing episode, Alice K. spent two days phoning a group of women friends for advice: should she give in to this growing feeling of being trapped and go see Mr. Danger and The Ice Picks of Love? Of course, Alice K. only chose a particular set of girlfriends for this mission: single girlfriends, girlfriends who didn't really know Alice K. all that well and who probably would have resented her departure into coupledom with Elliot M., girlfriends who would come down on the side of passion and adventure. (In other words, Alice K. did not phone her sister, Beth K.) She was also careful to word her descriptions in a way that would guarantee support for the foray away from Elliot M., a semiconscious tactic that involved taking no responsibility for her own conflicted feelings and blaming everything on Elliot M. instead.

It's not that I don't care about Elliot M., I really do, she told one friend, a woman she hadn't seen in more than a year. *But I'm just feeling—I don't know—like he wants too much from me.*

I just miss my independence, she told another (a former coworker from several years back; single and desperate about it). *Elliot M. is so . . . well, it's like all of a sudden we're spending every weekend together and he kind of expects us to act like this* couple, *you know, capital "c," and . . .*

103

And so on. All of the girlfriends, of course, told Alice K. to march right out and see The Ice Picks of Love. *It's not like you're* married *to Elliot M. or anything,* they said. *You* should *be jealous of your independence.* And although Alice K. was aware of the fact that she wasn't polling anyone like Beth K., anyone who understood that part of being in a relationship means living through times when you're doubting or bored, she ended all these phone conversations feeling buoyed and secretly thrilled. *I'll do it,* she thought. *I'll go.*

So now she lies in bed wondering if she really has the will to go through with it. Can she go see The Ice Picks of Love without telling Elliot M. what it means? If she does go, will she try to make contact with Mr. Danger? And then, suddenly, an even more frightening question leaps to Alice K.'s mind, something so scary it makes her sit bolt upright in bed.

Oh my God, she thinks. *What will I wear?*

One week later:

Alice K. lies in bed, writhing with guilt, anxiety, and confusion: it is a Sunday night, you see, and Alice K. has spent the previous Saturday evening with Mr. Danger.

Alice K. is feeling guilty about this, of course, because at the moment she is lying in bed with Elliot M., and this, in turn, makes her feel anxious: Alice K. invited Elliot M. to spend the night tonight because she felt badly about her foray to see Mr. Danger, and a part of her realizes this. But another part of her wishes that Elliot M. would get the hell out of her bed and go home so she could lie there and fret in peace. And this, needless to say, makes Alice K. feel confused.

Elliot M., of course, doesn't know anything specific about Mr. Danger. Alice K. merely told him that she was going out with Ruth E. which was only sort of a lie because she did, in fact, make Ruth E. accompany her to the bar where Mr. Danger's band was playing. Still, Alice K. realizes that she has crossed over some kind of line in the honesty-and-full-

Alice H.'s Wish List, Part 3
The Man-O-Mixer
Magic Personality-Meshing Machine

How many times has this happened to you? You fall for Guy A, who's sweet and kind and compliments you on your shoes, thereby making you feel safe and warm and comfortable. Then you meet Guy B, who's manly and virile and remote and unpredictable, and who makes you swoon one minute and feel eerily on edge the next. Drawn to both men, you see the two of them for a while and feel perfectly happy because Guy A meets your closeness and intimacy needs while Guy B meets your distance and space needs. This proceeds nicely for, oh, about six weeks, at which point you begin to feel torn in half, schizophrenic, duplicitous, and completely unable to sleep.

Sound familiar? Then what you need is the Man-O-Mixer Magic Personality-Meshing Machine. Based on the same principle as the common household blender, the Man-O-Mixer would combine specific, preselected elements of two competing but complementing men, allowing you (at last!) access to the extremely rare and enviable experience of having all your needs met at once.

Simply invite both men over to your apartment and ask them, one at a time, to step into the Man-O-Mixer, which resembles a large, metal, refrigerator-size box (don't worry, you'll find a way to get them in there). Lock both men in. Enter your special requests on the attached computer (Guy A's sense of humor, Guy B's forearms, and so on). Then press a button and—presto!—meet the men you've been waiting for all your life.

A Handy Alternative:
Ambiva-relent [caplets and pills]

Ambiva-relent caplets and pills would serve a related function—enabling you once and for all to rid yourself of the demons that torture you and your mate: those pesky mixed feelings, those dang internal conflicts, and that accompanying little problem you have with commitment.

So. Feel like your honey is just perfect except for that irritating noise he makes with his teeth? Feel like you'd love him to death if he had better taste in neckties? Relax. Help is just a caplet away. Simply pop an Ambiva-relent, swallow and wait. Within twenty-four hours you'll find yourself looking at him (or her) through entirely different eyes. Hey, you'll think, he may make hideous noises from time to time but at least I feel loved! Or, so what if he likes bow ties—he's a sweetheart!

disclosure department, and she's aware that that act carries a certain risk: it throws up the beginnings of a barrier between herself and Elliot M.

That, in fact, was already happening. For example, Elliot M. had spent Saturday afternoon at Alice K.'s apartment, watching videos, and Alice K. had sat beside him feeling paralyzed by conflict. On the one hand, there they were having a perfectly nice afternoon together, and it seemed pointless to Alice K. to spoil it by confessing that she'd developed this interest in some reckless-and-wild-seeming musician she barely knew. On the other hand, she was aware that her silence was in itself deceptive: to keep this information from Elliot M. was to keep him in the dark; to avoid discussion of Mr. Danger was to avoid bringing up the subject of her ambivalence.

So she merely sat there beside him on the sofa, nodding and smiling at his comments on the movie, and secretly obsessing about what to wear.

Elliot M. left late that afternoon, and some three hours and thirty-two outfit changes later, Alice K. found herself sitting in The Cave, the smallish, college-town-type bar where Mr. Danger's band was playing. Alice K. was on her third vodka and grapefruit juice, The Ice Picks of Love were throbbing away on a song called "The Ice Queen," the refrain of which seemed to be, "Baby, Baby, Baby, don't close the refrigerator door on me," and Alice K. was feeling a little dizzy.

Actually, she was feeling a little swoonish. Alice K. had felt wildly self-conscious when she and Ruth E. had first walked in: all the other women in the room seemed to have long, blonde hair and perfect figures, and black eye make-up, and thigh-high black boots, and Alice K. had leaned over to Ruth E. and whispered, "Oh my God, I'm the only woman in here who doesn't look like a graduate of Rock Chick School." But then they'd taken a table toward the front of the stage, and as soon as he'd caught Alice K.'s eye, Mr. Danger had grinned broadly and winked at her. Winked!

For a long time, she just sat there, trying to look nonchalant and struggling not to stare at him. *God he's cute,* she kept thinking. There was something so . . . so sexy about the fact that he was a performer, too. It suggested to Alice K. a quality of confidence and control, as well as a capacity for abandon that appealed to her profoundly. He looked so free up there, singing, so comfortable in his own skin.

Alice K. lies in bed, mulling over the details of what happened next. It's all a little fuzzy, but Mr. Danger's band finished up at about eleven-thirty and he and the lead guitarist from the band ended up joining Alice K. and Ruth E., and they had a few drinks, and then somehow Mr. Danger and Alice K. ended up going outside to the parking lot to get some air. Alice K.'s heart races a little when she thinks about this—literally skipping a little beat. They stood there, leaning against a wall, and talked for what must have been more than an hour. Alice K. liked Mr. Danger. She liked his confidence, his directness. He'd asked her a lot of straight, who-are-you-really-type questions—Why do you live where you live? What kind of music do you like?—and then he sort of stood back after she answered and nodded his head slowly, as if he were saying, *Ah, I see, you're that kind of person.*

Alice K. wouldn't say that he seemed impressed by her or anything, but she sensed that he liked her, that he approved of who she seemed to be. Lying there thinking about this, Alice K. also realizes that there was a hard-edgedness to Mr. Danger that she found very compelling. He was a little blunt, a little cocky, and she had an image standing there beside him of a kind of internal steeliness; the feeling that she could knock up against him and not get consumed. With Elliot M., the feeling was different: Elliot M. was so . . . well, so sort of *soft* emotionally, so available and empathic, and sometimes that gave Alice K. an almost paralyzing feeling of claustrophobia, as though the emotional boundaries between the two of them weren't delineated quite clearly enough, as though they could end up fused as a couple instead of merely close. Her problems became his problems. His problems became hers. After a while, she felt like she couldn't breathe.

Alice K. lies awake and steals a glance at Elliot M., who's sleeping peacefully beside her. He always looks sweet when he sleeps, innocent. *Isn't this part of what I should be dealing with* with *Elliot M.?* Alice K. wonders. *Isn't learning to be close to someone else without giving up your autonomy part of what relationships are all about?* After all, Alice K. realizes that part of what she finds compelling about Mr. Danger is the fact that he seems like the kind of guy you *couldn't* get too close to. He seems like the kind of guy who'd back off if he felt *you* getting too near, who'd take it upon himself to make sure the boundaries didn't get blurred. Mr. Danger, in other words, would create the kind of distance in a relationship that Alice K. struggles to create with Elliot M.

This thought makes Alice K. begin to despair. *What is it I really want?* she wonders. *Do I want to be in a relationship where I can be intimate with someone else, or do I want to be in a relationship where I can be* afraid of intimacy *with someone else?*

That, it seems to her, is the choice here. Should she risk the pain of closeness with Elliot M. or the pain of heartbreak with Mr. Danger? Love or unrequited love? And, in the end, would her actions answer those questions for her?

At the close of the evening, just before Alice K. and Mr. Danger went back into the bar, he'd stood directly in front of her and touched her hair. *Very pretty,* he said. Then he cupped the side of her face with his hand and, very lightly, brushed the skin below her cheekbone with his thumb. He smiled down at her.

Can I give you a call?

Alice K.'s knees felt weak. Elliot M. flashed through

her mind, his goodness and devotion to her, his kindness.

Then she opened her mouth. The word just came out: *Yes.*

One week later:

Alice K. lies in bed, writhing with anxiety and confusion. *Should she sleep with Mr. Danger? Should she really go ahead and do it?*

Alice K., you see, has had her first date with Mr. Danger.

She turns the evening over in her mind. Mr. Danger picked her up at seven o'clock, ostensibly to go see a concert with a group of his friends. He was wearing black jeans and a white t-shirt and brown suede cowboy boots, and he looked tall and rangy and swoon-inducing. He drove a Jeep Cherokee (also swoon-inducing), and as they pulled away from Alice K.'s apartment, he leaned over to her and said, "Let's fuck the concert, huh? I know a little place where we can get something to eat and then maybe go dancing instead."

Alice K. gulped and said, "Sure," as casually as she could, but inside, her heart pounded and she felt dizzy. *A night alone with Mr. Danger?? Argh!*

For this was not merely a first date with Mr. Danger; this was also a first serious step away from Elliot M.

Unable to sleep, Alice K. stares at the ceiling and considers this. *Was this a terrible thing to do,* she wonders, *to go out with Mr. Danger without telling Elliot M.? Am I a terrible person?*

In her heart, Alice K. believes the answer is yes, but something in her has been unable to resist Mr. Danger. That night, for example, they'd ended up in a tiny Italian restaurant on the outskirts of town and Alice K. had sat there feeling literally swept away just by the mere sight of him. She looked at his solid, manly jawline, and his solid, manly forearms, and the strand of thick, dark hair that curled against his forehead, and whatever guilt she felt about deceiving Elliot M. receded further and further into the background.

Mr. Danger seemed so . . . powerful. His very presence seemed to represent mystery, or challenge, or some vague promise of validation, as if acceptance from him would grant Alice K. membership in some club she secretly longed to belong to.

Alice K. and Mr. Danger drank Chianti and talked. Actually, Alice K. drank Chianti and Mr. Danger talked. He talked about The Ice Picks of Love, and he talked about his aspirations as a painter, and he talked about the wild week he'd spent over Christmas, partying in New York and then skiing in Vermont, and Alice K. sat there, attentive and eager and absorbed by his jawline.

Actually, thinking about it now, Alice K. realizes that she'd experienced a range of conflicting impulses over the course of the evening: a vague longing that Mr. Danger would express a softer or more emotional side (when Alice K. asked him about his family, for example, he'd merely shrugged and frowned and said, "Ah, they're a bunch of losers"), and an accompanying compulsion to keep her own emotional life under wraps. A little voice in her head offered instructions: *Don't talk about your own complicated feelings; don't mention the fact that you're in therapy; don't say anything threatening.*

Threatening? Shifting in her bed, Alice K. ponders that word. In contrast to Mr. Danger, Elliot M. was the sort of guy Alice K. could say anything to: she talked to him in tremendous detail about her feelings, and she leaned on him when she had bad days at work, and he seemed to know every little nuance of her emotional life, from how she'd react to a sad book to how she felt when she was about to get her period. He was that kind of guy, intuitive and in tune with feelings, almost like a woman.

Mr. Danger, on the other hand, was one of those live-in-the-present, don't-look-back kind of guys, the sort of person who steadfastly refused to look inside and who'd probably sneer at Alice K. if she told him about therapy, who'd think of it as a self-indulgent and unnecessary waste of time.

So why does that appeal to me?, Alice K. wonders. She thinks back to her evening, and how completely focused she'd been on Mr. Danger. They'd finished the wine, and then they'd gone to a little bar next door and drank some more and danced, and on some level, Alice K. realized, she had felt enormously relieved to be with someone so non-introspective; his presence—or, more significantly, his unspoken insistence that she focus on his presence—somehow freed her from the pressure to experience and examine her own feeling so keenly.

Still, this was a mixed blessing; it had to be.

Mr. Danger had driven Alice K. home that night and then, as if it were expected of him, he came inside. Then he'd spent a few moments idly wandering through her apartment, picking up things (a picture of Alice K.'s parents, a book on women and ambivalence) and putting them down, randomly and without comment.

Then he'd followed Alice K. into the kitchen, where she was pouring wine. Alice K. handed him a glass, he took it, then put it down on the counter and moved closer to her, practically right up against her.

Alice K., aware that Mr. Danger was about to kiss her, had a sudden and intense moment of panic. And guilt. Elliot M. flashed into her mind. She smiled at Mr. Danger nervously, then choked out the words, "You know . . . I should tell you . . . I've been seeing this guy . . ."

Mr. Danger smiled. "That guy? You mean the one you were with at the party? What, did he give you his fraternity pin or something?"

Alice K., trying to giggle, let out an embarrassed little choke. "No, it's not . . . I mean, I just thought you should know where I am."

Then Mr. Danger smirked just slightly. "Where you are," he said, "seems to be right here in your kitchen. With me."

Alice K. didn't know what to say. Mr. Danger kissed her—a deep, sexual, frightening kiss—and then he lifted his mouth from hers, gave her a little pat on the cheek, and stood back.

He said, "Why don't you cook me dinner one of these days, huh?"

Alice K., well aware that the prospect of cooking dinner for Mr. Danger was laden with sexual suggestion, felt fearful and slightly intimidated and, oddly, immature. And the words just came out: "Sure," she said. "Anytime."

Five days later:

Alice K. lies in bed, writhing with post-coital confusion.

It has happened, you see. Alice K. has slept with Mr. Danger.

Oh God, she thinks, lying there in the dark. *What have I done?*

It happened like this: Mr. Danger came over to Alice K.'s house for dinner, at his own invitation.

Alice K. had spent days worrying about this, preoccupied to the point where she literally could not work. She spent a full three days at her job making angst-ridden phone calls to Ruth E., poring over recipe books, and (of course) making lists of things she might wear or need to buy.

A part of Alice K. had deep and profound reservations about all this. After all, Alice K. was aware that there was a very big difference between feeling infatuated with someone from a distance and actually sleeping with him in the flesh. Alice K. was aware that sex with Mr. Danger would shift the balance in what had been a fairly benign flirtation, that it would up the ante, intensify her feelings of vulnerability. And, on a more pragmatic level, Alice K. was aware that sex with Mr. Danger would raise all kinds of complex and frightening questions:

Would he use a condom?

If he didn't, would she have the nerve to ask him to?

And what if he turned out to be the kind of guy who fled the room if you so much as uttered the word "tomorrow" after a sexual encounter?

Which, Alice K. suspected, is precisely the kind of guy Mr. Danger would be, and a part of her equated the impending date with a certain kind of psychic doom: she felt like the conquest-to-be, the next notch on Mr. Danger's belt, and she understood that giving in, submitting to him sexually, could quell his interest in her, rather than intensify it. He was (or so she imagined) that kind of guy.

And still . . . a part of Alice K. felt compelled to go through with it. Maybe it was because Ruth E., who was far more sexually daring than Alice K., kept urging her to go for it: "Do it, Alice K. What have you got to lose?" Or maybe Alice K. merely needed to get this infatuation out of her system, to set her Mr. Danger fantasies to rest so she could resume her relationship with Elliot M. without guilt or distraction.

For already, of course, the dalliance with Mr. Danger had thrown up a subtle but (to Alice K.) all too apparent wall between herself and Elliot M. She couldn't talk to him about it. She couldn't even talk to her sister about it: Alice K. knew that Beth K. would be disapproving and suspicious about her attraction to Mr. Danger, so she'd been avoiding calling her for nearly two weeks, occasionally leaving a vague message on her machine at times she knew that Beth K. wouldn't be home.

Alice K. was having a hard time talking to her therapist, Dr. Y., about this too, in part because she no longer felt she could assess her relationship with Elliot M. on its own terms; every interaction, every conversation and outing and sexual encounter with Elliot M. was loaded (on her side) with scrutiny and comparison, and at times this made Alice K. feel as though she couldn't think straight. While she was doing dishes in her kitchen a few nights ago, for example, Elliot M. had come up behind her and given her a big bear hug, and Alice K.'s mind flew right to Mr. Danger, who'd kissed her at that very spot the week before. *Elliot M. is not as tall and solid and manly-feeling as Mr. Danger,* she thought. *Not as rugged, not as . . . sexy.*

Mercifully, Elliot M. was out of town on business during the three days prior to Alice K.'s dinner with Mr. Danger, and wouldn't be back until the day following it. That, in turn, gave Alice K. three days of uninterrupted obsessing, and by the appointed evening, her refrigerator was equipped with three different possibilities for dinner (steak, salmon, or a pasta dish), her closets with two new shoe options, new underwear, and several of Ruth E.'s best-looking sweaters, and her bed (of course) with clean sheets.

Mr. Danger showed up a half hour late, at eight-thirty. He brought a single red rose. Alice K. (halfway through her second glass of pre-date white wine herself) poured him a drink and started to make dinner.

Mr. Danger positioned himself on the counter while she cooked, his cowboy boots dangling against her cabinets, and watched her with a wry smile. And somehow, Alice K. managed to put together a spread of baked salmon and green beans and new potatoes and French bread without (she hoped) communicating the fact that her heart was racing and she thought, several times, that she might actually faint.

Two hours later—Alice K. can't even remember what they talked about during dinner—Alice K. was clearing the last of the dinner dishes when Mr. Danger, still seated, suddenly grabbed her around the waist and pulled her toward him. "C'mere, K.," he said, drawing her onto his lap so that she was facing him, her legs straddled over his. And then he started to kiss her. And then he picked her up—literally, picked her up off the chair—and carried her into the bedroom.

Ruth E. would have called this a moment of great passion, and . . . well, in a way it was.

Mr. Danger was one of those incredibly confident, technically expert men who'd probably slept with five thousand women before her, and he played Alice K. like a musical instrument: touching this note, then that one; modulating tempo and speed; sweeping her away. Alice K., who was almost always paralyzed by self-consciousness during first sexual encounters, felt her thoughts recede further and further into the background under his touch . . . thoughts of Elliot M. . . . anxious thoughts . . . thoughts of safe sex (Mr. Danger provided his own condom!) . . .

This was physical, just physical, and Alice K., who rarely experienced the joy of escape from her own emotions, lost herself.

About half an hour later, Mr. Danger lay on the bed with his eyes closed. He didn't touch Alice K.; he merely rolled off her without a word and lay back. Beside him on the bed, Alice K. felt vulnerable and exposed, unsure what to say or how to act. She felt detached from her own body, her self-consciousness restored.

Time ticked by.

After about twenty minutes, Alice K. reached over and gently stroked Mr. Danger on the chest. "Jack? Are you awake?" she asked.

He stirred, murmured something.

"Jack?"

Another murmur.

"It's late. Would you like to stay over, Jack?"

Mr. Danger opened his eyes, gave Alice K. a dazed look, then sat up. "Huh?" he said. "Oh, shit. What time is it?"

Alice K. told him the time—one-thirty a.m.—and Mr. Danger stood up. Putting on his jeans, sliding on his t-shirt, he looked down at Alice K. and said, "Hey, sorry. I've got this big thing tomorrow, you know? But listen, some other time. Dinner was terrific."

Then he bent down, kissed her on the forehead, and he was gone.

The next day:

"So? SO? Tell me: how was it?"

Alice K. is sitting in a bar with Ruth E., and Ruth E. is being merciless. What happened?, she wants to know. What was Mr. Danger like? Did Alice K. . . . well, you know, how was it?

Alice K. is a loss for words. She has already divulged what, in her own mind, are the most relevant details: they slept together and then he left. Just left. And she hasn't heard from him all day. Not even a message on her machine.

To Alice K., this is a most agonizing turn of events, largely because the sexual side of the evening had been, in fact, quite astonishing. Alice K., you see, is the sort of woman who secretly believes she's the only woman in America who doesn't own a vibrator and who's incapable of multiple orgasms, so the idea of actually enjoying a first sexual encounter, of losing herself in the complete physical nature of it, has taken her completely by surprise. If the sex had been lousy, she understands, if Mr. Danger had just kind of slammed into her and left, then Alice K.'s emotions would have been a good deal simpler: she'd feel humiliated, then angry, and then over it, able to dismiss him as a mean-spirited, womanizing rat.

But Mr. Danger was so . . . well, Alice K. tried to tell Ruth E. about it, but she just blushed and smiled and choked on her words. "I guess it was pretty good," she said.

"You guess?" Ruth E. said. "What do you mean, you guess?"

At this point, Alice K. launched into a long and rather confused description about how unsettled she felt when she woke up that morning, about how it all seemed like a dream, and about how *weird* this made her feel, having passionate sex with a man but not really having any kind of emotional relationship, and how she didn't know what to do, and how . . .

"Alice K.! What is wrong with you?" Ruth E. had little patience for this. She continued: "Can't you just sleep with a guy without analyzing it? I mean, why does this have to be such a big deal?"

Alice K. had a terrible time responding to this. A part of her longed to say: *You're right, Ruth E., I am a modern woman. I know what's what. He fucked me and I fucked him and I can be just as cool and detached about this situation as a guy would be.* But another part of her didn't believe this for a minute. Or, at least, couldn't accept it. For as modern and liberated as Alice K. was on an intellectual level, another part of her had a very hard time separating sex from her emotions, or believing she was capable of acting out of lust alone, without love or tenderness.

Even more bothersome—and this is something she could not bring herself to discuss even with Ruth E.—Alice K. felt badly bruised on some level, convinced deep in her heart that Mr. Danger's vanishing act was a direct response to some kind of inadequacy on her part, as a person in general and as a lover in particular. *If I'd been that good in bed,* she secretly thought, *he would have stayed. If I were a wilder, less inhibited, more exciting person, he'd fall in love with me.*

Alice K. understood that this line of thought was irrational—Mr. Danger was clearly the kind of guy who didn't get emotionally involved with women, and his distance was no doubt a product of her availability, not her personality—but Alice K. could feel her self-esteem eroding all the same, diminishing with every hour that passed without a call from him. Each hour, he seemed a little more powerful, and, by contrast, Alice K.'s own life seemed a little more ordinary.

As if reading Alice K.'s mind, Ruth E. took a sip of wine and asked, "So, where's Elliot M. fit in with all this?"

Oh God, Alice K. thought. *Another impossible question.*

She looked up. "I don't know, Ruth E.," she said. "I really don't. He'll be home tonight."

Four days later:

Elliot M. knew something was up—he had to. For the first few days after he got home, Alice K. had felt so ridden with guilt that she'd thrown herself into the relationship with a kind of vigor she hadn't felt since their early days together: cooking him dinners, calling him at odd hours just to say hi, displaying more affection than usual. But as her guilt subsided, Alice K. found herself feeling more and more petulant in his presence—critical and claustrophobic—and Elliot M. was clearly picking up on that.

On his third night home, for example, Elliot M. had come over to eat dinner and watch TV, and Alice K. had felt a creeping sense of annoyance at his presence. After dinner, Elliot M. had put his arm around her while they were sitting on the sofa, and Alice K., feeling compelled to escape his touch, had immediately come up with an excuse to go into the kitchen; when she came back, she sat down further away. A little later, Elliot M. turned off the TV and said, "Alice K., is something wrong?"

"No," she said, a little too lightly. "What makes you think that?"

"I don't know—you just seem preoccupied these days.

Like sometimes you're here and sometimes you're a million miles away."

Alice K. mumbled something about getting her period, and Elliot M. didn't pursue the matter. But later, instead of suggesting that they spend the night together, Elliot M. stood up and said, "I think I'd like to be alone tonight." And then he kissed her—a weird, wistful sort of kiss, Alice K. sensed—and then he looked at her hard, and then he left.

Alice K. lay in bed that night, feeling a little alone, a little guilty (she knew she was taking Elliot M. for granted), and a little worried, for the first time, that their relationship might really be in jeopardy.

The following day, she tried to talk about some of this with Dr. Y.

Dr. Y. asked her one question—"You seem to be investing a lot of power in a man who doesn't seem to want to be involved with you. Why do you suppose that is?"—and Alice K. couldn't come up with an answer.

But on the phone with Ruth E. that afternoon, she brought the question up. Why *did* she feel so drawn to Mr. Danger? He obviously didn't care about her the way Elliot M. did. What in the world was compelling about that?

"I feel really bad about Elliot M.," she said. "He's such a good person, you know?"

Ruth E. snorted. "So? Just because you slept with Mr. Danger doesn't mean you have to abandon Elliot M., does it? I mean, it's not like the two of you are living together or anything."

Alice K. paused. "But . . . but I worry that I'm just confusing lust with love, you know? I worry that I'm going to let this guy break my heart and screw everything up with Elliot M. just because he's good in bed."

Ruth E. laughed. "Alice K., you don't have to 'let' him do anything. Just enjoy it, for God's sake."

Alice K. agreed, but inside she understood that it wouldn't be—couldn't be—that simple.

That night, Elliot M. took Alice K. out to dinner. He had something he wanted to talk about, he said.

Elliot M. took her to a small, bistro-like restaurant downtown, a romantic place with wonderful roasted chicken and expensive wine. They had a long, meandering conversation about things that Alice K. cared about—her job and her mother and Dr. Y.—and as the evening wore on, Alice K. found her anxiety about Mr. Danger dissipate, replaced with a familiar stab of fondness for Elliot M. Not sexual longing, but closeness, and comfort and caring.

Toward the end of the evening, Elliot M. leaned across the table and took Alice K.'s hand. "I've been thinking," he said. "This relationship with you has really made a big difference in my life. . . . I've—I've really been happy."

Alice K. smiled. That was actually a nice thing, making Elliot M. happy. And for the moment, she felt happy too, relaxed and warm toward him.

He continued: "But I've been thinking . . ."

He cleared his throat.

"I've been thinking . . . you've been really distant lately, and . . . well, I'm just getting this feeling that I'm more into this relationship than you are."

A wave of panic came over Alice K. and she sat up in her chair.

Elliot M. looked at her. He pointed out that they hadn't made love in several weeks (this was true). He pointed out that every time he mentioned going away for a weekend together, Alice K. changed the subject (also true). He said he'd been feeling less and less connected to Alice K. And he added that he was at a stage in his life where he really didn't want to be involved in a relationship that wasn't going anywhere.

And then he said something that caused the hair on the back of Alice K.'s neck to stand up, something that—for a brief moment—made Elliot M. seem as frightening and powerful as Mr. Danger.

"Alice K.," he said, "I'd like to start seeing other people."

5

HOW TO
FEEL GOOD
ABOUT
YOURSELF

alice k. in therapy, part i

Alice K. (not her real initial) sits in Dr. Y.'s office and thinks.

Alice K. is thinking about her relationship with Dr. Y.

Alice K. is thinking about how difficult it is to talk honestly and openly about your feelings when what you're really doing is sitting there secretly wishing that your therapist would stand up, race over to your side, and say, *"Alice K., you are absolutely brilliant and incredibly insightful and a true pleasure to work with. In fact, you are my very favorite patient and if I weren't so wise and well-adjusted myself, I'd probably fall in love with you—or at least, treat you for free."*

Why is this? Alice K. wonders. *Is everybody this preoccupied with being special to their shrink, or is it just me?*

For Alice K. understands the meaning of her wish pre-

cisely: it's a longing to be valued and respected by a male figure of authority, a longing for unqualified love and attention.
Freud, of course, would call it transference: Alice K. wants Dr.
Y., who she's been seeing for three years now, to give her the
sense of approval and belonging that Alice K.'s own father
never gave her. And this is why she often finds herself thinking about Dr. Y., and imagining that he's out there
somewhere—like God—watching her, monitoring her. And
(of course) beaming with pride.

Alice K. contemplates this phenomenon. It is very difficult to get anything out of therapy, she thinks, when your
whole being is oriented toward pleasing and impressing the
shrink. Toward hiding your ugly and less pleasant feelings.
Toward showing only your most introspective, thoughtful
sides. It has taken years for Alice K. to respond spontaneously to Dr. Y., to blurt out some thought or feeling without
sanitizing it first, or censoring it, or worrying instinctively
about how she'll come off sounding. And even now, although she struggles mightily to avoid that tendency, she still
finds herself sliding back into it, and this realization causes
Alice K. to despair.

If I can't even let my guard down with Dr. Y., she thinks, *will
I ever let it down with anybody else?*

She sits in her chair, pondering this question, and tears
well in her eyes. Dr. Y. leans forward and gives Alice K. one
of his sympathetic, encouraging shrink looks.

"What are you thinking about?" he asks.

Alice K. looks up, a little startled. "Oh . . . ," she says,
"Nothing much. . . . really. Nothing."

alice k's journal: an excerpt

Today, I am starting a journal.

This is my first entry.

I feel incredibly self-conscious.

No. Scrap that.

Today, I am starting a journal and for the first time, I am making a solemn vow to myself that I will *not* be self-conscious about what I write. I will free-associate. I will commit all my deepest, darkest fears and secrets to these private pages. I will use this journal to explore my feelings and express my most personal hopes and dreams, and it will be a marvelous, freeing experience, an exercise in passion and uninhibitedness.

Yes! I'll do it! I will no longer be prey to the secret terror that someone will find my journal and read every word of it out loud in the middle of a Barbara Walters special on prime time TV.

So here goes.

Today, I had this incredible fantasy about . . .

No.

This morning, I was lying in bed, thinking about . . .

Um . . . no.

Shit.

I realized this morning that my sexual feelings about . . .

I'll start tomorrow.

self-esteem made easy: alice k's guide to self-deception

Let's face facts: it's hard to feel good about yourself. If you are like Alice K., you begin each week resolving to read more, eat less, work harder, drink more responsibly, and take better care of yourself. And you end each week in a fit of self-loathing, having read nothing, eaten too much, fallen behind at work, under-exercised, and under-slept.

Worse, your resolve is probably shaky to begin with: you have that one extra cookie after dinner, or that one afternoon of procrastination at work, and you throw up your hands in despair. *What's the use?* you think. *I am a slothful lout and I might as well just accept it as my fate.*

This phenomenon is known as "psyching yourself out." You set yourself up for failure, live up to your own worst expectations, get in your own damn way.

Luckily, Alice K. has discovered a way to use this line of thinking to your own advantage. You merely need to learn how to psych yourself out in positive ways. You need special tricks, ways of fooling yourself into believing that you're a calmer, more controlled, more virtuous person than you really are. You need to learn the art of healthful self-deception.

Consider, if you will, the following:

"I am well rested." Set your clock ahead by one half hour. This way, when you have to get up at an ungodly hour like six-thirty a.m., you can set your alarm for seven—a much more reasonable time to rise. When you wake and look at the clock, you'll know it's really six-thirty, but never mind: the important thing is that you will feel as though you've gotten more sleep than you really have. (Note: this also helps if you oversleep: if the clock says eight-thirty and you have a meeting at eight forty-five, you can sigh with relief—it's really only eight and you can still make it to work on time.)

"I am virtuous." There are many, many ways to make yourself feel better than you really are. Practice them often.

The salad bar is your friend. Approach it with chin held high and stomach sucked in. Select delicate portions of romaine lettuce, spinach, and fresh vegetables, and then drown the whole plate with olives, nuts, garbanzo beans, and about three ladles of blue-cheese dressing. Never mind that a roast-beef sandwich would be less fat-saturated and more healthful. This is a "salad," and because it's a salad, you will feel good about yourself.

Half-glasses of wine are your friend, too. They allow you to say things like, "Oh, just give me a half-glass—I have to get up at six-thirty tomorrow," thereby impressing your friends (and yourself) with your abstemiousness. Pour them liberally. Even if you get really plowed, you'll still come out sounding a lot more controlled than you actually are.

When you go to magazine stands, be sure to pick up copies of the *Atlantic, Harper's, Scientific American,* and (for extra credit), *Daedalus.* You won't read them, but the mere process of purchasing them will make you feel intellectually ambitious. When you take these magazines home, stack them on top of (*i.e.,* hide) *Cosmo.*

A related trick: buy the *Wall Street Journal* daily, but only read the center column on the first page (the interesting one).

Never watch a whole episode of your favorite bad sitcom (*Roseanne, Married . . . with Children,* and the like). If you didn't see the whole thing, you didn't really watch it.

Likewise, never order dessert. Order a fork instead. You can eat as much of your companion's dessert as you like, but if you didn't order your own dessert, you didn't really have one.

Only eat ice cream out of the container. This way you "only had a spoonful."

Only bum cigarettes. Never buy a pack. Never even buy your friends who smoke a pack. That way you really don't smoke.

Only clean the surface of things. Cram stuff in closets. Store dirty dishes in the oven. It makes you feel tidier.

"I am incredibly well organized." Compile a list of things to do and be sure to add a few items that you've already accomplished. This way, you will fool yourself into believing that you're more organized, productive, and ahead of schedule than you already are. Extra benefit: full of neat little check marks, the list will look a lot less daunting than it would otherwise, thereby inspiring confidence.

"I feel good about my weight." Set the needle on your scale back five pounds. Or place it next to a sink, shelf, or window ledge in your bathroom, so you can subtly rest a hand on said surface and press down gently, thereby relieving the scale of a few extra pounds. You will know you're fooling yourself (it's hard not to), but remember: it's all in the mind. It's amazing how willing we can be to believe our own lies.

Only buy clothes from designers who inflate their sizes. Perry Ellis and Calvin Klein are good bets. If you wear a size ten, you'll probably wear a size six in Calvin Klein, and you may go down as low as a *two* in Perry Ellis, especially in coats.

Likewise, try to buy men's clothing when possible. The women's version of a medium-size men's shirt at the Gap will be sized "extra large," and you never want to buy something that refers to you as "extra large."

Always—*always*—take your jeans out of the dryer before they're completely dry. If possible, take them out when they're still damp. Put them on. Do knee bends. No matter how well jeans actually fit when they stretch back out, they always come out of the dryer feeling ludicrously small and this is bad for self-esteem. You must combat it.

"I am financially responsible." Only put $2 worth of gas in your car at one time. Never mind that you'll have to put $2 in every other day, and that in the long run you won't save a dime more than you would if you put in $10 worth of gas at one time. That's beside the point. Psychologically, $2 is a lot easier to part with than $10.

Apply this principle to the automatic teller machine, and only take out $10 at a time. Sure, you'll be back the next day (or the next hour) for another $10, and you'll end up taking out $100 over three or four days, but if you took the $100 out all at once, you'd feel terrible about yourself.

Decide to save money by not going out to dinner, movies, drinks, or concerts during the week. Stay at home for five nights in a row and swell with pride at your restraint. Then, on Friday night, go out and spend way more money than you have a right to on a fabulous dinner and an extra-special bottle of Burgundy. You will feel you've earned this, and while you sip your expensive wine (in half-glasses), you can justify your actions by vastly overestimating the amount of money you "saved" during the week.

"I am really happy with the way I look." Avoid fluorescent lighting at all costs, especially in your bathroom. Paint your apartment flattering colors (peaches and pale pinks are good). Try to find "thin mirrors," which make you look longer and leaner than you really are.

"I am a good friend." Only call friends or relatives you'd rather avoid when you're certain they won't be home. Leave a message, expressing glee at the mere thought of hearing their voice. Ask them to call back, then unplug your phone or screen calls on your machine. Do this several times in a row. When you run into them on the street, say, "Gosh, you're hard to reach. I've been trying to call you for *weeks!*" Voilà— guilt gets transferred to them and you can rest easy, safe in the knowledge that you're a good person.

Now go to sleep, set your alarm for seven a.m. and start all over again.

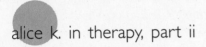

alice k. in therapy, part ii

Alice K. sits in the office of her therapist, Dr. Y., and thinks, *I need a therapy punch card.*

Isn't this a fine idea? After all, we have punch cards for just about everything else these days. Rent ten videos and get the next one free. Pump gas from the same station five times and get a free car wash. Buy ten cups of coffee from the same coffee shop and get a free refill.

So why not a therapy punch card?

Every ten sessions, Alice K. would march into Dr. Y.'s office, a small room she's occupied for fifty minutes every single Tuesday morning for the past three years, and she would present her therapy punch card, and say, "Okay, Dr. Y., I've been here ten weeks in a row, so now I get one free, right?"

And Dr. Y. would smile benevolently and say, "Certainly, Alice K. How about Thursday at nine? My treat!" Because she's been such a dutiful, long-term patient, perhaps he'd even throw in a pound of coffee beans as a bonus.

Alice K. squirms in her chair. Alas, it is not to be. No bonus cards for insight. No frequent flyer self-esteem miles. No free lunch.

And no free therapy, either. Alice K. thinks about that and she squirms again. Dr. Y., you see, has just raised his rates—Alice K. was informed of this in a very businesslike, neutral-sounding letter—and this explains why she is sitting there thinking about punch cards. Once again, the question of money has inserted itself into their relationship and it is easier to fantasize about therapy discounts than it is to bring the ugly issue up.

Dr. Y. breaks the silence. "Is there anything in particular

on your mind today?" he asks. "You seem a little preoccupied."

Alice K. doesn't say anything, but a response flashes through her mind: *Yes. I want to know why you won't treat me for free! Aren't I good enough? Aren't I important enough? Special enough?*

For that's what this is about, isn't it? That's why the issue of payment for therapy is so loaded and uncomfortable, even harder to talk about than sex. It reminds Alice K. that, at heart, therapy is a professional relationship, a business arrangement. It makes her think, *I pay this man to care about me,* and that makes her feel a little sick.

Suddenly, Alice K. is overwhelmed with a feeling of longing that she doesn't quite understand. She looks at Dr. Y., at his kind eyes. She thinks about the constancy of his presence over these past three years, about how he's always there, in person on Tuesday mornings, in a back corner of her mind the rest of the week.

Does the fact that she pays for this really mean anything? After all, even if their relationship is imperfect, even if it's inherently one-sided and incomplete, Dr. Y. still shows up for her, week after week after week. He's still there. He *must* care.

Right?

Suddenly, she recalls a conversation they once had, about this question.

"How do you know when someone cares?" Dr. Y. asked. "What makes you sure?"

Alice K. wasn't quite sure what he was getting at (Did he mean it isn't possible to know? Was this a rhetorical question or a specific one?), and she didn't know how to respond. She thought about Elliot M., and about how he looked at her sometimes with an expression of true affection. She thought about Ruth E. She said, "I guess . . . I guess it's just something you *know.* I guess it's just something you see in someone's eyes."

Dr. Y. didn't respond at the time, but sitting there now, Alice K. remembers that he was looking at her intently.

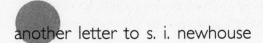

another letter to s. i. newhouse

Dear Mr. Newhouse,

Hey! How've you been? I still haven't heard from you about my proposal for *Stuck* magazine, but I have some more ideas for other publications that I think would benefit readers everywhere, especially those of us with self-image problems. I really think you'll really like them.

How about these:

The Obsessive-Compulsive Quarterly: the magazine by and for folks who just can't let go.
The goal of this periodical would be to help men and women who pine after unattainable others or refuse to get out of bad relationships feel better about themselves. After all, romantic obsessions can be a way of life—why not celebrate them? Regular features would include:

• Tips on fun things to do at four a.m. when you can't sleep because your mind is awhirl with the object of your obsession.
• Guides to pretending you're working when you're really at your desk writing the object of your obsession the latest installment in a series of forty-page letters that will finally "work things out."
• Handy lists of excuses you can use for getting

out of social obligations when what you
really want to do is go home and mope.
- A regular subscriber's contest, where readers
could battle it out to find out who's held on
to a bad relationship for the longest amount
of time.

Shy Times
Imagine the promotional material for this one,
S.I.:

Do you consider groups of more than two
people a "crowd"? Does the word "mingle" fill
you with panic and dread? Are you unable to
turn off the relentless, grating voice in your
head that insists that everything that comes
out of your mouth will sound boring and
inappropriate? You need *Shy Times*, the
magazine that reassures people like you that
it's perfectly okay to hole up in your
apartment for months at a time and speak to
absolutely no one.

Sample headlines: "Mail-Order, Voice-Mail,
E-Mail, and Faxes: Your Tickets to Total
Isolation"; "Re-runs: From the Brady Bunch to
Gilligan's Island, A Complete Guide to Fall
Fun"; and "Why I Love Ostriches: A Shy Man
Reports."

The Passive-Aggressive Times-Picayune:
The magazine for people who get what they want
without appearing to do a thing, this would
consist entirely of how-to tips. Among them:

- Saying no when you mean yes.
- Saying yes when you mean no.

- Saying maybe when you mean yes.
- Saying probably when you mean definitely not.
- Saying nothing at all when you make a mistake so you can blame someone else instead.
- Saying whatever you think another person wants to hear whether or not you believe it, because then you'll get to stew and seethe and feel secretly resentful later on.
- Saying bad things about other people behind their backs in order to make yourself feel better and then acting incredibly nice and subservient to those same people when you're in front of them.

What do you think, Mr. Newhouse? Real magazines for real people. What do you say?
    Looking forward to hearing from you.

                                    Sincerely,
                                    Alice K.

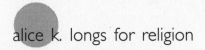 alice k. longs for religion

Sometimes, therapy makes Alice K. weary. Sometimes, she cannot stand all that probing and questioning and searching for insight. Sometimes, she wishes she could worship some other god instead.

For isn't that what therapy is? A form of religion? The gospel according to Freud? Alice K. thinks so.

Our subconscious who art in heaven, hallowed be thy name. Our impulses come. Our ego's will be done. In work as it is in love.

A real religion would be so much easier to manage; that's why Alice K. periodically longs for one. A real religion would explain things in simple, God-like terms, rather than complex, interpersonal terms. A real religion would provide structure and direction: Thou shalt not steal. Thou shalt not lie. Such simplicity! Dr. Y.'s commandments, by contrast, are so relentlessly intense. His rules, as Alice K. perceives them:

Thou shalt be angry at your parents because they didn't give you what you needed as a babe. Thou shalt repress that anger, turn it inward, where it will fester and grow and manifest itself as depression. Then thou shalt pick at the depression, the way you might pick at a scab. Thou shalt pick at your feelings, pick and pick and pick. Thou shalt relive the disappointment, experience the rage, feel the pain. And thou shalt "understand."

All that understanding. It's exhausting.

Late one night, exhausted with insight and unable to sleep, Alice K. found herself thinking about the Ancient Greeks. *The Greek gods,* she thought, *now* there *was a sensible approach.* A special god for every phenomenon, one to explain each source of angst or chaos in the world, one to correspond to every human wish. Why do we have war? Blame it on Ares. Tidal waves and deadly storms? Poseidon's fault.

Wouldn't that be wonderful? Alice K. thought, tossing in her bed. *Wouldn't it be far easier if I could march into Dr. Y.'s office and say, "Well, I've offered up a sacrifice to the god of Mixed Feelings, and all of a sudden my life is clear and focused!"*

And suddenly, at that very moment, Alice K. had an idea, something so brilliant it caused her to sit bolt upright in bed.

I've got it! she thought. *I'll come up with my own gods!*

---

alice k's greek gods for the '90s

Testicles (rhymes with Hercules), God of Male Chauvinism. A cruel god. Responsible for male insensitivity, excessive machismo, and such phrases as, "Check out those knockers!" and "Heeeeey, babeeee!" Men worship at the altar of Testicles in special, designated locations, known in some circles as "sports bars." Although women make many, many sacrifices on behalf of Testicles, they have not yet figured out how to appease him.

Procrastines, God of Wasted Time. Explains why your bills are unpaid, your work is languishing on your desk, and your apartment is a mess. Do not attempt to appease. This makes Procrastines angry, and he is likely to retaliate by loading you up with extra work or causing your dishwasher to break down. The best way to handle this god is to appeal to Apologes, God of Lame Excuses.

Infatues, Ambivales, and Whyareyoulyingtomes, the three Gods of Relationships. A most complex and mischievous trio. Infatues overcomes unsuspecting men and women during the first six weeks of a romance, imparting artificial feelings of bliss and ecstasy. This causes said partners to run around, smile insanely, and erode important, protective ego boundaries. At this point, Ambivales takes over, creating wild mood swings, sudden shifts of heart, and an extended dance known as "come here, come here; go away, go away." When Ambivales tires, Whyareyoulyingtomes steps in and creates sufficient tension, doubt, and mistrust to drive the pair apart.

Isosceles, God of Love Triangles. Often picks up where the previous three gods leave off. Generally makes a mess of things.

Meus (rhymes with Zeus), Goddess of Cellulite. A most cruel goddess. Causes thighs to bloat and puff to unnatural proportions, creates inexplicable cravings among women for Doritos and fudge, and erodes self-esteem in close to half the human population. Women spend their entire lives sacrificing at the altar of Meus, engaging in such bizarre, self-flagellating activities as Reebok Step Aerobics and the Ritual Drinking of Ultra Slim-Fast.

Accessores, Goddess of Hats, Scarves, and Handbags. A much kinder goddess. Provides women with temporary escape from worship at the altar of Meus.

Hermes, Goddess of Overpriced Hats, Scarves, and Handbags. Accessores's cruel sister. Attempt to avoid her—remember, the Greek Hermes was the conductor of souls to Hades.

Permes, Goddess of Hair Salons. Causes otherwise intelligent humans to engage in such bizarre rites as foil wrapping, scrunch drying, and obsessive application of mousse (not to be confused with Meus). A fickle goddess, sometimes kind and sometimes sadistic.

Herpes, God of Unfortunate Encounters. Self-explanatory.

Hyperboles, God of Politics. Also self-explanatory.

Whathaveyoudoneformelateles, God of Cruel Bosses. Explains why sometimes you come into work and your employer yells at you for no reason, fails to give you the raise you deserve, and otherwise deprives you of the respect, rewards, and professional success to which you are entitled. Very difficult to appease. Employees often attempt to offer sacrifices in the form of Ritualistic Brown-Nosing and False Flattery.

Raucchus, God of Bad Parties. Explains why we have fraternities. Impossible to appease, although keg bans help.

Telephone (rhymes with Persephone), Goddess of Utility Companies. Another mischievous god. Accounts for gas leaks, mysterious breakdowns in furnaces and air-conditioning systems, poor phone connections, and rampant bureaucratic inefficiency. Seems to respond solely to large sacrifices of cash.

Whataboutmes, Goddess of Self-Absorption. Causes selfishness, narcissism, and excessive focus on one's own problems. Is responsible for the prevalence of the phrase, "But what about *my* needs?" Also explains why we have psychiatrists.

Of course, Alice K. has a much longer list of other gods. There's Dermes, God of Bad Skin; Proctologes, God of Assholes; Syphilles, God of Sexually Transmitted Diseases; and Legales, God of Nightmare Attorneys.

Remember though: just as the ancient Greeks had Zeus, the Big Cheese of gods, Alice K. also has her own overlord, the god whose presence in the world truly explains why her life is the way it is: angst-ridden and confusing and unfathomably complex. His name?

It's obvious: Neuroses.

alice k.'s journal: another excerpt

Why is it so hard to be honest and forthcoming in a journal? Why is it so hard to really let go? Is it because the experience of rereading an old journal is always so incredibly embarrassing? Is it because you always read back and think you sounded so flat and stupid and preoccupied with trivia?

This morning I looked through a journal that I kept the first year I got out of college. Unbelievably boring.

Sample: Today, I started swimming. I'm making a promise to myself: I am going to swim four times a week. I promise. Four times. It felt good. I was a little embarrassed at first, standing in my bathing suit before I got into the pool, but I figure if I swim four times a week, I'll get much more toned, and I'll be a better swimmer, and . . .

Jesus! It went on like that for four pages!

But maybe this is why I'm having such a hard time starting this one. No one ever talks about this in journal-writing classes, but I think it is genetically impossible to keep a diary without banking on the idea, somewhere deep in your soul, that someone, someday will read it. Like, during that Barbara Walters special on prime time TV. So there's all this pressure to be incredibly eloquent and insightful, and to have this brimming, fantastic inner life. To sound like an artist, you know?

See? "You know." I just wrote "you know" as though I am talking to a real person, not just writing down thoughts as they come to me. I'm not sure who this "you" is. Dr. Y.? Elliot M.? Barbara Walters? But the point is I imagine that someone like Virginia Woolf or Edith Wharton would never write "you know" in a journal. That they'd never feel bogged down by self-consciousness or inhibition. Words and thoughts and expressions would just flow from their pens like . . . (I'm trying to think of a really poetic analogy here) . . . like sap from a maple tree.

No.

Like water coursing through the clearest, most babbling brook.

Damn.

Like . . . like . . .

Fuck it. I'll try again tomorrow.

alice k.'s journal: a final excerpt

Okay. Here goes.

Words would flow like lava down the side of a mountain.
No.

Words would flow like blood coursing through an artery.
No.

Words would flow like traffic down a superhighway, after
rush hour.

Fuck it. Maybe I'll try art therapy.

the fantasies of alice k., part i

Alice K. is sitting in Dr. Y's waiting room when—
suddenly!—it hits her: a fantasy, a brilliant idea, a way to
make therapy not only more productive but more entertain-
ing and fun as well!

She thinks: What if therapy were a really, really fun
game show?

She thinks: What if Dr. Y. played Monty Hall and I
played the contestant?

She imagines:

Let's Make a Treatment!

(The scene: Dr. Y. and Alice K. use his office as a stage.
He is dressed as Monty Hall and Alice K. is dressed as a
homemaker from Fort Wayne, Indiana. She wears a fun
costume—in this case, a hilarious Anna Freud disguise. [Ha,
ha! Get it?] To play, Alice K. must choose between two prizes,
one of which is concealed from view in a box.)

DR. Y.: "Okay, Alice K., are you ready?"

ALICE K.: "I'm ready, Monty."

DR. Y.: "Are you sure? You look a little nervous."

ALICE K.: "No, Monty, I'm ready to play!"

DR. Y.: "Okay, I have here in my hand a $500 bill. That's

$500. Now, you can either take this $500 bill and apply it toward your next five sessions of psychotherapy, or you can choose what's in the box. What'll it be, Alice K.?"

ALICE K. (wringing her hands): "Oh, gee, Monty . . . um . . . I'll take . . . oh, I'll go for the box!"

DR. Y. (gesturing toward lovely assistant): "Carol, shall we take a peek?"

CAROL (opening box with a flourish): "Ooooooh! It's Prozac!"

DR. Y.: "Hey! Prozac! Don Pardo, let's tell Alice K. what she's won!"

DON PARDO: "Alice K., you've won a two-year supply of Prozac, one of America's best-selling antidepressants! Manufactured by Eli Lily, each twenty-milligram dose comes in an attractively packaged green-and-cream-colored capsule, guaranteed to pick up your spirits and chase away those depressive symptoms within weeks! And best of all, Alice K., at $2 a pop retail, this two-year supply is worth almost $1500!"

(Alice K. jumps up and down in the office/stage with glee, clutching arm of Dr. Y.; audience roars.)

therapy nightmare ————————————————————

In the dream, Alice K. is sitting on the couch talking to Dr. Y. It is forty minutes into the session and she is discussing her feelings of ambivalence toward Elliot M. She is discussing her fear of losing him, and her fear of committing to him, and the long conversation she'd had the other day with Ruth E. about him, and about this one time, several months ago, when she and Elliot M. had had dinner together, and he'd been wearing this blue shirt (or maybe it was a white shirt, Alice K. can't quite remember), and about how—

Suddenly, Dr. Y.'s phone rings and when he leans over to pick it up, the notebook in which he has been scribbling furiously falls open on his lap.

Alice K. peeks.

Alice K. sees a drawing.

Alice K. sees a drawing of a young woman who looks a lot like Alice K.

The young woman is sitting on a sofa that looks a lot like Dr. Y.'s sofa.

The young woman is wearing a muzzle and a gag.

Alice K. wakes up in a fine sweat.

the fantasies of alice k., part ii

Again, Alice K. is sitting in the waiting room of Dr. Y. when it hits her:

I've got it, she thinks:

The $20,000 Psychopyramid!

(The scene: a fabulous celebrity such as Morgan Fairchild is seated opposite Alice K. [who, this time around, is a dental hygienist from Flint, Michigan]. The fabulous celebrity is equipped with a screen upon which a single word or phrase is printed. By offering a series of clues, Morgan Fairchild must try to get Alice K. to figure out what that word or phrase is. Dr. Y. hosts; he stands there, beaming, as the action begins.)

MORGAN FAIRCHILD: "Okay, first clue. Um . . . she makes you angry . . . um, she provokes guilt . . ."

ALICE K.: "Your boss?"

MORGAN: "No . . . um . . . she makes you feel guilty. Guilty. And hostile. Oh, and she's nosy!"

ALICE K.: "Your younger sister?"

MORGAN: "*No!* Guilty! Nosy. Um . . . and she's *critical!* . . . Critical of your haircut! Critical of your boyfriend!"

ALICE K.: Your *mother!*"

Bing! Bing! Bing! (audience roars).

the fantasies of alice k., part iii

Alice K. and Dr. Y. are sitting in his office.

Alice K. says, "Dr. Y., are you ever—ever—going to tell me what the 'Y' stands for?"

Dr. Y. looks at her kindly. He smiles. He says, "Absolutely not."

ALICE K. IN LOVE, PART III: CHAOS

Twenty-four hours later:

Alice K. (not her real initial) lies in bed, writhing with fear, jealousy, and confusion.

Elliot M. wants to see other people. Elliot M. wants to find someone new! How could he do this to me?

Of course, this is a relatively new feeling on Alice K.'s part, this jealousy and torment. When Eliott M. actually delivered the news, a part of Alice K. sat there feeling awash with relief. After all, she was well aware that a good part of the reason Elliot M. had decided to take this big step back from her was that he'd sensed her drift away as her interest in Mr. Danger grew.

So at first, when Elliot M. delivered his speech (he was at a point in life where he wanted a relationship with a future; he wasn't sure Alice K. shared his commitment; he thought some time out would be best), Alice K. sat there looking sober and a little surprised, but inside a little voice was shouting, *Yes! I'm free! Free to pursue Mr. Danger!*

But soon, that little voice faded away. Or, at least, changed its lyrics. Eliott M. sat there at the table, looking at Alice K. His expression was very serious and very sad, and gradually, Alice K. became alarmed: perhaps this was a prelude to a genuine breakup. Perhaps Elliot M. meant he wanted to see other women *instead* of Alice K., not just in addition to her. Perhaps—oh my God—perhaps she was being *dumped.*

Alice K. cleared her throat. "Elliot M.," she said. "Are you saying you think we should stop seeing each other altogether?"

Elliot M. looked pained. "Alice K. . . ."

Then there was a long pause. And then Elliot M. began to talk some more: he talked about how much he cared about Alice K., and about how when they'd first started seeing each other, he'd really felt like this was *it,* like Alice K. was a woman he could really share his life with. He talked about how difficult it had been over these past weeks to feel her drifting away from him, and about how many times she'd seemed reluctant to talk with him about what was going on.

And the longer Elliot M. talked, the clearer it was to Alice K. that she'd been overestimating him. Overestimating his tolerance for her shifts in mood and affection. Overestimating the security of her position. And, on the flip side, *under*estimating his wish to be in a committed relationship.

Later, when Alice K. told Dr. Y. what had happened, she got very teary and said, "I just figured that, you know, in every relationship one person loves the other person a little more than they get loved back. And I guess I figured that the one who gets loved is . . . well, that they're not the ones who get left."

Dr. Y. was quiet for a while, and then he said something about power: he wondered why Alice K. seemed to need to experience relationships in terms of who had the upper hand and who didn't, and he wondered what she made of that. Alice K. had just sat there at the time, choking back tears, but now, as she lies tossing in her bed, she thinks about the rest of that night with Elliot M. and Dr. Y.'s question comes back to her.

Elliot M. and Alice K. had left the restaurant and driven back to her apartment. Then (this was typical; Alice K. could have predicted it), they spent two-and-a-half hours sitting in Elliot M.'s car having one of those grueling conversations (his needs, her needs, this problem, that issue) that leave you incredibly drained but don't really resolve anything.

As they sat there in the car, it occurred to Alice K. that she'd barely given Mr. Danger a second thought since he first popped into her mind at the start of Elliot M.'s speech. Alice K. had slept with Mr. Danger shortly before Elliot M.'s announcement, and she'd been obsessed with him—literally obsessed—for days. And now . . . well, it amazed Alice K. how you could be so completely preoccupied with someone one minute and so oblivious to them the next. *Danger, Shmanger,* she'd practically thought, sitting there next to Elliot M. *He was going to turn out to be a rat anyway.*

She lies there and contemplates this. *Was that change of heart all about power? Did Mr. Danger recede from her mind simply because Elliot M. had made this sudden display of independence, of control over his own life?*

She'd tried to raise that question with Ruth E., but Ruth E. (damn her, sometimes) responded with simple logic: "Listen, Alice K.," she said. "I don't know why you're making such a big deal out of this. You're seeing someone else, why shouldn't Elliot M. go out with other people, too?"

"But that's different," Alice K. said.

"How is it different?"

"I don't know. It just is."

Alice K. shifts in her bed. Elliot M. had finally turned to Alice K. in his car that night at about two a.m. and said, "Listen. It's late. We really ought to get to sleep." Hoping—hoping—that he meant they ought to get some sleep together, Alice K. had looked up and said, tentatively, "Do you want to stay here?"

Elliot M. had smiled sadly and kissed her briefly on the cheek. "I wish I could, Alice K., but I can't."

Alice K. has spoken to him only once since then. One phone call (she called him) and a tentative plan to get together the following weekend (she said she needed to talk some more). But that's it.

She looks at the clock: it's one-thirty a.m. Alice K. does some quick calculations: one week ago at this very hour, she was lying there in her bed curled up next to Elliot M., sleeping quietly.

She sighs, recalling this. Then, all of a sudden, Alice K.'s phone rings. She sits bolt upright and reaches for the receiver: *It's Elliot M.*, she thinks, *it must be Elliot M.*

Alice K. answers the phone.

"Hey, K.," she hears. "It's Jack S."

One hour later:

Alice K. lies in bed, her heart pounding with astonishment.

Oh my God, she thinks. *I have just told Mr. Danger to go to hell.*

Well, actually, this is a bit of an overstatement. Alice K. didn't exactly say those words—"Go to hell, Mr. Danger"—but she did manage to rebuff him and, to Alice K., this represents an alarming turn of events.

This is what happened.

She heard his voice on the phone. "So, K.," Mr. Danger said. "How've you been?"

Alice K., taken completely by surprise, was at a loss for words. She choked something out—"Um . . . ah . . . fine, I guess"—and then she sat there as Mr. Danger, sounding as though it was perfectly ordinary to pick up the phone at one-thirty a.m. and call up someone you'd slept with and then totally avoided, proceeded to chat. To chat!

He chatted about The Ice Picks of Love, who'd been on the road ("Sorry I didn't call earlier," he said. "It's been nuts with the band, you know?").

He chatted about some new song they'd written ("It's called 'Revenge of the Ice Queens.' It's great, you gotta hear it").

He chatted about this, that, and the other thing, and although Alice K. sat there saying "Mmmm-hmmm" and asking polite questions at appropriate moments, inside, she was aware that her blood was slowly beginning to boil.

I am sick of this, Alice K. thought. *I am sick of being nice to men who aren't nice back. I am sick of feeling like an emotional chameleon.*

For that is precisely how Mr. Danger was making Alice K. feel: like an emotional chameleon, like a woman who would be accommodating and sweet and uncomplaining simply because he expected her to be so, like a spineless pea brain who didn't have the guts to sit up and say, *"Listen Jack S., who the hell do you think you are, avoiding me like that and then calling up at one-thirty in the morning as though nothing ever happened."*

As Mr. Danger talked, you see, Alice K. could imagine perfectly what would happen next: Mr. Danger would keep chatting for a while, and then he'd say something noncommittal about getting together, and Alice K.'s instincts would tell her to be a good girl, to just roll over and play dead, and she'd say, "Sure, whatever you want."

And this image infuriated Alice K. *Where is that going to get me?* she thought. *Abandoned again? Screwed and then avoided for another two weeks?* And slowly, almost against her will, Alice K. felt a powerful kind of rage build up inside of her, a feeling that made her throat tighten and her heart pound.

It was rage at Mr. Danger for making her feel so power-less, and it was rage at Elliot M. for seeming to abandon her so suddenly, and it was rage at all the hours she'd spent lying awake in the night tossing and turning and obsessing about how some man was treating her. It was even rage at Ruth E., who kept telling Alice K. to relax about the whole situation, and (perhaps above all), it was rage at herself, for being so weak and so confused and so easily bandied about by other people's reactions to her.

Perhaps all this fury was the result of Dr. Y., who'd looked at Alice K. during her last session and asked, "What do you do with all the anger?"

At the time, Alice K. had just sat there, blinked, and asked, "What anger?" She didn't know what he was talking about. But as Mr. Danger continued to chat away, Alice K. began to realize that, yes, she was angry. She was very angry. *I am thirty-three years old,* she thought. *I do not need this. I do not deserve this. I should not be sitting here on the phone at one-thirty in the morning being polite and forgiving to a guy who slept with me and then disappeared and caused me to fuck up my relationship with Elliot M.*

Suddenly, in the midst of this line of thought, Alice K. heard silence on the line and realized that Mr. Danger had asked her a question.

She asked him to repeat it.

He laughed. "Boy, I guess you are tired," he said. "I asked if you wanted to come see the band this weekend—we're playing at The Point."

Alice K. was quiet for a moment. And then, amazingly, she felt herself swallow hard and she heard herself say, "Um . . . I don't think that's such a good idea."

Mr. Danger appeared slightly taken aback. "What, you mean you're busy?" he asked.

Alice K. felt her heart race. *I have to do this,* she thought. *I have to make myself say no.*

"It's not that," she said. "I just ... Listen. I just don't think I'm interested, that's all."

Mr. Danger paused for a moment and Alice K. swallowed again and then she heard him say, "Oh." And then one of those incredibly awkward moments followed when no one really knows how to end the conversation, and somehow, they hung up.

Alice K. sat there for a minute in the quiet, staring at the phone.

I should feel proud of myself, she thought. *I should feel good and strong and self-respecting.*

But then she thought about Elliot M. wanting to see other women. And then she thought, *No more Mr. Danger.* And then she thought about the coming weekend and about how she had nothing to do on either night. And then she thought about the weekend after that, and the one after that, and about this whole horrible business of looking for a relationship that felt right, and about going through the loneliness, and about dealing with all the disappointments, and about her terror that she was looking for some kind of perfection in a man that simply didn't exist.

And then Alice K. flipped out the light and curled up on her side and started to cry.

Two weeks later:

Alice K. lies in bed, writhing with jealousy and confusion.

Alice K., you see, has just made a shocking discovery: Elliot M. is seeing someone new. *Someone new! Someone who is not Alice K.!*

Alice K. cannot believe this. She is absolutely stunned. And humiliated. And crazed with panic.

This is what happened:

It is a Thursday night. That evening, Alice K. left her job with some friends from work and went to Pete's, a nearby

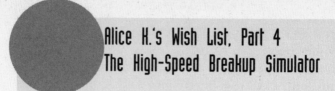

Alice H.'s Wish List, Part 4
The High-Speed Breakup Simulator

It's sad but true: ending even the worst, least healthy relationships can leave you with many feelings of anger and disappointment, and—worse—a long period of rehabilitation in which you regularly feel you want to throw up. This can go on for months. Even years in some cases.

Enter the High-Speed Breakup Simulator, a machine that would allow you to go through all the phases of separation anxiety and post-breakup trauma in less than an hour, leaving you mercifully free of hurt feelings and able to get on with your life.

Like the Man-O-Mixer Magic Personality-Meshing Machine, the Breakup Simulator would resemble a large refrigerator, and it would be equipped with a control panel/computer into which you would put your own, individual symptoms. Plagued by feelings of rejection and abandonment? Simply press the handy "R&A" button. How about guilt? Hit "G." Have more specific feelings, problems, or sources of angst? Just enter them on the computer keyboard. Some sample entries: "I cannot believe he left me for *her*," "Every time I drive past her apartment, I want to throw up," "My confidence is shot," and "I am filled with hopelessness and despair and feel I will never fall in love again."

All the feelings punched in, you simply enter the machine, hit the "on" button and wait. Within minutes, you will experience an intense rush of feeling that, depending upon the length of the relationship and the difficulty of the breakup, would last anywhere from several minutes to an hour. In a nutshell, the simulator would allow you to experience all the bad feelings at once rather than dragging them out for long periods of time. You emerge feeling restored and refreshed, unphased by the fact that he still has all your records, or that he's dating that blonde, or that he ruined your summer vacation plans, or whatever other piece of information was torturing you beforehand.

And there you are with a clear head and a calm soul, ready to forge ahead into new romantic territory and safe in the knowledge that, should it happen again, at least you'll have the proper equipment to deal with it.

restaurant. This is a place that Alice K. and Elliot M. had often frequented together (*together!*), a nice, low key, bar-and-light-food kind of place where they'd often go to have burgers and beers before going home to Alice K.'s to watch TV.

Accordingly, Alice K. had sat down toward the back of the restaurant, in a booth, feeling a little wistful. She missed Elliot M.

Since he'd announced that he wanted to start seeing other people, Alice K. had seen him on only a handful of occasions: two long "talks" about their relationship (neither of which really resolved anything), and one dinner at her apartment (she'd invited him; he didn't spend the night). So much to Alice K.'s dismay, they'd entered one of those ill-defined, no-rules-no-expectations-let's-just-see-how-it-goes phases of a relationship, and the less certain of her place in his heart that Alice K. became, the more she yearned for him.

Ruth E. thought this was ridiculous.

They'd had lunch the day before and Ruth E. had practically started yelling at Alice K. "Do you have a memory, or what?" she kept saying. "Think back just three weeks ago. Think about how ambivalent you were feeling about Elliot M. *Think about Mr. Danger!*"

Alice K. rolled her eyes. "Mr. Danger is a rat."

"Right," said Ruth E. "And that's exactly why you liked him."

Well, Alice K. acknowledged, that was probably true, but what difference did it make?

She took a bite of salad and looked at Ruth E. "Mr. Danger is the one who caused all the problems with Elliot M. in the first place. If I hadn't been such a jerk, taking Elliot M. for granted, and obsessing over him—"

Ruth E. interrupted. "Then you probably would have been obsessing over someone else."

Sitting in Pete's, waiting for a beer, Alice K. was pondering that very exchange with Ruth E. when all of a sudden—from the booth directly in back of her—she heard the sounds of two people laughing. A man and a woman. And the man was Elliot M.! She was sure of it!

Alice K. froze. She shushed her friends at the table, forced them to listen, and then issued a series of surveillance commands. "Is that Elliot M.? Look and see. No! Don't stand up! *Jesus!* Don't be so obvious! It *is* him? Oh my God, who's he *with?*"

Alice K. lies in bed, contemplating what happened next. Initial surveillance reports indicated that Elliot M. was with a blonde. A reedy blonde of about twenty-five. A reedy blonde of about twenty-five who was wearing a black velvet shirt with a low scooped neck.

At one point, Elliot M. got up to go to the bathroom and Alice K. managed to steal her own glance, peering discreetly around the edge of the booth. What she saw caused her heart to pound with fear and indignity: this blonde, this twenty-five-year-old reedy blonde in the black velvet shirt, looked like an *aerobics instructor,* and Alice K. didn't necessarily mean that in the kindest sense of the word.

How could Elliot M. do this to me? Of course, the evening became interminable: desperately afraid that Elliot M. would find her sitting in the next booth and further humiliate her by introducing her to his date, Alice K. was forced to cower in Pete's for two-and-a-half hours, waiting for them to leave first.

They didn't leave. They talked about Elliot M.'s job, and although she couldn't hear a lot (the restaurant was loud), Alice K. did hear this aerobics instructor look-alike say to Elliot M., "Wow, you know a lot about computers, don't you?" She heard them laugh out loud a few times (the reedy blonde had a high giggle). And finally, just as they were getting up to leave, Alice K. heard Elliot M. say something about Letterman being on in twenty minutes. She couldn't prove that Elliot M. and the aerobics instructor look-alike were actually going off to watch Letterman together, but Alice K. spent the next two hours in a frenzy of obsessive imagination, picturing Elliot M. on his sofa, giggling with an alien blonde.

When she got home that night, Alice K. immediately phoned Ruth E. and told her what had happened. Ruth E. sighed and told her not to get so bent out of shape.

"Alice K.," she said, "you don't know who this woman is—it could be some idiot from work. It could be his cousin from out of town. It might not be anything."

She continued. "And besides. Even if it was a date, why shouldn't Elliot M. see other people? You did."

Obviously, Ruth E. didn't understand. Now, staring at the ceiling, Alice K. tries to determine why, exactly, this display of independence on Elliot M.'s part upsets her so. For that's precisely how it appears to her: as a display of independence. A statement. A way of telling Alice K. that he really doesn't need her after all, that he's perfectly capable of taking care of himself without her.

And that's not at all how Alice K. feels about Elliot M.— at least not right now. She needs him, she thinks, and this is especially true since she said goodbye to Mr. Danger. She feels she needs him to give her life clarity and shape and definition. Why, just that day, Alice K. had seen Dr. Y., and she'd spent the hour in tears, talking about how empty she felt without Elliot M., how afraid she was that he'd abandon her completely.

Dr. Y. had looked at Alice K. and made a remark about how insubstantial Alice K. seemed to feel on her own. "Why does there have to be a man?" he asked. "What's the fear?"

Alice K. hadn't been able to answer that question and now, lying there in bed, she still can't.

The image of Elliot M. and the reedy blonde churns in her mind and she is overcome with a wish to call him, a wish to call and talk to him and hear some kind of reassurance in his voice.

She looks at the clock: twelve-thirty a.m. Another five

minutes pass. Finally, as though she cannot stand it any-more, Alice K. turns on the light, picks up the phone by her bed, and dials his number.

The phone rings. Elliot M. has an answering machine, but it doesn't come on.

Alice K. sits in bed, horrified, and the phone just rings and rings.

One week later:

Alice K. lies in bed, writhing with feelings of betrayal and confusion.

What a night, she thinks. *What a goddamn nightmare.* This is the kind of night that makes Alice K. wish it were three years from now, so that she could look back and shake her head in wonder. But it is not three years from now, so Alice K. is lying there in mid-trauma, without the benefit of hindsight.

This is what happened:

The day after Alice K. saw Elliot M. in Pete's with the reedy blonde, after she'd tried to phone him in vain, after she'd spent the whole night lying awake and picturing Elliot M. unplugging his phone and message machine so he could lie in bed with this reedy blonde undisturbed, she finally reached him at work. She told him she needed to talk and asked if they could get together, and he agreed.

And then, Alice K. made the first in a series of tactical errors: she spent the next few days stewing and obsessing about Elliot M. and the reedy blonde, and by the time she arrived at his apartment on Friday night, she was secretly seething with rage.

Ruth E. had warned her about this: "Don't act like a wounded woman, Alice K.," she'd said on the phone. "Elliot M. has every right to see other women. He was up front about wanting to. He was honest, and that's more than you can say about you and Mr. Danger."

Alice K. knew Ruth E. was right, but she couldn't help it. She walked into Elliot M.'s living room, stiff with anger.

She kept her coat on and didn't sit down. Elliot M. asked her, "What's wrong?" and (tactical error #2), she adopted a haughty tone.

"Nothing," Alice K. snapped. "What would be wrong?"

Elliot M. tried to make small talk for a few minutes, but then, almost against her will, Alice K. exploded. Just totally exploded.

"Don't pretend like nothing is going on, Elliot M.," she said. "I saw you in Pete's the other night with that . . . that *blonde*." She paused. Elliot M. was staring at her. Alice K.'s heart was pounding and her hands were shaking and although a part of her realized that this accusatory, betrayed tone was both unfair and counterproductive, it was too late to shift gears, too late to settle down and talk rationally. She heard herself continue, propelled forward on her rage.

Alice K. launched into a tirade (tactical error #3). She demanded to know what was going on. She claimed she "didn't understand" his behavior. She said, "Two weeks ago, everything was just fine between us and then, just like that, you announce that you want to see other women, and you tell me there have been all these problems between us, and you don't even give us a chance to figure things out together."

Alice K. was aware, in mid-speech, that she was rewriting history to her advantage. Alice K. understood that everything was not "just fine" between them a mere two weeks ago. On a deeper level, Alice K. also knew exactly what she was doing: she was attempting to deflect her own feelings of guilt onto Elliot M., to make him feel responsible for their troubles rather than accept her share of the blame. After all, Alice K. was the one who'd strayed from the relationship, who'd taken Elliot M. for granted, who'd *slept with Mr. Danger.*

But she couldn't help herself. She went on. "And then I see you in Pete's with this blonde, and then I try to call you at twelve-thirty in the morning, and there's *no answer.* How do you think that makes me feel?"

Now, lying there in bed, unable to sleep, Alice K. realizes that in launching into this tirade, she'd been betting on Elliot M.'s dislike of confrontation: if she seemed sufficiently angry and betrayed, she'd been hoping, Elliot M. would soften, Elliot M. would come running to her side, Elliot M. would make everything between them all right again.

That was tactical error #4.

Elliot M. just stood there, a hurt look in his eyes. And when Alice K. finally stopped talking, he just shook his head.

"Listen, Alice K.," he said. "I am not going to take all the heat for this." He told her she had no business asking about the woman in Pete's. He reminded her that he'd been perfectly honest about his intentions to see other women. He said, "I don't need this." And then he told her he thought she should leave: "I am not going to get into this while you're in this kind of state, Alice K.," he said.

And then he turned around and walked out of the room.

Alice K. was stunned. And humiliated. *I don't need this.* The words sounded so . . . so brutal.

Alice K. stood there. She didn't know what to do. She contemplated her options: run after him? Try to instigate a more rational dialogue? Apologize? Her heart was still pounding. She felt too confused to think. And then, feeling too humiliated to change her tone or point of view, she just turned around and walked out, slamming the door behind her. And then she got in her car and sped home.

It was nine o'clock when Alice K. got in. She made a beeline for the phone and called Ruth E. No answer. She paced in her apartment. She contemplated calling Elliot M. but acknowledged that, at this point, that would be a tactical error of historic proportions.

She paced some more. She poured herself a large glass of wine and sat down on the sofa.

A part of Alice K. felt enormously guilty—and stupid. A part of her knew that Elliot M. was absolutely right—he *didn't* need all that venom, he didn't deserve it. A part of her respected his reaction, and a part of her wanted to take back the last few hours, to start over, to *fix* things instead of bungling them so badly.

Instead, Alice K. poured herself another glass of wine. And another. She tried to call Ruth E. several more times. No answer again. *Where the hell is she?* she thought.

And then, angry at Ruth E. for not being home, angry at Elliot M. for not stopping her before she lost control, angry at herself for everything, Alice K. worked herself into a defensive, drunken frenzy.

An hour later, she sat there on the sofa with her fists clenched. *Fuck Elliot M.,* she thought. *Fuck him.* She recalled his words: "I am not going to get into this while you're in this kind of state, Alice K." *How condescending.* Then she sat and forced herself to think about all the things she didn't like about Elliot M., all the things that had bored her, and made her feel suffocated, and made her feel drawn to Mr. Danger in the first place. *I didn't want him in the first place,* Alice K. thought. *Fuck him.*

And then, at about midnight, Alice K. found herself picking up her coat and her car keys and heading out the door, slamming it behind her again.

This is crazy, she thought at the time, but she did it anyway.

She drove to The Point, the bar where Mr. Danger's band often played.

She pulled into the lot and checked her hair in the mirror.

And then, just as she was about to open the car door and get out, Alice K. looked up and saw something so horrifying, so completely shocking, it caused her heart to skip a beat.

There, coming out of The Point and walking toward his Jeep was Mr. Danger.

He had his arm around a woman, and the woman was Ruth E.

7

HOW TO
LIVE IN
THE FEMALE
BODY

reading the fashion mags

Alice K. (not her real initial) lies in bed, writhing with anxiety.

Once again, you see, Alice K. has spent the better part of the evening engaged in that very special form of female self-torture: reading the fashion magazines.

Ever since she landed on the *Glamour* DON'T page, Alice K. has studiously avoided this activity: *DON'T go near them*, she has told herself, standing in line at the supermarket. *DON'T spend the evening leafing through seventeen pages of Naomi and Rachel and Christy. DON'T immerse yourself in images of women with better legs and breasts and skin and hair than you. It is bad for the self-esteem. Bad, bad, bad, DON'T.*

But something happened. (Alice K. suspects it was the

cover hype on one of the mags—"Celebrity Penises: Who Really Measures Up?") Somehow she ended up with a whole heap of them and now she is lying in bed, writhing with anxiety.

Alice K., you see, is the kind of woman who's never been able to make sense of a cosmetics color chart. The kind of woman who cannot wear hats, or figure out how to use a lip pencil. After all these years, Alice K. still does not know if she is a summer or a spring or a chilly evening in the third week of October, and this turns a cruise through the fashion magazines into an especially painful experience. All that daring and fashion savvy. All those pouty lips and expertly lined eyes. Alice K. understands that many of these images are artificial—manipulated and staged and air-brushed—but she also understands something else: some women in this world are simply equipped with a sense of style, an innate sense for what looks best and what doesn't. And Alice K. is not one of them.

The style thing has been a major life struggle for Alice K., a road pock-marked with multiple fashion disasters. Bad haircuts. Countless mail-order errors. Frightening experiments (don't mention the word "sarong" to Alice K.; she will have to leave the room). Alice K. estimates that she's spent $9500 on cosmetics in the past five years alone and the only thing she's really learned is that purchasing makeup is an alarmingly expensive process of trial and error in which you buy approximately forty thousand different shades of lipstick before you hit on the one perfect color that the company is about to discontinue.

Alice K. often has no clear idea what she looks like. She means this quite literally. "I don't know what I look like," she'll say to Ruth E., standing in front of a mirror in a clothing store. "I don't know what looks right or what looks wrong." What she is referring to is the persistent sense that she doesn't have an *image,* that she can't boil her appearance down to a few critical descriptive details. Ruth E. is funky and ethnic-looking. Beth K. is earthy and all-natural. But Alice K.? Sometimes she just doesn't know.

"It can be so uncomfortable to be a woman." Alice K. says this to Ruth E. a lot, too. So hard to stop linking self-esteem with appearance. So hard to lose the self-consciousness, the certainty that everyone else in the world is as focused on the one flaw in your appearance (today's unsightly blemish, tomorrow's premenstrual bloat) as you are. And so hard to look at magazines that make it appear as though such difficulties don't exist—or, at least, as though they can be successfully overcome with a makeover or a see-through blouse.

Alice K. tosses in her bed and sighs. *Perhaps this is the price of being female,* she thinks. Perhaps she should just accept it: accept that fashion magazines are dangerous and insidious, swear them off, and start reading *Popular Mechanics* instead.

And then suddenly Alice K. remembers something, something so heartening—so utterly uplifting—it causes her to sit bolt upright in bed. She flips on the light. She sifts through the stack of magazines, pulls one out. Then she settles back down against the pillow, the magazine propped against her knees and a glimmer of delight in her eyes. Ah, yes:

Celebrity penises.

 **eighties** flashback

It has happened again. Alice K. is wending her way through the drugstore aisle on a summer afternoon when, all of a sudden, she finds herself reaching, almost instinctively, for a bottle of Johnson's baby oil.

Oh my God!, she thinks. *What am I doing?*

Just then, for a split second, Alice K. had been cata-
pulted back into the past, back to her days as a sun slave.

Remember that? Remember waking each and every
summer morning secretly longing to lounge in bed with the
papers, but knowing deep in your soul that you had to heed
that ultraviolet call? That you had to get out there, slather
up, and roast?

Alice K. hated it. Early in the season before the beaches
opened, she and Ruth E. would drag their chaise lounges
out into the driveway, position the chairs with the precision
of brain surgeons, load on the oil, and then lie there stiff as
corpses in quiet, unarticulated misery: bodies sticky, chins
pointed toward the sky, eyes shut tight. Every twenty minutes
or so, Ruth E. would sit up, pull back the strap on her bathing suit top, and examine her skin for signs of progress: "Am
I getting anything?" she'd ask. "Am I getting anything?"

If Alice K. had had an ounce of common sense at the
time, she'd have sat up and snapped back, "Yes, you're getting a savage case of melanoma and facial skin like a cowboy
boot." But no. She'd merely mumble something reassuring
and lie back to sizzle some more.

Sweat, sweat. Sizzle, sizzle. This was ridiculous. And it
got worse when beach time rolled around. Weekend after
weekend, Alice K. would rise at some ungodly hour, stumble
into a bathing suit and pair of shorts, pack up her beach
towel and assorted oils and little red cooler full of Diet
Pepsi, then drive an hour and a half through nightmare traffic to a huge public beach where seventeen million people
had already paid $125 plus their firstborn child in order to
park and fourteen million others were lined up waiting for
the one, single public bathroom that existed within forty
miles. Then, after handing over half her week's salary to the
surly, teenage parking attendant, she'd trudge several miles
onto the beach, wishing all the while that she hadn't had
that second cup of coffee because she really, really had to go
to the bathroom but didn't want to spend the next two and

Alice K's Medicine Cabinet

- tube of "Paprika" lipstick; too orange
- tube of "Kiss of Watermelon" lipstick; too pink
- tube of "Sexual Frenzy" lipstick; too red
- six bottles of nail polish so old and crusted that Alice K. can no longer remove the tops
- nail polish remover
- seventeen emory boards (sixteen withered and unusable)
- tube of "Gale Force Protection" styling gel, which took Alice K. a week to wash out of her hair
- one box of Today contraceptive sponges (only one sponge has been used, and Alice K. spent six panic-stricken hours in the bathroom on a hot morning in June trying to extract it, convinced that she was about to pull out her cervix. She keeps the remaining sponges as a cruel reminder)
- tube of Preparation-H (very bad memory having to do with ill-advised laxative experiment; don't ask)
- "Sweet as Morning Dew" douche, which Alice K. is afraid to use
- foot scrub
- neck gel
- body polisher
- purse spray
- Prozac

Elliot M.'s Medicine Cabinet

- toothpaste
- mouthwash
- dental floss
- razor and blades (Gilette Sensor)
- shaving cream soap-and-brush kit

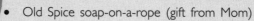

- Old Spice soap-on-a-rope (gift from Mom)
- Band-Aids
- toenail clipper
- Desinex athlete's foot powder
- calamine lotion
- cold sore medicine
- aspirin, ibuprofen, Tylenol
- condoms

Mr. Danger's Medicine Cabinet

- toothpaste
- mouthwash
- razor blades (disposable)
- Ex-ess hangover pills
- Brut aftershave (leftover from the '70s)
- English Leather aftershave (leftover from early '80s)
- Gray Flannel aftershave (leftover from late '80s)
- Chaps aftershave (currently using)
- Tenax
- massage oil
- condoms (ribbed; extra long; two boxes)

a half hours waiting in line. Once she actually got on the beach, she'd spend another forty-five minutes seeking out the sole two-by-four-foot stretch of free sand that didn't happen to be located too closely to an enormous gang of teenagers playing bad music on a boom box. And then she'd lie down, oil up, and prepare to sweat.

And these were the good days. On bad days, the wind would pick up and Alice K. would spend half the afternoon trying to pick off the particles of sand that collected like fungus on her greased-up skin. Or the weather would be sweltering but the water too cold to jump into. Or she'd run out of Diet Pepsi and lie there, dying of thirst and scoping out unattended coolers, wishing she had the nerve to go steal something. Or she'd have a horrible, drug-induced depression from too much cocaine (remember, this was the '80s), and she'd lie there secretly wanting to slash her wrists. Or she'd *really* have to go to the bathroom, and not just to pee.

Alice K. stands in the drugstore, shuddering at the memory. It's not that she doesn't like the concept of the beach—she loves the ocean, she loves the feeling of sand beneath bare feet, she loves the sea breeze in her hair. What she hated was the feeling of being trapped there like an animal, suffocating in 99 percent humidity with the teeming masses breathing down her sweating neck. What she hated was all that pressure to get out there and have *Fun*.

Thank God that's all over, Alice K. thinks. The heat, and the sand in your lunch, and the screaming children and their screaming parents, and the errant Frisbees, and the lying there, your pale, imperfect thighs spread out for all the world to see while your boyfriends inspected the much-better-looking-than-yours breasts of every woman who walked by.

Oh, it was just too much. By midsummer, Alice K. secretly relished rainy summer weekends because she could go to the movies or stay inside and read a book without feeling guilty. And by late September, she breathed virtual sighs of relief at the prospect of chilly, gray autumn days.

But now, she thinks, it's all different. These days, when Alice K. sees people on the streets with deeply tanned skin, she already finds herself sneering to herself and thinking, *Hah, an uneducated fool who wouldn't know an SPF from a CFC. A bimbette, no doubt, who probably snaps her gum and teases her hair and wears a lot of polyester as well.* The tan, Alice K. thinks, has become downright middle class.

Alice K. contemplates this and smiles. Finally, she thinks, it is hip to be pale! Finally, it is becoming perfectly acceptable to spend sunny weekends holed up in darkened theaters and restaurants. And finally, it will become chic to wear long, flowing clothes that not only protect you from the sun's harmful rays but cover up unsightly cellulite as well.

Then, suddenly, Alice K. has a vision, something that practically makes her squeal with glee. She sees it, a fashion solution for the '90s, a way—finally—for women to be in style, to be sensible, and still feel good about themselves.

They'll make a comeback, she predicts, picking up a bottle of SPF 36 sunscreen and moving on down the aisle. *And I can't wait. Muumuus.*

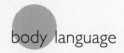

body language

One day not long ago, Alice K. was leafing through a magazine when she came across an ad for a douche.

Douche, she thought. *What a stupid word.*

And then she thought, *The word* douche *would never be applied to a male product or activity. If men used douches, the product would have a clinical, tough, manly name, such as "Power Wash." Douche sounds prissy.*

And then, thinking some more, Alice K. realized that the English language is peppered with stupid, ugly words, the vast majority of which apply to body parts, body functions, or body products. That evening on the phone, she discussed this with Beth K. and they came up with a list.

Panty. A miserable little word. Can you imagine a man using the word panty to describe his undergarments? *"Honey, have you seen my panties?" "Dammit, I can't find my blue panties."* *Panty* is one of those offensive, infantilizing little words that sounds pink. It's a male word, designed by men to satisfy some weird sexual fetish. Why can't women just wear underwear like everybody else? Related miserable words and phrases: panty liners, panty shields, panty hose.

Vagina/Penis. Couldn't we come up with something just a tad more dignified? Those are two very ugly words, aesthetically unpleasant, full of harsh sounds. Wouldn't it be far nicer if we had some truly pretty words to describe the sexual organs? Think of a word like, say, nuance. Much prettier.

Other sexual reproductive organs. Scrotum: terrible word. Pubus: awful word. Vulva: *who came up with these?*

Coitus. Talk about an unromantic word. Can you imagine anything less sexy? Want to ruin a romantic moment in about three seconds? Use the word "coitus." Or "coital." Ditto the words we've designed for oral sex. Fellatio? Cunnilingus? Where do those come from?

Any venereal disease—gonorrhea, syphillis, herpes. Ugly words. They even look ugly on the page. And what an indignity to have to use one. If you must suffer from a venereal disease, couldn't you at least have one that didn't sound so vile? Say, symphony. "I have symphony" would be much less unpleasant. (Chlamydia, on the other hand, is rather nice. Sounds like a flower.)

Plebiscite. Not a body part (it means "vote") but it sounds like one. It is also unnecessarily ugly. Vote is a pretty word, a nice, declarative word. Plebiscite sounds like a bacteria.

Most German words—gestalt, zeitgeist, liverwurst, weiner-schnitzel, rottweiler. Ditto: not body parts, but they sure sound like ones. Who invented this language? Who was the genius who decided to make the word "fahrvergnügen" the center-piece of a Volkswagen ad campaign?

Phlegm. Looks German.

Pus. Enough said.

Lint. Don't ask why. Alice K. just doesn't like it, especially when applied to belly buttons (another phrase she doesn't like).

Belch. Okay, it sounds like what it describes, so it might be a useful word. But it's a very, very ugly word, especially when used to describe inanimate objects, such as factories. "The factory belched out smoke."

Spew. See "Belch."

Bowels, as applied to buildings. Bowel is a bad enough word in reference to things intestinal, but when it's applied to infra-structures ("the bowels of the church," "the bowels of the subway system"), it becomes exceptionally ugly and gratui-tous, don't you think?

Old fart. Fart is ugly, but "old fart" is stupid. Why describe someone as an old fart? Think about the concept for a moment. What does this really mean? Stupid and gross.

Piping as an adjective. Not a body part or function but worth mentioning. It is a truly stupid word which can only be applied to the word hot, as in "piping hot." Have you ever heard the word piping applied to anything else? Piping smart? Piping mad? A ridiculous word.

Urinal. A cold, harsh word. Self-explanatory.

Bidet. Another rather unseemly word, possibly because Alice K. finds the concept a little unnerving. Don't ask.

Any synonym for the word vomit. Vomit is a very unpleasant word, both aesthetically and as a concept, but the synonyms are worse. Puke. Upchuck. Blow lunch. Hurl. Heave. Terrible words.

Gum as a verb. Consider it. "He gummed his oatmeal." "He gummed his toast." Descriptive perhaps, but gross.

Some just plain ugly words. Stench. Stool. Caucus. Pulp. Bulge. Hump. Mucus. Saliva. Ooze. Gurgle. Flagellate. Flatulence. Smear. Buttafuocco.

the guilt and shame of wearing black

Do you find yourself walking into clothing stores these days feeling like a stranger in a strange land?

Do certain words send chills up your spine? Words like "pastels" or "chartreuse" or even "earth tones"?

And when you walk out of the house in the morning, do you feel a vague sense of paranoia, an uneasy feeling that everyone thinks you're dressed for a funeral?

If you answered "yes" to the above questions, Alice K. understands you. You are suffering from the Guilt and Shame of Wearing Black.

Yes, it's true. Alice K. knows it. Alice K. is aware at this very minute that thousands of otherwise healthy, happy young women are staring mutely into their closets, uttering the words, "But I hate bright colors!" Thousands more are out on the street, muttering softly: "Prints? Florals? I can't *stand* it!" Still others are simply stymied, paralyzed by the chilling question: Is there life after black clothing? Can there be?

Alice K. has a simple answer to this question: No.

Sometimes, she has horrible flashbacks, painful recollections of the days (when was it? the late '80s? early '90s?) when it looked like black was being swept down the great fashion drain.

Alice K. remembers it well. Slowly, she began to notice that women were showing up at work in odd and foreign hues—pale peaches, mint greens, bright, neon things. She was alarmed. Then, one day in the early '90s, Alice K. went shopping and her blood pressure rose another notch. Sleeveless little A-line dresses covered with bursts of psychedelic color hanging right there where all the black skirts used to be . . . little pastel bolero jackets . . . '60s-style medallions . . . capri-length stretch pants with Pucci prints . . . retro bell-bottoms and see-through blouses and the beginnings of (gasp) grunge.

Alice K. was shocked. Shocked! And, of course, very sad. After all, black had been Alice K.'s color of choice for nearly a decade. A perfect color. The ideal fashion solution.

For one thing, black just happened to look good, and back in the '80s, when scads of women like Alice K. were entering foreign and strange new worlds, it came in very handy to have a wardrobe full of stuff that made them feel chic and svelte and possibly even vaguely mysterious.

For another thing, black made women look thinner than they really were, thus improving self-esteem while hiding the widespread failure to make use of their expensive health-club memberships even *once*.

Even more important, as Alice K. knew well, black served a vital role in maintaining self-image. Equipped with nothing more than a few basics (the black skirt, the black sweater, the cool black shoes), all that dark, impossible-to-mismatch clothing provided a critical way to cover up the fact that, deep in her heart of hearts, Alice K. knew absolutely zip about fashion. Felt intimidated by it. And simply didn't have time to learn about it because she was so busy running around trying to Have It All, or Be It All, or Do It All, or whatever else she was supposed to be doing as one of those on-the-go women of the '80s.

In short, black made Alice K. look like she had a sense of style even when she couldn't dress her way out of a paper bag. It allowed Alice K. to fake it.

And now, today, while everyone else in the world seems to be zipping around in earth tones and pinks and puces and what have you, Alice K.'s black clothing hangs in her closet, secretly testifying to her fashion failure: to the fact that after all these years, she still finds this question of what looks good on her and what looks bad inordinately confusing. That when it comes to style, she still prefers the easy way out. After all, even when it's worn badly, black affords the wearer a certain inconspicuous anonymity, something that's a good deal harder to pull off if you're wearing a see-through blouse with a magenta-colored camisole.

But take heart. If you, like Alice K., suffer from the Guilt and Shame of Wearing Black, there are steps you can take.

You could pierce your nose, stop washing your hair, and acquire a new group of friends.

You could adopt a new role model ("I just happen to really like Johnny Cash, okay?").

Or you could do what Alice K. does: walk into your local women's clothing store, purchase a bright yellow skirt or a pastel blouse, take it home with your head held high, and promptly die it black.

yet another letter to s. i. newhouse

Dear S.I.,

Still haven't heard from you re my earlier proposals, but a few other ideas have come to mind in the meantime, so I thought I'd pass them along. How about these?

Depressionwear Daily.

I envision this as the ultimate guide to fashion savvy for today's angst-ridden woman. A slick, elegantly photographed, glossy publication, this would feature the latest in clothing with vertical stripes, clothing with dark colors, and other outfits that hide unsightly bulges incurred by depression-related bouts of overeating. In addition, there would be regular spreads on fashion eyewear to hide bloodshot and swollen eyes. A significant portion of each issue would be devoted to spreads of fantastically ugly clothes that make other people look pale, stressed, sad, washed out, and otherwise horrible, thereby making today's angst-ridden woman feel significantly better about herself.

I won't bother you with more details right now, but suffice it to say I have a number of well-developed ideas for special quarterly supplements, including a fabulous guide to cooking with antidepressants. I'll fill you in on the details if you're interested.

And if you don't like that one, how about this:

Sloth Magazine.

Don't you love it?

A slightly more mainstream publication than the other ones I've mentioned, this would contain the kinds of regular-feature departments found in other magazines, only they'd be devoted in this case to helping lazy, procrastinating slobs feel less guilty about their lives. For instance:

• "Slothful Decor" would include successful laundry-aversion techniques; ways to disguise dust bunnies, rotting refrigerator contents, and unsightly buildups of books, magazines, and floor wax; as well as regular profiles of especially slothful individuals ("MAN IN FLINT, MICHIGAN, HASN'T MADE BED IN 17 YEARS— AND LOVES IT!")

• "Slothful Health and Fitness" would be devoted primarily toward helping the slothful find ways to avoid exercise and healthful nutrition. Sample headlines: "Ooooops! Forgot My Gum Bag Again!" "Whaddayamean Cheezits Are Bad For You?" and "I Really Would Exercise, but I Hurt My Knee Skiing in 1962 and My Doctor Says I Can't."

• "Slothful Style," finally, would celebrate the wonderfully streamlined and simple joys of slothful dressing; we'll call it the All K-Mart approach to fashion.

What do you think, S.I.? Can I count you in?
Look forward to hearing from you!

Sincerely,
Alice K.

P.S. I hope you don't mind me calling you S.I.;
I kind of feel like I know you by now.

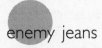

enemy jeans

Alice K. sits on her sofa, squirming with discomfort.

It is one of those days, you see. Alice K. is wearing enemy jeans.

Do you have those days, too? Do you know how Alice K. feels?

She feels miserable. Full of self-loathing. Intensely uncomfortable. Trapped in enemy jeans.

I hate this, Alice K. thinks. *I hate this feeling of total self-consciousness. I hate this feeling that my identity is inextricably linked to the size and shape of my thighs. Why must I be such a jerk about food and weight and body image?*

Ah, the $64,000 question. Of course, Alice K. already knows the answer. She is a jerk about food and weight and body image because she is a woman and women are genetically, culturally, and socially programmed to be raving fools when it comes to food and weight and body image.

True? True.

Alice K. knows this. She knows it in her soul. Alice K. has read all the books—books on eating disorders, and books on diets, and books on the connection between fat and fear of fat and feminism. She has had scores of dialogues on the topic with other women, endless dialogues (often over dinner) about food and food games, about the complete futility of dieting, about the tremendous resentment they feel at living in a culture that holds out such unattainable ideals of beauty for women, that puts such a ridiculous premium on slenderness. Alice K. has struggled and struggled to feel good about her body just the way it is. She has fought to attain the level of self-acceptance and self-love that, as she understands it, will diminish her anxiety about food and weight.

And yet . . . she can't help it. When Alice K.'s jeans become her enemy, all of her feminist logic and better impulses go straight out the window and she finds herself stuck on the sofa, not knowing if she wants to go on a diet or go into the kitchen and eat seventeen pounds of Ding Dongs.

Should I give in to this cultural tyranny and starve myself or should I resist it and binge? Should I drive myself nuts one way or torture myself the other?

For that's what happens when your jeans are your enemy: there's no way to win. Food becomes a terrible, powerful symbol of everything that's wrong with you (you're a failure, a grotesque mess, a miserable excuse for a grown woman); food ceases to be a nurturing substance, a fuel, a source of pleasure, and becomes, instead, an implement of self-torture.

This is how Alice K.'s mind works when her jeans are her enemy:

Here I am, sitting in a restaurant. I can feel my thighs encased in my jeans. Too tight. I can feel the waistband digging into my stomach. Ick. I feel bloated and gross, but I have to eat something or I'll die. Okay, let's see. What I really want is a hamburger. A fat, juicy hamburger with cheese and bacon and a heap of fries. . . . But I can't get a hamburger because I'll feel slothful and filled with self-loathing, so I'll get the Greek salad. The puny, boring Greek salad with not enough feta cheese and only two measly olives. But that will make me feel sad and deprived, and I'll overcompensate by ordering eleven pieces of cake for dessert, so maybe I'd better stick with the hamburger. Or maybe I should get something in-between, like a turkey sandwich. Or maybe I should just skip dinner and go straight for the eleven pieces of cake and then go to the gym afterward and work out like a maniac for three hours straight because I feel guilty. Or maybe . . .

Get the idea? Basic decisions about food become impossible. Meals and snacks become hopeless trade-offs: *If I eat these cookies now, I won't eat that piece of pie later. If I skip lunch, I can have a huge dinner. Deny, deny; reward, reward. Calculate, scheme, rationalize.*

Alice K. does not know one woman—not one—who doesn't play these games at least on occasion, and the ones who say they don't are lying.

"Are we crazy? Are we insane to do this to ourselves?" She asks Ruth E. this question on a regular basis and Ruth E. merely nods soberly and says, "Yes."

Mercifully, Alice K. is not nearly as weird about food as she was back in her early twenties, when she (along with about fourteen million of her peers) was engaged in a furious routine of binging and starving that caused her to gain and lose the same ten pounds about thirty-seven times over a three-year period. Since then, she's learned the hard way that she needs to eat a certain amount of food in order to stay sane, that she needs to exercise a certain amount in order to feel comfortable in her own skin, and that dieting is really nothing more than an institutionalized form of masochism, something that's so fundamentally at odds with basic human needs and desires that it's almost guaranteed to backfire. Over the years, Alice K. has even learned to like healthful, low-fat foods and most days, she gravitates instinctually toward things like fish and chicken and pasta dishes without heavy cream and butter sauces.

Still, every once in a while, something will crack. Alice K. will get a bad case of premenstrual bloat. Or she will be too busy to exercise for too many days in a row. Something will happen, and all of a sudden Alice K.'s clothes will feel too tight, and her self-consciousness about the size of her thighs will intensify, and—yes—it's inevitable: she will find herself sitting on her sofa, trapped in enemy jeans.

Sitting there now, Alice K. shifts uncomfortably, stares down at her legs, and sighs. She contemplates her options. Should she go work out? Should she try to forget about her thighs, eat a normal dinner, and wait for her jeans to restore themselves to a friendlier state? Should she spend the evening pondering this women-and-food thing, struggling to attain some greater level of insight and peace of mind?

She closes her eyes and prays. She says, "God, please let me be normal about food and eating. Please take away this excruciating self-consciousness. Heal me, God. Heal me."

She pauses, considers something else, then speaks again. "And while I'm at it, God, thank you for inventing sweatpants."

step aerobics

"And *one!* And *two!* And *right!* And *right!* And *left!* And *left!*"

Alice K. is in the middle of step aerobics. The instructor, a perky, muscle-bound redhead with a high ponytail and a pink Latex leotard, is leading the group in a series of warm-up maneuvers which involve standing with the feet apart, leaning forward slightly from the waist, and punching at the air: *right* punch, *right* punch; *left* punch, *left* punch. A bad Donna Summer song from the '70s is blasting on the radio, and Alice K. feels like a total idiot.

A *total* idiot.

Why am I here? she thinks, punching, punching. And then—*oooops!* Alice K. forgot to switch from her right punching arm to her left punching arm and she nearly nailed the woman next to her.

I am too uncoordinated for aerobics, Alice K. thinks. *I find it too confusing.*

This is true. Alice K. tends to get tied up in knots, aerobics-wise. There's something about standing opposite an aerobics instructor, trying to mimic her actions, *plus* trying to remember which is her right and left and which is your right and left, *and* trying to anticipate which move or motion is coming up next, *and* trying to maintain some semblance of rhythm and balance that just gets her all cloudy in the head. *Right, right, left, left, arm, arm, leg, waist, wait! Where am I?*

Alice K. is the sort of aerobics-class member who's always falling just a tad out of step, always struggling to keep up, and always hip-hopping awkwardly from one foot to the other in order to compensate for her errors.

She thinks, *This is supposed to be fun? This is not fun.*

Alice K. hates the competitiveness of the aerobics class. Who's wearing what? Who's thinner than who? Who looks more toned? Who has snazzier sneakers? It is a subtle and insidious kind of competitiveness, full of sly glances and little sneers, and it brings out the worst in women. For her part, Alice K. likes to blend into the background. She wears the most nondescript aerobics attire she can find (black leotard; black sweats or gym shorts), she stands in the back row, as far away from the other members as possible, and she watches with amazement as other women jockey and preen and practically wrestle each other for a place right in front of the instructor, or right in front of the mirror, or both.

These are the Studettes. They put on lipstick before class, and they wear little midriff things over their unitards, and they continually steal little looks at themselves in the mirror during class, and they wear *thongs.*

Thongs. What is this thong thing? Alice K. would really like to know. Once, in a very secret experiment that she didn't even share with Ruth E., Alice K. actually tried on a thong bathing suit in a department store. A horrifying experience. *Disgusting!* She stood there, this thick, braidlike thong cutting like a knife between the cheeks of her rear end, her butt all white and exposed and kind of pear-shaped on either side—not at all perfectly round and tan like the ones you see in the *Sports Illustrated* swimsuit issue—and Alice K. thought she was going to die.

I would not wear this thong bathing suit to the beach if you paid me a million dollars, she thought, and tore the thing off as fast as she could. *Thongs belong on the feet, not the female rear end.* Accordingly, when Alice K. actually sees a woman in an aerobics outfit with a thong—in other words, a Studette— she registers shock and disbelief. A part of her wants to run up and ask questions. *How can you stand it? Doesn't it* hurt? But another part of her figures that it's not worth the effort. As Alice K. understands, a woman who parades around in a thong (and there's no other way to wear one; you either parade around in it or you tear the thing off as fast as you can) is so different from Alice K. that she might as well be from another planet.

Yes, she is a Studette and I am not; it's not worth attempting to communicate. That's what Alice K. thinks. Studettes make her angry and contemptuous and resentful. Their preoccupation with their appearance and clothing and bodies confuses her, not because it's foreign to her (it isn't at all), but because it's manifested in a way that makes her uncomfortable, a way that raises ugly, difficult questions about what women are really like and how they respond to the world around them.

Questions like this: Does a woman wear a thong because it makes her feel good about herself or because it elicits gawks from the men in the gym? And if it's the latter, is that a bad thing or is it okay?

Is all this attiring and posturing and checking out of other women a part of the female nature? Are these women just being a little more obvious than Alice K., or are they genuinely more superficial or self-absorbed?

And what is Alice K. herself doing in there, punching and stretching and huffing and puffing? Is she exercising because it makes her feel calmer and stronger? Because it allows her to eat? Because it helps her maintain her weight and thus feel more attractive to other people? Or all three?

Alice K. contemplates this last question. Her relationship with exercise has been long and complex. Alice K. failed miserably at competitive sports in high school and gave athletics up entirely until the early '80s, when the fitness cabal forced everyone into running shoes and leotards. Since then, she has tried just about everything. Running (too boring, too hard on the knees). Squash and racquetball (too much hand-eye coordination required). Bicycle riding (too dependent on the weather). Swimming (too wet).

Today, now in something like her eleventh health-club membership, Alice K. has actually settled into a routine that she can live with. She goes at lunchtime, when the place is nearly empty and she can work out without feeling exposed or self-conscious. She uses the rowing machine, which makes her sweat hard (and Alice K. has discovered the joy of sweating hard: it feels good). She does some free weights, which make her feel strong. She does stretches and sit-ups and often takes a long sauna afterward. But occasionally, if she can't make it to the gym during the day or the weight room is too full of beefy men, Alice K. will take an aerobics class. She secretly hates them, but it makes her feel less guilty than doing nothing, and it helps Alice K. keep her finger on the pulse of womanhood.

"And *one!* And *two!* And *lift* that leg! *Lift* that leg!"

The class has moved on to leg lifts. Alice K. is on her hands and knees lifting her leg up and to the side, up and to the side, up and to the side, like a dog with a serious urinary problem at a hydrant.

Alice K., huffing slightly, looks up and sighs. *Oh, well,* she thinks, *it could be worse. Dr. Y. could be watching.*

hair

Alice K. is standing in front of the mirror, can of mousse in one hand, styling brush in the other, wrestling in vain with her hair.

Alice K. has been here for forty-five minutes.

She stares into the mirror. It is one of those days. Her hair looks stringy, plastered against her head. A few strands stick out in unlikely places, resisting the combined forces of spray, gel, and gravity. The color seems all wrong. So does the texture. So does the way it falls about her face.

Worse, it looks pouffy.

Pouffy. As Alice K. well knows, only a woman in the throes of hair trauma can fully appreciate a word like "pouffy." It's a devastating word, rife with negative associations.

"It's all pouffy! Can't you see it? Right over there! Look! It's *POUFFING!*"

This is the kind of thing an otherwise intelligent, articulate woman will say when she is standing in front of a mirror in mid–hair crisis. She will look fearful and aghast. She will point to the offending pouff as though it were symptomatic of a dread disease. Sometimes, she will weep.

Alice K. and Ruth E. discuss this frequently. "Why are we like this?" Alice K. asks. "Do men do this?"

"Only if they're losing their hair," Ruth E. answers, "in which case they're worse than us. But ordinary bad hair? Men don't obsess the way we do, at least not straight men and not to the same extent."

Alice K. agrees. A man might feel a private pang of despair or embarrassment at a bad haircut, but he won't call up all his friends for support, he won't stand in the men's room at work for three straight hours trying to force his hair into some position it doesn't want to go, and he won't burst into tears when his friends, worn down, finally concede that the haircut is in fact terrible by uttering those devastating words: *"Don't worry, it'll grow back."*

So what is this? Alice K. wonders, standing there in her bathroom, mid-mousse. *What is it about a bad haircut that can attack the self-esteem with such devastating force? Why is it that a good haircut can be a life-altering event? And why is that for so many of us, finding the right haircut can be as hard (and as terrifying) as finding the right job, the right apartment, the right boyfriend?*

Of course, Alice K. already knows the answers: If eyes are the window to the soul, hair is the measure of the ego: it's one of the most self-defining aspects of a woman's physiology, more so than large or small breasts, fat or thin thighs, long or short legs. It's something you can change, use to good or ill effect. And as all but the most fearless women know, to be brave about hair is to be brave about life: cut it, color it, change it dramatically, and you call into question your very sense of self.

This is why Alice K. can spend hours with other women debating the merits of mousse versus gel, spray versus spritz, perms versus body waves, bangs versus no bangs, beer rinses versus vinegar rinses, hot oil treatments versus deep conditioning, and on and on. Alice K. would never admit this in therapy, but beneath all that fussing and spritzing and tinting, her self-esteem is on the line. Her fantasies. Her wishes to look—and so to feel—better, more sophisticated, more self-possessed.

This is also why, for Alice K., a trip to the hairdresser tends to be such a frightening event. After all, when you walk into a salon and surrender your head to a stylist, you are really surrendering your ego. No matter how intelligent and well-reasoned you may feel inside, you carry with you the hope that you will walk out a different woman. Alice K., for example, has straight, dark brown, shoulder-length hair and for this reason, she has spent years and years marching into salons equipped with photos clipped from magazines of women with curly, blonde, waist-length hair. "Hi," she'd say. "I'd like something a little like this."

Then came the surrender phase. This took place during the '80s, around the time when hairdressers started calling themselves *stylistes* and salons started feeling like the headquarters of cults. Chrome and blasting music and exotic chemical treatments. Artistes wielding scissors and spray. Alice K. would walk in, surrender her head to the snooty *styliste,* and then listen to her verbal skills deteriorate, specificity giving way to vague and fearful abstractions. She'd stammer, "Um, well . . . I want something different but not too different, you know? I mean, I'd like it to kind of fall *this* way, not *that* way, but I don't want it to be flat on top, and I'd like it to have more body, but no frizz, I definitely don't want frizz, and . . ." Finally, *styliste* poised with scissors in hand, Alice K. would bow her head and issue silent prayers to the Salon Gods: "Please, Gods," she would pray, "please giveth me a good cut, please giveth me a cut that falls just so about my jawline and always looks good in the morning, a cut that just needeth to be washed and shaken in order to fall into place, a cut that doesn't require that I spend forty-five minutes each morning trying to beat it into submission with a blow dryer. Please, oh God, please, please."

This was hopeless, futile. She might as well have walked into a clothing store and said, "I'd like to fit into a size four dress even though I wear a size nine, okay? And while you're at it, I'd like to have longer legs and bigger breasts and a smaller waist, too."

But still Alice K. persists. She hopes and longs. She spritzes and sprays and mousses and sometimes, her worst fears are realized and—Oh, evil Gods!—she enters the land of the truly bad haircut.

Alice K. stands before the mirror (she has abandoned the mousse and deployed an alternative strategy involving barrettes), and contemplates the truly bad haircut. The kind of haircut that makes you spend the next forty days and forty nights moaning, "Why? Why, oh why did I ever do this to my-self?" The kind of dead-wrong style that causes your sense of self—your sense of sexuality, of attractiveness to others—to drift downward to the floor with each maiming snip.

Alice K. has had three. The first took place shortly after she graduated from college, and several months after she had (quite daringly, she thought) changed her center-parted, waist-length hair to center-parted, shoulder-length hair. She went to a *styliste* downtown. She uttered a set of amazingly brave words: "Just do whatever you think would look best—I want something completely different." And two hours and a vast sum of money later, she walked out with some gruesome, layered affair, stubs of hair sticking out about her head like needles on a porcupine. Alice K. imme-diately went to her car, sat on her glasses, tore home, ran over a squirrel on the way, and spent the next three days in the bathroom with Ruth E., sobbing.

The second involved something with bangs and wings. It looked okay, but it required a phenomenal amount of daily styling and maintenance, and it caused Alice K. to de-velop a severe mousse dependency that lasted for nearly two years.

The third involved a bad perm. Today, Alice K. has suc-cessfully repressed the memory of the bad perm and will not discuss it, except to say that she spent the next four years en-gaged in a furious, daily battle that involved blow dryers, a curling iron, and a great deal of experimentation with hats. These days, *stylistes* constantly tell Alice K. that bad perms are a thing of the past, that the chemicals they use today are "re-ally gentle" and "really natural." She doesn't believe this for a minute.

But then again, Alice K. does not abandon hope, either. Why, just the other day, she ran into a colleague in the la-dies' room at work and noticed something . . . different. Al-ice K. couldn't quite place it, but she looked more sophisti-cated, more self-possessed.

Alice K. asked, "Did you cut your hair?"

The co-worker smiled. "Yes."

Alice K. admired the new look, and said it was the kind of haircut that really changed her appearance without screaming *New Haircut!*

The co-worker smiled again. "Well, I really wanted a *change.*" She emphasized that last word, as though she meant it in far more than the physical sense.

Then Alice K. said something about how that must have been a really big, life-altering event. The woman looked serious and nodded, and they both knew it was true, that the haircut represented some profound internal shift, as well as an external one. Then the co-worker left and Alice K. stood there, shaking her head. An amazing thing, the perfect haircut.

the male body, part i: gross men

Alice K. and Ruth E. are talking over drinks. Ruth E. has been in a meeting for the better part of the day, and she has come to the following conclusion: Ruth E. knows a lot of men who do gross things in front of other people.

"It's really unbelievable," she says. "I'm sitting there looking around the conference room, and this one is picking his teeth, and that one is picking his nose, and that one is also picking his nose, and, I mean, it's *disgusting.*"

Alice K. nods seriously. Disgusting. And then she tells Ruth E. about loaning her boss her pen in a meeting, then sitting there watching as her boss took the pen, wrote something down, then stuck the pen in his ear. Then he twisted the pen around, pulled it out, and looked at it. Then he stuck it back in, twisted it some more, and looked at it some more.

"This is a true story," Alice K. says.

"Disgusting!" Ruth E. says.

"Gross!" they both say.

Later, Alice K. ponders this phenomenon. She realizes, of course, that not all men are so indiscreet when it comes to personal hygiene and bodily functions. Elliot M., for example, would find the idea of borrowing a woman's pen and twisting it in his ear as appalling as she does. But Alice K. also knows a lot of gross men. Or seems to.

What is this behavior? she wonders. *What makes someone uninhibited to the point where public teeth- and nose-picking seems utterly natural? Why are some men so . . . so gross?*

Seeking answers, Alice K. called her Aunt K., a wise woman. She asked her, "Aunt K., do you know a lot of gross men? Men who do disgusting things in public?"

Aunt K. said, "You mean, like farting?"

Being discreet about such matters, especially with her older relatives, Alice K. did not pursue that line of inquiry in great detail. But she did relate the pen-twisting story. Aunt K. turned out to be unfamiliar with that mode of behavior, but she did have a fair amount to say about belching.

"It's really awful," she said. "You'll be sitting there at an expensive restaurant and some man will let out some horrible sound." She made a feeble attempt to imitate the sound—something like "blrrrrecccch"—but it wasn't necessary. Alice K. knew what it sounded like and she knew it was gross.

Aunt K. continued: "Women do not do that. They do not belch like that in public."

Alice K. nodded into the phone. Indeed. Most women she knows would no sooner let out a ripping belch at an elegant restaurant than they would stand up and brazenly attempt to adjust a sanitary napkin that had slipped out of place in their underwear. They just wouldn't.

Later, she calls up Ruth E. with another perplexing observation: "Here's something else," she says. "Men seem to be a lot more preoccupied with their bowels than women are—and they're a lot more public about the activities of the lower tract."

Aunt K. described this as a generational thing—in her day, a lot of women were equally obsessed with their bowels. They would talk about it, and think about it, and if they did not "produce" each day (that's Aunt K.'s word; she's very delicate), they would panic and take measures: enemas, high-colonics, and such.

Women, Alice K. thought at the time, seem to have evolved beyond that state, but she also knows that the bowels are a topic of endless fascination for a lot of men. She knows men who actually brag about their morning "production." She knows men who compare notes, kind of a digestive counterpart to who has the bigger dick, an "I'm more regular than you are" thing, heh, heh, heh.

"Isn't this weird?" Alice K. asks Ruth E. "Why *is* this? Are men just naturally less inhibited about bodily functions than women are? Am I just being a prude?"

Ruth E. doesn't think so. "Just look at all the stuff men do!" she says. "It's gross!"

They run through a list:

- Neither Alice K. nor Ruth E. has ever seen a woman blow her nose into a tissue and then open up the tissue and look at it to see what came out. But they have both seen men do this, plenty of times. In public. In meetings. On the *bus*.
- Neither Alice K. nor Ruth E. has ever seen a woman blow her nose *without* a tissue. Like out on the street. Just block one nostril with a finger and then—honk!—let 'er rip, right there in public.
- Likewise, neither Alice K. nor Ruth E. has ever heard a woman engaged in that grotesque kind of sucking-and-smacking tooth thing that they've seen (and heard) men doing to get stuff dislodged from their teeth. Or make that horrible throat-clearing, retching sound and then lean over and spit some large specimen of phlegm into the sink or on the street.

"We may do some of these things," Ruth E. says. "I won't pretend women are *that* delicate—but at least we do them in private."

Then Ruth E. evokes evolutionary theory. "Have you ever seen a documentary about apes?" she asks. "You know how they'll sit around picking at themselves and grunting? They look suspiciously like men, don't they?"

Alice K. nods. Interesting idea, she thinks, but it doesn't quite explain how, or why, women may have evolved differently.

Later, she calls up her sister, Beth K., and asks for her opinion. "I think it's that men seem to think they're invisible," Beth K. says. "Especially in cars. They think they're the only person on the road. That's why you can drive past a guy and his finger will be buried in his nose up to the second knuckle. It's gross, but they don't care because they assume no one is watching."

They assume no one is watching. This phrase sticks in Alice K.'s mind and she decides it is key.

Unlike women, she thinks, who are told from a tiny age that everyone on God's green earth will notice if so much as a hair on their heads is out of place, men are raised with a much more liberating set of assumptions: no one will see. No one will notice if you pick your nose in public or twirl a pen in your ear. And—best of all!—no one will *care*. So when a guy is sitting in a meeting, he may be preoccupied with power and posturing and one-upmanship and all those other guy dynamics, but at least he doesn't have to worry about what's hanging out of his nose or lodged between his teeth.

She shares this theory with Ruth E.

Ruth E. ponders it carefully and nods. Then she says, "Of course, there may be a simpler explanation too: Maybe men are just gross."

Alice K. isn't sure, but she does know one thing: From now on, she's keeping her pens to herself.

the male body, part ii: men and their dicks

"So what is it with men and their dicks?" Alice K. says. "I really want to know."

Alice K. and Ruth E. are talking over drinks again, and Alice K. is most perplexed.

"They *name* their dicks," she says. "The average man must have at least twenty-seven names for his dick."

She runs through a list: weenie, and wang, and tool, and member, and pecker, and war club, and love muscle, and love gun, and meat pole, and (her personal favorite) one-eyed trouser snake. And on and on and on.

"I know a guy who calls his 'Persuasion,' " says Ruth E. "And another who calls it his 'Résumé.' "

Alice K. shakes her head. "Why do they do this?"

Next, they move on to the subject of male masturbation. Men, Alice K. points out, also have forty-seven ways to describe masturbation. Choking the chicken. Flogging the dolphin. Buffing the musket. Slappin' it. Flappin' it. Wackin' it.

She says, "Women are so much more discreet about their reproductive anatomy. See? We call it 'reproductive anatomy.' We are so genteel in our descriptions we're almost prissy."

She pauses. "Remember how we used to talk about our periods when we were fifteen? Remember how we'd whisper? *'I have it.'* That's what we called our periods: 'it.' "

Ruth E. rolls her eyes. "Or 'my friend.' Remember that one? 'I have my friend.' "

Serious nod: "Oh, yes. Your *friend.*"

Men would not talk this way, Alice K. thinks. She remembers reading a column by Gloria Steinem about what would happen if men menstruated: they'd brag about it. They'd run up to each other in the schoolyard and say, "Hey, man, I am *on the rag!*" They'd boast about how many tampons they went through in a day.

Once, a month or two into their relationship, Alice K.

tried to discuss this phenomenon with Elliot M., a conversation that made her realize that despite their apparent love affairs with their dicks, men can be surprisingly reticent about the subject.

"I am not going to talk to you about men and their dicks," Elliot M. said. "I am not going to get into this. I refuse."

Alice K. poured him a glass of wine and waited for him to soften. She said, "A woman has a very hard time saying the word *cunt*. To women, this sounds crass and grotesque. It makes them visibly uncomfortable. So why is it that men can use a phrase like 'one-eyed trouser snake' and think it's funny?"

"Because it is!"

Then Elliot M. loosened up a little and segued into a somewhat familiar train of thought about how male genitals are external and female genitals are internal and how because of this difference, men have an easier time talking about things sexual in objective, external terms while women are more prone to think about them as internal matters.

"Maybe," Alice K. said, "but I don't think it's all physiology and hormones."

"Well, if you had this thing hanging there between your legs," he said, "you'd probably have a different attitude about it, too." Then he started free-associating about what it was like to be a sixteen-year-old boy sitting there in math class and getting a screaming erection for absolutely no apparent reason and having to stand up at the end of class and . . . well, how it's just pretty hard to be a guy and not be wildly conscious of your sexuality at least 98 percent of the time.

As Alice K. sat there listening, she began to notice the presence of an odd feeling. At first she felt defensive, as if she wanted to say, "Okay, I am sick of hearing about you boys and your hormones and how ridiculously horny you get just sitting there in math class." But then the feeling evolved into something more like . . . jealousy. No, not penis envy. Alice K. has never once in her life had the desire to have several inches of

rather unremarkable-looking flesh influence her entire outlook on life and love. She meant something else.

She was jealous because her memory of being sixteen years
old and sitting in math class is so decidedly less sexual. Back
then, she recalls, she sat there and worried about zits. Or about
what she was wearing. Or about why some particular boy she
liked hadn't looked at her that day even once. Probably he was
too focused on his screaming erection to look at Alice K., but
she didn't know about those things back then, so she figured it
was her fault; she wasn't interesting enough, or pretty enough.

And that, she thinks now, is precisely the point. It would
be so much easier to grow up male and to be so in touch
with your sexuality and sexual impulses, to have your whole
being dominated by that singular wish: to get laid.

She discusses this with Ruth E. the following day. "It's an
equation," she says. "You have a dick, you want sex. And you
are taught from an early age that this is okay, the way it should
be."

Ruth E. agrees, and they get into a long discussion
about the kinds of things you are taught when you grow up
female, about how many weird messages you get. "We are
taught that our vaginas are dangerous and scary and dirty,"
Ruth E. says. "If you're a man, you're taught to see sex as a
goal; if you're a woman, you're taught to avoid it. So of
course we don't think about sex—or talk about it—with that
kind of bravado."

Alice K. nods soberly. *Yes,* she thinks. *Our sexuality gets de-
flected onto all those annoying externals: How we look and what
we're wearing, and how we behaved every single time a boy came
within spitting distance in the cafeteria.*

She feels sad, thinking this. "When you grow up female," Alice K. says, "you get saddled with all the burdens of
being attractive and very few of the pleasures of being *attracted.* Is this not true?"

Ruth E. agrees. She says, "Yes. And beyond that, even if
you happen to be attractive naturally, you're not allowed just to

sit back, wallow in the attention, and learn to enjoy your sexuality. This may be the '90s, but, as a man might say, I'd bet my left nut that boys will still call you a slut if you sleep around."

That night, lying in bed, Alice K. ponders that thought and feels sadder still. It's hard enough, Alice K. believes, to have the kind of anatomy that doesn't scream sexual messages at you the way male anatomy seems to. It's hard enough to grow up in a culture that sometimes equates sex with deep, romantic love and sometimes makes the two seem mutually exclusive. But when you add a million mixed messages into that stew (Be attractive! Not too attractive! Be sexual! Don't sleep around!), it's no wonder that women get all weird when they talk about their own bodies. It's no wonder they come up with eleven different names for stupid, trivial things (lipstick is "lip gloss" is "lip color" is "lip blush") instead of meaningful, important things.

She tosses in her bed. *When you're taught that something isn't valuable in its own right,* she thinks, *you don't give it a name.*

And then, suddenly, Alice K. has a brilliant idea, a revelation. She sits bolt upright in bed.

I know, she thinks. *From now on, I'll call mine 'Martha!'* "

ALICE K. IN LOVE, PART IV: CRUEL REALITIES

Twenty-four hours later:

"So why were you there in the first place?"

"What do you mean, why was I there? I go to The Point all the time!"

"Yeah, but . . . Ruth E., why did you leave with Mr. Danger? I mean, what is going on?"

Alice K. (not her real initial) is sitting at a restaurant with Ruth E., and she is writhing with feelings of confusion and betrayal. An omelette sits on a plate before her, uneaten, and she keeps suppressing the wish to scream. This is the morning after, you see. The morning after The Incident.

Ruth E. does not understand why Alice K. is so upset. Ruth E. claims that Alice K. is being ridiculous. Ruth E. claims that this is a simple misunderstanding.

She'd gone to The Point with a group of friends, Ruth E. says, and Mr. Danger and some of the members of his band joined them at the table and drank for a while. Then, Ruth E.

claims, toward the end of the night she got a screaming head-ache and wanted to leave, but none of her friends were ready to go. So when Mr. Danger stood up and said he was taking off, Ruth E. asked him for a ride. That, Ruth E. says, was that.

Alice K. is having trouble accepting this. "But . . . well, then why did he have his arm around you?"

Ruth E. rolls her eyes. "Because that's the kind of guy he is. He's a die-hard flirt and he's probably genetically inca-pable of being with a woman for more than thirty-five sec-onds without coming on to her."

"So he *did* come on to you?"

"Alice K.!" Ruth E. is practically shouting. "Give it a rest, would you?!"

But Alice K. cannot give it a rest. She simply cannot. It's not that she doesn't believe Ruth E. about the facts—she be-lieves that Ruth E. had a headache and wanted to leave; she believes that Mr. Danger drove her home; she even believes (and Ruth E. swears this is true) that he didn't invite himself in, or try to kiss her, or ask her out. But there is something about the whole thing—something about the image of Ruth E. in the parking lot with Mr. Danger, something about her al-lowing him to put his arm around her and flirt with her and drive her home—that bothers Alice K. to the bottom of her soul, and she doesn't know what to do about it.

She sits back in her seat and pushes the omelette across the plate with her fork. She doesn't know what to say.

Ruth E. adopts a softer tone. "Alice K., listen. Nothing happened, okay? Nada. Can we just forget about this and, like, go shopping or something?"

Alice K. nods, but it doesn't feel convincing. She feels betrayed. She feels confused. And underneath it all— underneath this attempt to discuss the evening with Ruth E., and to sort out the events as they unfolded—Alice K. feels as though some hidden edge of competitiveness or mistrust in their friendship has been exposed, a feeling that's lain there, dormant and waiting, for years.

"I guess . . ." Alice K. has something to say, but she's not sure how to put it. She swallows hard and starts over. "I guess . . . I mean, it just makes me feel weird. It makes me feel really weird that I'm having this big fight with Elliot M. and I'm all upset and meanwhile my closest friend is driving around with this guy who's obviously a womanizer, and who I once slept with, and who—"

Ruth E. interrupts. "Jesus Christ, Alice K. It was a ride. A *ride*. We didn't exactly elope to Las Vegas, you know. I mean, come on!"

An uncomfortable moment passes before Ruth E. breaks the silence. "Plus, so what if you slept with him? What difference does that make?"

Alice K. responds instinctively. "It makes a difference," she says. "It just does."

Sitting there, feeling like she's about to cry, Alice K. ponders this. Why *does* it make a difference? After all, Mr. Danger is a rat, a womanizing rat. She knows this. So why *should* she feel so bothered that this man—this discarded piece of Alice K.'s past—gave Ruth E. a ride home?

She answers the question herself: *This isn't about Ruth E. and Mr. Danger,* Alice K. thinks. *It's about Ruth E. and me. I am jealous of Ruth E. and I hate it.*

For that's the truth of the matter. That's what kept Alice K. awake the previous night. Ruth E. is spontaneous and tough and hard-boiled; she speaks her mind and she doesn't give a whit what other people think of her, and somewhere, in a deep corner of her heart, Alice K. has always suspected that these qualities make Ruth E. more attractive to men than Alice K. is—especially to men like Mr. Danger. And that's why the image of Ruth E. in the parking lot with Mr. Danger makes Alice K. so uncomfortable: it reinforces Alice K.'s suspicions and it fills her with despair and rage, jealousy's evil twins.

Ruth E. fumbles in her purse for a cigarette and Alice K. steals a glance at her. Ruth E. is so damn confident. Alice K.

hates her for this sometimes. She has beautiful skin, and thick hair that looks good even when it's just tossed back in a careless ponytail, and her lipstick never seems to fade or smear, and sometimes Alice K. wants to choke the life out of her.

Jealousy, Alice K. thinks, *is a poisonous emotion. It brings out the absolute worst in people.*

She hates feeling jealous of Ruth E. She loathes it, but sitting there, contemplating how different she and Ruth E. are, a part of her can't help it.

Ruth E. is so much less obsessive than I am, Alice K. thinks. *She's so much less fearful and introspective and prone to lying in bed at night writhing with fear and worry.* Sometimes those differences seem to complement Alice K., but other times, like now, they make her feel resentful, as though Ruth E. has it easier than she does, as though by some arbitrary luck of the draw, Ruth E. just got to be free from so much anxiety and soul-searching and self-doubt.

A line comes to Alice K.'s mind, something Dr. Y. once said about the connection between jealousy and mistrust, about how they usually exist in tandem.

Alice K. contemplates that thought: Perhaps that's what's gnawing at her; perhaps this incident has raised an accompanying question about whether or not Ruth E. is trustworthy.

Ruth E., Alice K. thinks, *is the sort of woman who probably would have slept with Mr. Danger if that's what she felt like doing at the time. If her impulses said go for it, she'd go for it and that would be that.* There was a selfishness to her, an ability to move blithely through the world, and Alice K. reacted to these qualities with an odd mix of envy and rage.

Just then, Ruth E. interrupts her train of thought. "Listen, Alice K.," she says. "I really think you're making a mountain out of a molehill here. Nothing happened, all right? Can we please just drop it?"

Alice K. looks across the table at Ruth E. and nods.

"Okay," she says, "let's forget it." But inside, Alice K. knows that she is lying.

Two days later:

Alice K. lies in bed, struggling with the concept of female intimacy.

I thought this was supposed to be the easy stuff, she thinks. *I thought your girlfriends were the ones you never had to worry about.*

But this is proving not to be true.

Never mind Ruth E.'s reassurances. Alice K. left their breakfast feeling that their friendship had been altered in a way she couldn't quite describe, and then she went home, a little lonely and a little depressed and not at all interested in spending the rest of the day with Ruth E.

That feeling of aversion has persisted. The day after their conversation, Ruth E. called up Alice K. to ask if she wanted to go to a movie, and Alice K. actually told a lie. "Um . . . I can't," she said. "I promised this woman from work I'd meet her for a drink." And then she wrapped up the conversation quickly, feeling awkward and confused.

The fact of the matter is, Alice K. is still angry at Ruth E. When she thinks of Ruth E. walking across that parking lot with Mr. Danger, she still feels betrayed, as though Ruth E. had violated some kind of unwritten rule: THOU SHALT NOT FLIRT WITH A MAN YOUR BEST FRIEND HAS SLEPT WITH FOR A PERIOD OF NO LESS THAN FIVE YEARS. There was an intimacy to the image, and the fact that Ruth E. engaged in that intimacy made Alice K. feel hurt and estranged.

Even Ruth E.'s attempt to dismiss the incident bothers Alice K.; it feels like an attempt to dismiss Alice K.'s feelings, and that, she thinks, is not something a best friend should do.

Earlier in the day, Alice K. tried to communicate some of these feelings to Dr. Y., but Dr. Y. didn't get it (or so it seemed to Alice K.).

"I guess we're just really different in some ways," Alice K. said. "Ruth E. has always had this selfish streak that sort of bothers me. She's much more impetuous than I am, and I don't think she's the kind of person who'd necessarily consider how I'd feel about her being with Jack S."

Dr. Y. looked sort of blank. "Well, is that such a bad thing?" he asked. "Isn't it okay for the two of you to be different?"

Alice K. merely shrugged at the time, secretly annoyed at his lack of sophistication about girlfriends. But now, staring at the ceiling, she contemplates his comment. In a way, she thinks, this whole episode with Ruth E. has made her feel the way she feels when a boyfriend does something hurtful. It gnaws at her, and makes her feel misunderstood and mistreated, and this makes Alice K. wonder if maybe she's expecting too much from Ruth E.

Dr. Y. had wondered that, too. "The way you describe Ruth E.," he'd said, "reminds me a little of the way you've described Elliot M.—the same wish for an ideal companion, the same wish for someone who's incapable of disappointing you."

Alice K.'s eyes had welled up with tears at that comment. It made her think about how long she'd known Ruth E. (since college!), and about how much she'd relied upon her friendship, and about how that relationship had helped sustain her through all her other disappointments: with men, with bosses, with her family.

She'd looked at Dr. Y. and sniffled. "But Ruth E. *did* disappoint me," she said. "I feel really hurt."

Dr. Y. had fallen silent for a moment, and then said, softly, "I know. It happens sometimes."

Alice K. shifts under the sheets and sighs. On the one hand, she still feels upset with Ruth E., and confused, and angry. And on the other hand, she knows that Dr. Y.'s comment is true: Hurt and disappointment are facts of life. Alice K. may have a harder time tolerating disappointment than some people, but in her rational mind she knows that she can't avoid them, that she must learn to accept these ebbs and flows in relationships, in trust and intimacy and closeness.

Maybe I am holding Ruth E. to higher standards than everybody else, she thinks. *Maybe I am doing the same thing I do in relationships with men: freaking out when things don't feel perfect, freaking out at any sign of a flaw.*

Alice K. lies in bed for a while longer, contemplating this and struggling to be rational. *Maybe Ruth E. is right,* she thinks. *Maybe I am making a mountain out of a molehill. Maybe I should just chalk this up to intimacy problems and try to let it go.*

About ten minutes later, the phone rings, and Alice K. sits up in bed.

The thought flashes through her mind—*It's Ruth E.! Ruth E. reading my mind and feeling as badly as I do and wanting to talk!*—so Alice K. is most pleased and relieved to hear Ruth E.'s voice on the line.

"Did I wake you?"

"No ... no ... what's up?" Alice K. has flipped on the light at this point, in preparation for a long friendship dialogue with Ruth E.

Ruth E. clears her throat and says she has something to discuss. There is an edge of discomfort in her voice. "Listen, Alice K.," she says. "I got a call tonight and I need to talk to you. Jack S. asked me out."

Sixteen hours later:

"I told him the same thing you did: adios. Sayonara. Hasta la vista, baby."

"You did?"

Alice K. is sitting in a restaurant with Ruth E., and a feeling of relief and joy is washing over her.

"Yup. I told him, 'Look, Jack S. You were nice enough to give me a ride home the other night, and I appreciate that, but I am not interested in going out with you. No, thank you.' "

"You *did?*"

"I did. And I also told him that I did not appreciate the way he had treated my best friend, Alice K., and I told him that I thought men like him should periodically be hung upside down by their toenails in order to give them some lessons in basic human feelings, such as pain."

"Ruth E., you are the best."

Ruth E. smiles. "I know."

Thank God, Alice K. thinks. *What a relief.*

Following Ruth E.'s phone call, after all, Alice K. lay awake for hours thinking the worst. *Oh my God,* she thought. *Ruth E. is going to tell me that she is going out with Mr. Danger, and I will never be able to trust her again, and I will have lost not only Elliot M., who hasn't called me since our last big fight, but also my best friend!*

For that is the one clear resolution Alice K. had made about the situation: Friends do not go out with their friends' ex-boyfriends. Period. End of discussion. They just don't. Alice K. could maybe—*maybe*—forgive Ruth E. for flirting with Mr. Danger (and, truth be told, she was still a little ambivalent about that concept), but she could not tolerate anything beyond that. When it came to female camaraderie, he was off limits.

So resolved, Alice K. had shown up at the restaurant after work all prepared for a showdown with Ruth E. She had rehearsed her lines, stockpiled her emotional ammunition, even ordered a large glass of Scotch for good measure, in case she lost her will. And when Ruth E. sat down and announced that—just like Alice K.—she had told the womanizing rat to take a hike, Alice K. just sat there in a state of awe and gratitude. *Thank you, God,* she thought. *Thank you, Ruth E.*

Now, the two of them halfway into a long gab and a bottle of wine, Alice K. sits there and marvels. *Ruth E. can be selfish and impetuous and crazy,* she thinks, *but she is on my side, and that's the important thing.*

Those qualities, Alice K. realizes, are also the things she loves about Ruth E. She may be a little brash and a little insensitive, and she may go through life blithely, not always considering the way her actions affect other people. But she's also the kind of woman who can look a Mr. Danger straight in the eye and tell him to go hang upside down by his toenails, and Alice K. regards this with genuine awe.

Alice K. recalls a recent therapy session in which Dr. Y. talked about how difficult it often is for Alice K. to tolerate ambiguity in relationships and shifts of feeling and moments of disappointment. She had that problem, in spades, with Elliot M., a problem that manifested itself in a near inability to stand it when he didn't measure up to her vision of what a relationship should be, and Alice K. finds it reassuring to think she's managed to live through a period of uncertainty and disappointment with Ruth E.

Dr. Y. is right, she thinks. *If you can tolerate those moments, things usually do have a way of resolving themselves. Maybe I am actually learning something here.*

She sits back and looks across the room. For a brief moment, Alice K. realizes, she has a feeling of peace—a rare sense that she's capable of managing relationships, of tolerating the bad times and appreciating the good.

And just then, a man walks into the restaurant, someone Alice K. hasn't seen in years. Alice K. notices him and begins to stare, her mouth agape.

"Oh my God," she whispers.

"What?"

"Over there . . ." She stops. Alice K. is practically speechless.

"That guy, the one in the leather jacket. I can't believe it's him. I haven't seen him in *years.*"

Alice K. gestures in his direction and Ruth E. steals a look. "Nice," she says.

Next, Alice K. turns and stares straight at Ruth E. She can feel her face reddening and her hands begin to tremble.

"Don't you recognize him?" she asks. She looks at him again. "That," she says, "is Mr. Cruel."

Two hours later:

Alice K. lies in bed, writhing with anxiety and disbelief.

He is back, she thinks. *Mr. Cruel is back.*

Alice K. is astonished.

Mr. Cruel was Alice K.'s boyfriend for four years, her moody and complex boyfriend for four long and excruciatingly difficult years. She met him the year after she graduated from college and she has always considered him one of her first adult relationships—or, at least, one of the first relationships that taught her anything about being an adult and being in a relationship at the same time.

"Mr. Cruel was about anger and power and control."

Alice K. has often said this to Dr. Y.

"Mr. Cruel was about being in a relationship where you don't get what you need, and where you refuse to accept that, and you refuse to give up, and you refuse to do anything but relive the same drama, over and over and over. Mr. Cruel was Mr. Danger with a brain."

She shudders. When Alice K. talks about the moody and complex Mr. Cruel to Dr. Y., her heart still races.

Oh, the memories. The trauma. Alice K. stares at the ceiling and thinks back.

At one point, toward the end of their relationship and for close to a year afterward, Mr. Cruel dominated virtually every aspect of Alice K.'s life. Her self-esteem rose and fell like a barometer, depending on how he reacted to her. Her moods improved or disintegrated along with his. Mr. Cruel had so much power over Alice K. that she felt like a piece of clay in his presence: malleable, mush-brained, willing to mold herself into any shape he desired. That's why she called him Mr. Cruel (his real name is Johnny D.; real pseudonym, fake initial). Alice K. felt like she lived in the palm of his hand, and that at any moment, Mr. Cruel could smash his hands together and crush her like a bug.

It has taken Alice K. years to piece that part of her past together, to understand why she was so drawn to Mr. Cruel and to figure out what went wrong.

She met him at a dinner party, thrown by mutual friends. She didn't like him at first. Alice K. thought Mr. Cruel was good-looking and rather charismatic but also opinionated and arrogant; she remembers thinking he was an insecure man, someone who overcompensated by showing off how much he knew. But Mr. Cruel pursued Alice K. intensely, with a vigor and a level of sophistication that made Alice K. feel special and valued in a way she'd never felt before. Mr. Cruel wooed her, seduced her, pushed all the right buttons.

Most of those buttons, Alice K. realizes in retrospect, were marked with words like *confidence* and *validation* and *security*. At that time in her life, fresh out of college and terribly uncertain about who she was and where she was going, Alice K. was searching desperately for solutions, for something (or someone) to help her feel adequate and mature and sophisticated and safe in the world. And Mr. Cruel appeared: a boisterous, lively, seemingly self-assured artist, a few years older than Alice K., and a man possessed with a far more fully developed persona.

In effect, Mr. Cruel presented himself as the solution Alice K. needed (or she perceived him that way; she's still not sure if there's a difference), and within a matter of months, she had surrendered to him, surrendered her ego and her future and every ounce of her self-esteem.

Create me! Invent me! Tell me who I am! Lying there in bed, Alice K. thinks she might as well have been wearing t-shirts at the time emblazoned with those words. The problem, of course, was that despite her neediness, Alice K. understood on some level that no one had the power to "invent" a life for her, not even Mr. Cruel. On some level, she understood that life was not a board game, that she couldn't just skip over the three quarters of the board marked GROWING UP and land, without so much as a flinch, in the square marked ADULT.

So even as Alice K. invested Mr. Cruel with power over her life and feelings and future, she knew that it was false; the tactic was bound to backfire.

And backfire it did.

Mr. Cruel, you see, was exciting and decisive and full of bravado, but he was also a controller, and he was only too willing to help invent Alice K., to re-create her, to tell her who she was. Her first instinct was correct—Mr. Cruel was terribly insecure, and he tried to mold Alice K. into someone, or something, that would reflect well on him, someone who would bolster him and look good walking down the street on his arm. Sometimes, lying there in Mr. Cruel's apartment, Alice K. thought that if she had a dollar for every time Mr. Cruel used the word "should," she'd have been fabulously rich.

"You should go to art school."

"You should dump those girlfriends from college."

"You should get some exercise, cut your hair, stop wearing this and start wearing that instead."

The part of Alice K. that longed for guidance and validation was desperately attracted to this; she wanted to believe that Mr. Cruel knew what was right for her and, even more, she wanted to please him, to become the person he seemed to want her to be.

But another part of her saw these "shoulds" as conditions—you become this and I will accept you—and she resented them profoundly. "Why can't you just accept me the way I am!" She would stand in Mr. Cruel's apartment and scream this sometimes. "So what if I don't exercise! So what if I have friends you don't like! What difference does it make?!"

Of course, Mr. Cruel couldn't accept Alice K. the way she was, in part because Alice K. herself couldn't do the same, and in part because (she now suspects) he was incapable of that kind of love in the first place.

Dr. Y. often encourages Alice K. to look at relationships in terms of dances: who leads, who follows, who determines the tempo and speed and music. When she thinks of her relationship with Elliot M., for example, Alice K. thinks about a nice, easy two-step: not too passionate, not too hard to master, but comfortable. The music is pleasant and no one steps on anybody's toes.

With Mr. Danger, Alice K. never quite figured out the music.

And with Mr. Cruel? Emotional slam-dancing: *Boom!* His wish to control her slamming up against her wish for independence. *Crash!* Her wish for someone to tell her how to lead her life slamming up against his inability to accept her. *Slam!*

Alice K. has not seen Mr. Cruel for years. Ultimately, he moved to New York to pursue his painting career, and after a tremendous amount of agonizing Alice K. chose not to accompany him. "Best decision I ever made," she has repeatedly said to Ruth E. "A terrible relationship. A disaster."

But a part of Alice K. has always wondered: If they had met at another time, would things be different? If she felt more grounded in her own life and he felt more secure, could it have worked out? At his best, Mr. Cruel seemed to combine Elliot M.'s intelligence and sensitivity with Mr. Danger's elusiveness and allure. She has never met anyone, before or since, who has so overwhelmed her.

And now, Alice K. thinks, *he's back.*

She loved Mr. Cruel. She hated him. She is dying to see him.

Three days later:
"What's the fear? What's the worst that could happen?"

Alice K. is in the midst of a session with Dr. Y., and Dr. Y. is questioning her about Mr. Cruel.

Alice K. does not know what to say. In fact, Alice K. is in something of a panic. For tonight, Alice K. is meeting Mr. Cruel for dinner.

Alice K. will not say this to Dr. Y., but right now her most pressing concern is not her fear of what might happen with Mr. Cruel. Right now, she is not worrying about what kinds of old angers or memories or feelings this meeting might stir up. Right now, she is primarily concerned with a much bigger question:

What the hell am I going to wear?

In her mind, Alice K. is digging through her closets in a frenzy, searching for the outfit that says, "I am over you, Mr. Cruel. I have become a wise and mature and extremely desirable woman, and you are going to take one look at me and you are going to think of how you used to treat me and you are going to wish that you could take a dagger and plunge it straight into your heart, right then and there."

Ruth E. is voting for a little black Donna Karan dress with a low neckline, but Alice K. thinks that would be too much.

Dr. Y. interrupts this train of thought. "What do you imagine will happen?" he asks.

She ponders that. What does Alice K. imagine? The fantasy, of course, is about revenge: She wants to waltz into the restaurant and say to Mr. Cruel, "Hah! See? I didn't need you after all. I turned out just fine without you. And now I'm going to make you want me as much as I wanted you, and then I'm going to reject you, and then—finally!—you will know how horrible it feels to be in that position."

But Dr. Y. is asking about reality, not fantasy: What does Alice K. truly imagine will happen?

"I don't know," Alice K. says. "I honestly don't know." A

part of her can imagine one of those nostalgic, bittersweet reunions: They'll sit and catch up and admire each other and recall all the reasons they fell in love and leave feeling wistful and warm and wise. And another part of her can imagine all the old baggage simmering beneath the surface: old resentments, old hurts and jealousies.

I think I'm kind of hoping that he's miserable. I think I'm kind of hoping that his painting career is stagnating and that he's in a terrible relationship and that he hates New York and that . . .

Alice K. thinks all these things but she cannot say them aloud to Dr. Y. They sound so . . . so vengeful and meanspirited.

He asks her another question: "Are you hoping for some kind of reconciliation? Is there a romantic fantasy?"

Alice K. allows herself to respond to that one: "Yes. Definitely. A part of me is hoping that we just, you know, fall back into each other's arms and recapture all the good stuff without any of the bullshit."

"And does that seem reasonable?"

Alice K. shakes her head. "No. I doubt it. It seems impossible."

Later that afternoon, Alice K. sits on her sofa and contemplates that exchange. *Recapture all the good stuff;* that's what she told Dr. Y. a part of her hoped for.

But what was the good stuff, exactly? It wasn't really compatibility or companionship; she and Mr. Cruel fought all the time. No, it was something more visceral; it was a feeling of excitement mixed with desperation; it was the presence of hope, embodied in Mr. Cruel.

In retrospect, Alice K. understands that she was asking for the impossible from Mr. Cruel: she was asking him to give her life shape and definition, asking him to transform her from a needy and insecure young woman into a confident and self-assured young woman. And the thing that made the relationship so utterly seductive was that sometimes—*sometimes*—that actually seemed possible. Mr. Cruel would look at Alice K. just so—with a certain look of tenderness and approval, with a certain pride in his eyes—and an odd feeling of victory would wash over her, as though she'd made it, as though she'd taken some extraordinarily difficult test and passed.

She remembers one fleeting moment from early on in their relationship, when she and Mr. Cruel were cooking dinner together in her apartment. Alice K. was stirring a sauce and Mr. Cruel came up behind her and kissed her on the neck. She turned and saw him looking down at her with that look in his eyes—validating, content—and Alice K. was flooded with a feeling that (she now realizes) she spent the rest of their relationship trying to recapture: a feeling of safety, a feeling that she had landed in a place she was meant to be, a sense that struggle and ambivalence and complexity—all the things that characterized Alice K.'s inner life—would vanish if she could just stay there, stay there in that kitchen with Mr. Cruel.

Alice K. sighs, thinking about this. She had that same feeling at the very beginning of her relationship with Elliot M.—that feeling of warmth and acceptance, that feeling that a battle was over and she had won—but it had seemed to disappear, and Alice K. still isn't sure why.

She'd mentioned that to Dr. Y: "Maybe it was because Elliot M. didn't keep testing me," she wondered. "Maybe it was because that constant feeling of having to struggle to win someone's approval wasn't there. There was no fight, no battle, so there wasn't the same excitement either."

Now, sitting there on the sofa, Alice K. ponders this. *Do I really need that? Does a relationship have to be such a big, huge struggle in order to feel real? In order to be exciting?*

For a fleeting moment, Alice K. feels a pang of longing for Elliot M., sweet, kind, responsible Elliot M., to whom she hasn't spoken since their last big fight.

But she pushes the feeling out of her mind—she doesn't understand it, doesn't want to contemplate it—and rises from the sofa. Bigger challenges call: Alice K. must find the right dress.

9

LIFE
IN
THE
OFFICE

alice k. longs to be italian

Alice K. sits at her desk, longing to be Italian.

This is not a frivolous or passing thought. Alice K. has longed to be Italian for some time. She loves pasta. She loves Italian wine. But mostly, Alice K. has come to believe that if she were Italian—or at least had an Italian temperament—she would not find the '90s so woefully upsetting.

Consider, for example, Alice K. at her job. Like most of her peers in these tough economic times, Alice K. spends about fifty hours a week at *Green Goddess* magazine and about forty additional hours worrying about it.

She worries about whether she's doing a good enough job, and she worries about where her career is going, and she worries about whether the economy will ever improve and whether she'll ever be able to get another job in a different field. She worries about being overworked and she worries about being underpaid and she worries about whether or not she's satisfied doing what she does.

After work, she goes out with her work friends for drinks (only one!—remember, this is the '90s), and they talk about work. When she goes home, she either does more work or she goes to sleep because she's so tired from working.

If she were Italian, Alice K. thinks, she would have a far more manageable attitude toward work. She would go to her job, she would go home, and—*presto!*—that would be that. She would eat large, lavish dinners with friends and family. She would drink wine. She would stay up well past midnight and then sleep until a reasonable hour the next morning.

A few years ago, Alice K. went to the wedding of a friend who married an Italian. A man she met there, who'd had a nervous breakdown working as an investment banker in New York City during the '80s and subsequently moved to Rome, spoke to her about the difference between the Italian and the American approach to work.

"It sounds like a cliché, but it's true," he said. "Americans live to work and Italians work to live."

Alice K. nodded and smiled, but inside, she silently smirked. At the time, Alice K. had just launched her career in journalism, and she was full of ambition, full of dreams of fortune and fame. Work to live? Hah!

But like most of her friends these days, Alice K. is beginning to realize that she has spent the better part of the past decade doing nothing but working and working and working. Even though she is relatively happy at *Green Goddess* magazine, she realizes she really hasn't had a life in all those years. Barely a vacation. Hardly a romp by the seashore. And nary a good night's sleep.

How much better, Alice K. thinks, to be Italian, to believe in your bones that life is something you live each day and not just once in a while on Saturday when you can make the time.

She doodles on a pad at her desk and sighs. Ah, she thinks. To be Italian. To laugh and cavort and speak Italiano! To be in *amore*. And best of all—yes, Alice K. gets shivers just thinking about it—to feel free to explode with emotion and fury and rage.

Ah, how Alice K. longs to explode with emotion and fury and rage, like the Italians. As it is, being a responsible, mature woman of the '90s, Alice K. maintains a very tight rein on her emotions, and she deals with the strongest of them the way she would deal with, say, a bad case of hemorrhoids.

Quietly. Secretly. In the privacy of her own home.

This was not quite so true in the '70s and '80s, when everyone was in therapy and could explode with emotion and fury and rage at her or his therapist. And it certainly wasn't true in the '60s, when exploding with emotion and fury and rage was downright *de rigueur*—all that marching in the streets and chanting and burning of brassieres.

But here in the '90s, Alice K. thinks, there's no permission to explode with emotion and fury and rage anymore, no place to let loose. People are so worried about losing their jobs that they don't speak up for themselves at work. People are so worried about saying the correct thing in social circles that they either talk about safe things (work) or they say nothing at all. And people are so disenchanted and fatalistic about relationships that they figure it's just not worth it to explode with emotion and fury and rage at their partners—it won't change anything, so you might as well keep your feelings to yourself. So Alice K. and her friends walk around looking tired and repressed, and no one says anything provocative.

All this would be different, Alice K. suspects, if she were

Italian. She would have a fiercely passionate husband, and together they would have a fiercely passionate family of fiercely passionate children, and they would sit there at the dinner table over huge bowls of pasta and scream at one another from dusk to dawn.

Whaddayamean, you aren't going to college? Smack! Whaddayamean, you didn't use a condom? Smack! They'd scream and scream, and then they'd cry and hug and confess their love to one another in a flood of fiercely passionate tears, and everything would be all right.

How different this would be from Alice K.'s current dealings with people, the majority of whom are terrified of their emotions, who walk around suppressing their hostility and ill will and acting passive-aggressive instead.

Alice K. does this, too, and she admits it. When she gets angry at work, she runs into the ladies' room and cries. When she gets angry at co-workers, she clams up and acts hostile and cold for weeks at a stretch. It's not that she doesn't have negative feelings, it's just that her way of expressing them is to let them seep out in all these ugly, gradual, unpleasant, insidious ways. She ponders this.

The afternoon drags on and Alice K. grows despondent. Why couldn't she have grown up on some lovely Tuscan farm? Why couldn't she have fiercely passionate blood coursing through her veins instead of timid, repressed blood? Why must she be so . . . so *American?*

But then, suddenly, Alice K. brightens. She has a brilliant idea. There is, after all, one realm in America where you don't have to work so obsessively, where you can be downright vapid and still become a success. There is one realm in America where it's still possible to explode regularly with emotion and fury and rage. There is one realm in America where all this and more is possible.

She sits up in her chair, smiling. That's it! Perhaps Alice K. will go into politics.

the sniffer

The offices of *Green Goddess* magazine, where Alice K. works, have no windows.

That's one problem.

They also have no air. Another problem.

But Alice K. can live with that. She can live with the horrible ventilation and the sense of enclosure and confinement. She can live with fluorescent lighting and sterile, faceless cubicles. What she has a harder time with—a much harder time—is . . . the Sniffer.

Do you know the Sniffer? Is there one in your office, too?

The Sniffer is that big, lurking lunkhead of a guy who has a crush on you but is too awkward and socially inept to do much about it except hang around your cubicle, launch conversations that go nowhere, compliment you too obviously, and generally sniff about like a big, hungry dog who keeps coming back and coming back because he thinks one of these days his luck will change and he'll actually find you in heat.

"Um . . . Hey, Alice K., so . . . um, how's it going?" (Sniff, sniff)

"So, um . . . didja see Letterman last night?" (Paw, paw)

"Um . . . that's a really pretty sweater." (Snort, snort)

The problem with the Sniffer, of course, is that his awkwardness catapults you right back to the eighth grade, when you were every bit as socially inept and obvious about your crushes as he is now, so when he lumbers over and actually tries to talk to you, your hair practically stands on end, the associations are so horrible.

This is why it is virtually impossible to respond to the Sniffer with anything more than a two-word answer.

"Gee, Alice K., that's really nice nail polish you're wearing. What color do you call that?"

"It's red."
[awkward pause]
"Oh . . . So, um, what are you working on?"
"A memo."
[awkward pause]
"Oh . . . So . . ."

Anything longer than a two-word answer will encourage the Sniffer and cause him to hang around your cubicle for hours, making you intensely guilty and uncomfortable. Once, early on in her tenure at *Green Goddess* magazine and before she learned to keep the Sniffer at bay, Alice K. actually ended up talking to him for twenty consecutive minutes about mousse.

The Sniffer had lumbered over to pay her an absurd compliment. He said, *"I really liked that write-up you did about . . . what was it?"*

Alice K., feeling compelled to be polite as a new employee who didn't yet know who was worth being nice to and who wasn't, racked her brain. She'd been new-products editor at *Green Goddess* magazine for only two weeks and the only words she'd written were three lines about a new kind of banana-scented mousse.

She said, *"You mean the thing about the mousse?"*

The Sniffer looked grateful. *"Yeah. Yeah, the mousse. That was it. Now . . . is that, like, really good mousse or something?"*

And thus ensued a twenty-minute dialogue about how the mousse company gets the mousse to smell like bananas, and whether that's a good thing or a bad thing, and how some women might rather have their hair smell like, say, peaches or limes, and . . . well, about five minutes into this conversation Alice K. became acutely aware that the Sniffer was, in fact, a sniffer, and then she became intensely self-conscious, and then she spent the rest of the dialogue worrying that her co-workers, who didn't yet know her very well, would think she was a complete and total loser because they'd seen her talking politely to the Sniffer for twenty consecutive minutes about mousse.

Working in an office is a lot like being in the eighth grade, is it not? Alice K. contemplates this frequently, and the lurking, looming presence of the Sniffer is a constant and unpleasant reminder. The divisions. The ever-present, unarticulated popularity contests. The office-wide consensus about who's up, who's down, who's in, who's out, who's special, and who's just plain weird. It's all played out with a tad more subtlety because the people involved are allegedly adults, but it's really the same thing. Eighth grade all over again.

This is why starting a new job is always such an agonizing process. In her first two weeks at *Green Goddess* magazine, Alice K. didn't really worry about whether she'd be able to do the work, or what her actual job responsibilities would be, or whether she'd be able to figure out the computer system. No, her far more pressing worries had to do with things like what she'd wear on her first day, and what she'd do for lunch, and whether anyone would ask her out for drinks after work. She worried, in other words, about *whether the other kids would like her.*

This, Alice K. believes, is one of the great unspoken explanations for lost productivity in America. *Does the Secretary of Labor have any idea how much time people spend worrying about their office social lives and their office status? Do the Teamsters know about this? Shouldn't somebody tell them?* She lies awake at night and contemplates these questions.

It took Alice K. a full six weeks—six weeks—to feel comfortable enough in the office to actually begin getting any work done. Six weeks of acting just humble enough so that people wouldn't think she was socially aggressive, and just friendly enough so they wouldn't think she was a snob, and just hardworking enough so they wouldn't think she was a slacker, and just laid back enough so they wouldn't think she was a nerd. Six weeks of edging toward a sense of camaraderie with the other women in the office, of asking them about their hair and their shoes and their boyfriends, of sharing just enough information about herself in return—not too much or they'd find her pushy, not too little or they'd think she had something to hide. Six weeks of lunches here and drinks there and small conversations in the ladies' room and key little exchanges by the coffee machine.

And what's a little pathetic about this, Alice K. thinks, what makes it so closely resemble the eighth grade, is that someone—someone—always gets sacrificed in the process. Someone just doesn't fit in, someone's just a little too nerdy or awkward or inept, someone has to be disliked in order to throw the accepted status of the rest of the group into sharper relief.

Someone, in other words, has to be the Sniffer.

He lumbers over. He sniffs. He says, *"Hey, Alice K. . . . so, um, seen any good movies lately?"*

Alice K. pretends to be very, *very* busy. She looks up vaguely. *"Me? No."*

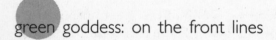

green goddess: on the front lines

Here are some of the projects Alice K. has overseen in her tenure as new products editor.

Sunscreen body-parts protectiveness test. Alice K. is forced to apply seven different brands of sunscreen to seven parts of her body (calf, thigh, forearm, and so on) and then spend an entire day lying in the sun on the roof of *Green Goddess* magazine. Results: Alice K. ends up with a perfectly white left forearm and right upper arm; a moderately burned chest; a slight burn on her right leg; and a burn on her left thigh so severe it requires a trip to the emergency room. Alice K. cannot go to the beach all summer as she resembles a patch-work quilt. The story, however, is a success.

Lip therapy report. Alice K. tests a different lip-protection product every day for twelve days. She tries Chap-Stik; Lip Silk; Lip Gel; Lip Gel-'n'-Go; Super Moisture Lip Coating; Moisture PLUS! For Lips; Love Your Lips, *Really* Love Your Lips; Lip-Smackin' Lip Treatment; Extra Protection Lip-Smackin' Lip Treatment; Hyper-Dewey Lip Gloss 'n' Sheen; and Huey, Dewey, and Louey Lips for Life. She completes her report but requires three extra sessions with Dr. Y.

Female condom test. It came out on the market last year. Alice K. still cannot figure out how to get it in.

Hair removal: *A Green Goddess Special Report.* This took Alice K. a full year. She accumulated nine different hair-removal products, including a rotary nose-hair clipper and a frightening-looking device called NippleClean: Hair Removal Just for Breasts. She tweezed and plucked and electrolysized. She bleached her upper lip, waxed her bikini line, and her bathroom smelled like depilatory cream for a month. She shaved the six or seven hairs protruding from her right nipple and NippleCleaned the six or seven hairs from her other one, then took copious notes charting the progress of regrowth (results: NippleClean works better but it hurts). Several times over the course of the year, Alice K. found herself in a vague fog, daydreaming about becoming a lesbian.

Tampon Absorbency: How Does Your Brand Stack Up? Alice K. fought and fought over this one. "Please. Can't we use a water test? Can't we just immerse the different brands in little cups of water and find some way to measure how much they absorb? Isn't that what the tampon companies do?" Alice K. lost. Today, she will not discuss the absorbency test in detail except to say (angrily) that *Green Goddess* magazine would not reimburse her for the underwear.

the boss

Alice K. has a recurring nightmare about work, a truly horrifying nightmare that causes her to wake in a cold sweat, gasping for breath.

It's always the same. She's at a party. All her co-workers are there. And all of a sudden she realizes: She is playing Naked Twister with her boss.

Can you imagine anything more horrifying?

All right, Alice K., right foot on red, left hand on yellow, left foot on green, right hand on blue, your boss is right there with you, and you're BOTH STARK NAKED!

What is this? Do other people have this nightmare? Alice K. would like to know.

Actually, what Alice K. would really like to know is this: Do other people have such complex feelings about their bosses? Do other people project all their feelings about authority and control onto their supervisors? For that's what the dream is about, is it not? Transference in the workplace. The boss as blank screen onto which Alice K. projects her fears.

Alice K.'s boss, the editor in chief of *Green Goddess* magazine, is a tough, erratic, sometimes explosive man in his forties named Frank E. (no relation to Ruth). He is capable of being charming and wise and extremely amusing, but often he is hostile and withholding.

"Alice K.! Get me a caption for that nipple hair thing!"

"Alice K.! Where's that write-up about exfoliation!"

"Alice K.! What's the status of that goddamn tampon report!"

That's the hostile part. The withholding part is reflected in the fact that you never—never—know what Frank E. is thinking. Alice K. will ask him to read something and he will sit there and stare at the paper, and stare at it, and stare at it, and then he'll say something like "Hmmmmm," and she'll have no idea if she's about to get fired or about to get an A.

Which, of course, is one of Alice K.'s problems at work—not Frank E.'s withholding nature but her wish for the A, her feeling that some part of her is still stuck in high school, equating success with good grades and gold stars. Alice K. is often struck by the power of the feelings Frank E. can evoke. Because she thinks of him as very smart, a simple compliment from him—"Great job on the lip report, Alice K.," "Thanks, Alice K."—can make her heart swell, can fill her with the conviction that she's genuinely capable and competent, something she rarely believes on her own. And a single disdainful look, a sense that she's caused him irritation or frustration, can do just the opposite. *I'm a failure. He hates me. He's in a bad mood—it must be my fault.*

So Alice K. spends a lot of time at work feeling terrified of Frank E. Terrified, really, of his power. *Am I doing okay? Am I doing okay?* When she is in a meeting with Frank E., Alice K. is often aware that her eyes are begging that question. *Tell me I'm smart. Tell me I'm measuring up.* She hates this but she can't help it. It's in Alice K.'s nature to look to others for approval, and this tendency is magnified when the other in question is in a position of authority.

Once, early on in her tenure at *Green Goddess* magazine, Frank E. took Alice K. out to lunch, a rare attempt on his part to establish office camaraderie. She worried the entire time about whether she had stuff stuck between her teeth and to this day she cannot remember what they talked about. She had the first Naked Twister nightmare that night, and they've recurred about once a month ever since.

Why the naked part? she often wonders. Is there a sexual edge in this dream? A sexual fear? She thinks there probably is, although after more than a decade in the workforce, Alice K. has gotten rather used to the presence of sexuality as a leitmotif, a strange and unspoken element in relationships between male bosses and their female employees. She has gotten rather used to worrying about the fine line between being attractive and being sexual. She has learned the rules (no fishnets; no plunging necklines), she has learned to accept her own sexual fears as part of the nature of things. She still worries (are the men in this meeting looking at my breasts, or what?), but she doesn't let the worry overwhelm her.

What Alice K. has *not* learned to do is to use her sexuality, to translate it into her own sort of power. Other women at *Green Goddess* do this; she sees other women engaged in the kind of sophisticated, subtle flirting that only the most sexually confident woman can pull off, a kind that disarms even the hostile and withholding Frank E., and, accordingly, usually yields results. A kind of sexually charged banter. A look here, perhaps even a touch there. Alice K. watches such women with a combination of envy and awe and despair; it is the kind of behavior that causes her to lie awake at night and worry about the nature of female power: Does it have to be sexualized? Is it possible to be powerful just by being smart and productive and sure of yourself? She is still not sure.

Other questions: When, Alice K. would like to know, did the workplace become such an intimate setting? Was it always this way? This is another thing about growing older that's surprised Alice K.: The way her image of work as a relatively safe and emotionally sterile environment has shifted over the years, the way *relationships* develop in the office, real relationships that evoke all the same feelings, inspire all the same struggles as relationships with lovers and friends and family members.

But this, she supposes, explains the Naked Twister nightmares. The fear of exposure and entanglement. The uncertainty about how Frank E. really sees her. The ambivalence about female sexual power. And the terror of doing something that will cause him to lose respect for Alice K., something truly humiliating, such as ending up naked on a Twister mat.

Sometimes Alice K. thinks she would do less projecting, less approval-seeking, if her boss were a woman, but she's not sure. This way of thinking seems to have less to do with gender than it does with respect and admiration and imbalances of power. Alice K., after all, is a boss herself; she supervises two young copy editors, both in their twenties, and she often notices the way they look at her, the same doe eyes, the same unspoken questions: *Am I doing okay? Do you like me? Do you approve?*

This can make Alice K. desperately uncomfortable, to be on the receiving end of other people's insecurities, and she often finds herself struggling for the right managerial approach, the right balance: to be enough of an authority figure that they respect her, enough of a friend that they like her, that they feel they're on equal footing. The boss part of her tries to praise them when they deserve it, and tries to be direct about where they're making progress and where they need to improve. The friend part of her takes them to lunch from time to time and invites them over to her apartment for dinner every three or four months. And only once—only once—did Alice K. flirt with the idea of exploiting her own potential power.

It happened during one of those dinners at her apartment. Alice K. had had a bad day—the kind of really bad day that involves several computer breakdowns and numerous

221

untimely interruptions and (eventually, inevitably) a verbal beating from Frank E. in the middle of a meeting. Alice K. had come home feeling dejected and stung. And when her two employees arrived and settled into chairs in Alice K.'s living room, she'd had a terrible, evil impulse. She'd looked at them, the two young things so eager to please, and her eyes had narrowed just slightly.

"So," she said. "How about a game of Twister?"

 office weasels

This is what Alice K. likes best about Frank E: he may be hostile and withholding, but he is not passive-aggressive.

"Why are there so many passive-aggressive people in offices?" Alice K. asks Ruth E. at least once a week. "Is it that there just happens to be a lot of passive-aggressive people in the world, or is there something specific about the workplace that brings it out?"

Office weasels, that's what Ruth E. calls them. There are dozens of them at *Green Goddess* magazine. They weasel out of work. They weasel credit for other people's ideas. Weasel, weasel, weasel.

The worst weasel is a guy who sits near Alice K. and does nothing—absolutely nothing—until he sees Frank E. approach. Then he will pick up his phone and, without dialing it, begin speaking loudly into the receiver, issuing commands, taking fake notes, saying things like, "Ah . . . I see . . . very good . . . well, we'll get back to you on that."

How do people like this end up with jobs?

Here are some of the other weasels, and protoweasels, at *Green Goddess* magazine. Do any of them sound familiar?

The annoyer. This is the woman in the company who embodies every single annoying human characteristic there is.

She clicks her fingernails against the desk when she's on the phone. She slurps her coffee and smacks her lips. She often eats carrot sticks at work, is a chronic hummer of high-pitched, tuneless little hums, and has an annoying nasal whistle. She is also a prime weasel: lazy and complaining and exceptionally good at finding reasons not to do the work she's supposed to do. (Sample: "Well, I can't start this project now because it's already three o'clock and if I start it now I'll just have to stop at five o'clock and that won't make any sense because when I come in tomorrow morning I won't remember where I was and . . .").

Some guy named Jim. This is one of those employees who exists out of the mainstream and whose name Alice K. can never seem to remember. ("What's that guy's name? Oh, right. Jim.") Alice K. has no idea if he is an actual weasel or not (perhaps he's a protoweasel), but he looks like one—thin and sort of shriveled, the sort of person who always disappears into the background. He makes Alice K. intensely uncomfortable, though; Alice K. usually goes for months having virtually no contact with him until, in a highly awkward moment, she finds herself standing behind him in the food line at the office Christmas party with absolutely nothing to say.

The office cheapskate. The financial weasel. Always present when someone in the office is having a birthday and there's a cake; never there when someone in the office is leaving and an envelope is passed around to collect money for a goodbye present. Hoards office supplies. Steals pens. Never offers to get anyone else coffee but will appear in path of co-workers as they go out for coffee and say, "Hey, would you mind picking up a large with extra cream for me?" He will then say "I'll catch you later," but he will never pay you back.

The woman with the boundary problem. The social weasel. Truly believes the rest of the office really wants to hear the intimate details of her love life, medical health, personal hygiene habits, her weight, the new rug she bought on sale over the weekend, what she had for dinner last night, how she was up half the night with indigestion because of the beans, and the huge fight she had with her mother on the phone about any or all of the above. (Tip: Do not ever—*ever*—ask her to describe the plot of a movie. Likewise, if she begins a sentence with the phrase "I had the strangest dream last night . . ." you should run and hide immediately.)

The overcompensater. The emotional weasel. Usually, but not always, a woman, she is so desperately insecure about everything (appearance, intelligence, professional status) that she spends the bulk of her energy reminding everyone around her, at every possible opportunity, how important and valuable she really is. A weaseler of compliments. Will always take advantage of the opportunity to tell you about praise she receives, and struggles mightily to convince you that she has a more interesting social life than she actually has ("God, I had the busiest weekend, you wouldn't *believe*"). Also a master of the backhanded compliment ("Your hair looks really different. Did you *dye* it or something?").

an open letter to corporate america

Not long ago, in a fit of disenchantment and fatigue, Alice K. sat at her desk and typed the following letter to corporate America.

```
Dear Corporate America,
     Hello. My name is Alice K., and as a repre-
sentative member of the American workforce, I
```

thought you might like to hear some of my thoughts about how you might conduct your businesses in these, our tough economic times.

As you know, the good times are long gone, and the perks we enjoyed during the '80s are disappearing faster than you can cut a budget. Fat expense accounts? Gone. Fifteen-percent raises? Hah. Unlimited personal use of such office services as Federal Express and long-distance phone calls? A thing of the past.

Recessionary times do little for the morale of your many employees. We sit at our desks and fret about pink slips. We hear the gloomy economic forecasts and our dreams of a better standard of living wither and die. Overworked and underpaid, we toil through the day, then look at our checkbooks and think, "Oh, shit. We're still not rich." Our little hearts sink.

But there is something that you, corporate America, can do about this. Ways you can improve our lives that don't involve huge expenditures of cash. Small kindnesses that can brighten our days and soothe our souls simply by reflecting your boundless empathy and compassion. Herewith, recessionary perks for the '90s.

On-Site Laundry

You may not be aware of this, but a tremendous amount of productivity in corporate America is lost because employees are sitting at their desks feeling preoccupied with their laundry. They have no clean socks. No clean shirts. Worse, they are so busy knocking themselves out in these, our tight economic times, that

they have no spare energy to wash said socks
and shirts.

This is bad for everyone. A messily clad employee is an unhappy employee, and those of us
who are forced to work side-by-side with a colleague who hasn't washed his or her socks for a
month are none too pleased either. On-site
laundry would vastly improve this situation.
Think about it. Employees would race to work in
the morning, determined to get a free machine
before anybody else. They'd throw their stuff
in the machine, hustle to their desks, work,
work, work, then leap up to nab the first
available dryer. Adrenaline would flow, morale would soar, and offices everywhere would
emanate with the clean, uplifting scents of
Tide and Cheer.

Mandatory Errand Days

Fat vacation packages are a thing of the past.
We don't expect to have three or four weeks off
a year anymore, and even if we did, we couldn't
afford to go anywhere. That doesn't mean, however, that we don't need some spare time for
non-recreational purposes. In fact, our time
has become so dominated by work that our lives
outside of the office are on the verge of
chaos. We don't have time to get our cars tuned
up. We don't have time to pick up our dry cleaning. We don't have time to pay our bills, or get
our parking stickers renewed, or have our
teeth cleaned, or stock up on groceries and
shampoo and coffee and toilet paper and
stamps, and in fact, when we get to the office
in the morning, we're often frantic because

our last pair of panty hose has run, and we've run out of toothpaste, and we haven't eaten breakfast because we haven't had time to buy Wheaties in a *month*, and, well, you get the idea.

Which is why mandatory errand days make a tremendous amount of sense. Every six or eight weeks, on a rotating basis, each employee in a given company would be asked to draw up a list of the errands in his or her life that need doing. He or she would present said list to his or her supervisor, then be excused from work for the day and expected to accomplish as many of the items on the list as possible. As a special incentive program, employees who ticked off the most items from their lists would receive small errand-related prizes—a dry cleaning coupon, for example, or a quart of motor oil.

Is this not a fine idea? During the working day, we would all rest much, much easier. And hosts of ancillary businesses (car repair shops, drugstores, post offices) would flourish.

Mental-Health Days

Same principle, but employees wouldn't be allowed to do anything except sit quietly at home on the sofa, watch daytime talk shows in their bathrobes, and eat bonbons.

Nap Rooms

Self-explanatory. We're tired. Let us rest from time to time.

Soundproof Designated
Personal-Phone-Call Cubicles

Anyone who works in corporate America knows
how hard it is to maintain a personal life when
you work upwards of fifty hours a week, and
anyone in that situation gets confronted
from time to time with that most awkward of in-
teroffice scenarios: attempting to have a
fight with your boyfriend/girlfriend/mother/
spouse over the phone at work. This is very
difficult. You have to lean far forward in your
chair and *hiss* into the phone. You have to communicate complicated, delicate thoughts
("Just because I didn't want to have oral sex
does not mean I am selfish!") in whispers. And
you have to pray that the embarrassing details
of your personal life do not inadvertently
wend their way into the company newsletter.

Soundproof cubicles would give employees
the luxury of complete privacy. They could go
in, shut the door, and scream at their spouses
with abandon. An added benefit: This would
free women from the humiliating business of
having to hightail it to the ladies' room to
have a good, post-fight cry.

Company Masseurs

Also self-explanatory. Our necks and shoulders begin to ache when we sit at our desks for
hours at a time. Help us out a little.

Are you getting the picture? Are you beginning
to realize that we, the folks who slave and toil
for you, are actual people with actual lives

that are actually in the process of falling
apart? Have a little empathy, all you CEOs and
presidents. Take a hint from your old kindergar-
ten teachers. Put cots in our cubicles, and
serve us cookies and juice. Let us out for re-
cess now and then. And once in a while, call for
a companywide nap, wherein everyone would take
out a blanket and rest comfortably on the floor
for thirty minutes. Yes, times are tight, but,
to resurrect an old phrase from long, long ago,
that doesn't mean we can't have a kinder, gen-
tler work place. Does it?

Sincerely,
Alice K.

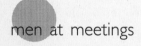

men at meetings

Alice K. sits in the meeting, glancing furtively at her watch.

The meeting began at ten a.m.

It is now twelve forty-five, and the meeting shows no
signs of winding down.

The meeting is being run, you see, by a man.

It doesn't matter which man—it could be some guy
named Jim, it could be the janitor who vacuums at the end
of the day. Alice K. understands this as a central fact of corporate life: If a man is running the meeting, it will take eighteen times longer than it would take a woman.

"This is absolutely true," says Beth K. She works in a
much larger company than Alice K. does, with many more
policies and rules and meetings, and she says she spends half
her working life in meetings run by men. "Just last week.
Two hours. Two hours to discuss the company policy about
throwing birthday parties."

Alice K. nods soberly. She can imagine. The other day, she spent forty-five minutes in a meeting talking about who was responsible for buying more coffee filters for the coffee machine when they ran out.

Why is this? What is it about the male character that makes a meeting drone on and on and on? Is it a difference in organizational skills? A difference in the male and female sense of time? Is it simply that men so like to hear the sound of their own voices that they'll ramble on indefinitely if given the chance?

Alice K. believes it's all three. Today, this particular meeting is devoted to a discussion of the correct use of semicolons in *Green Goddess* magazine, and this is how the man is talking: "Now let me say that when we're talking about semicolons—and in this case I mean semicolons as opposed to colons or as opposed to commas—when we're talking about semicolons what we have to do is talk about the *utilization* of semicolons and not just the proper application of semicolons in the context of, say, current grammatical theory. . . ."

Alice K. would like to slap him. Why can't he just say "Use semicolons in this case but not in that?" Why can't he make a simple list of rules? Why must issues like this become so convoluted?

Oh, she knows why. Because he's a man. The idea that women are feelings-oriented and men are action-oriented is a bunch of hooey when it comes to life in the office. Alice K. believes this in her soul. The real truth has to do with different notions of success and accomplishment, and how best to attain them. Alice K. tends to associate accomplishment with productivity. If she's being busy and efficient and engaged, if she has just ticked nine out of ten items off her list of things to do—*that* makes her feel successful. Diligent. Deserving of reward. But most of the men she works with seem to associate success with presence, with being seen and heard and felt.

If I can force nine people to sit in a room and listen to my voice for two and a half hours, then I must be successful.

If I can turn what should be a three-minute conversation about coffee filters into a forty-five-minute dialogue, then I must be important.

If I can find nine ways to say the same thing about semicolons and fourteen ways to use big words such as context *and* utilization, *then I must be really smart and I'm probably equipped with a huge dick as well.*

The meeting goes on. And on.

Alice K. looks at her watch again and sighs. Testosterone poisoning. It's a terrible thing.

Alice K.'s Wish List, Part 5
Virtual Reality for Virtual Identity Crises

Alice K. seems to read a lot about virtual reality these days and this is what she thinks: virtual reality? Who needs it? Who needs to strap on a pair of glasses and gloves and walk around a virtual garden or look at a virtual moon? What Alice K. really needs is virtual reality with real-life applications. Virtual reality for people who are dissatisfied with their lives and want to experience something different. Virtual reality for people who hate their jobs and want to experiment with a career change.

Example: When Alice K. is sitting at her desk having an identity crisis because she is in her mid-thirties and still hasn't gotten married or had children, she needs to be able to strap on a virtual apron and hold a virtual baby with virtual colic who will emit virtual spit up on her shoulders and cry virtual tears at two o'clock in the morning, thereby giving Alice K. a good case of virtual insomnia that lasts a virtual three or four months. This would help her settle down and get back to work.

another open letter to corporate america: goods and services for working girls

Dear Corporate America,

Still haven't heard from you about my idea for perks for the '90s, so I assume you're still mulling that one over.

In the meantime, I've come up with a list of products and services that might be useful for those of us out here in the working trenches.

Here is the issue:

In these, our tight economic times, thousands and thousands of us workers are overworked, overtired, overstimulated, and overextended. We spend so much time at our jobs that we simply cannot find the time to do the things we need to do. Our social lives have been reduced to dim memories. Our love lives are in disrepair, and so is our mental health.

Given the emphasis among you, the members of corporate America, to provide us with so many useful, time-saving devices to help us manage the physical world (instant breakfast, express mail, fast food, cellular phones), it surprises me that none of you have come up with a way to develop comparable goods and services to help us in our personal lives.

Which is why I think you ought to come up with a line of goods and services designed specifically for the lifestyles of busy professionals.

233

To get you inspired, I have come up with the
following examples, complete with representa-
tive advertising copy:

Social-Life-in-a-Can

How many times have you shuffled home from work
at the end of the day, thrown yourself upon
your sofa, and thought, "Oh, my goodness, I've
been spending so much time at the office, I
forgot to have friends!"

Nearly every day, right?

That's why you need Social-Life-in-a-Can.
For just $49.95, you can have all the benefits
of a real personal life, full of laughter, fun,
and friendship, with absolutely no strings
attached—no planning, no ugly compromises, no
disappointments. And so easy! Just uncap
Social-Life-in-a-Can, aim the small nozzle at
your face, close your eyes, and spray. Within
minutes, you'll be filled with the *sensation*
of a social life. Memories will flood you: that
fabulous two-week vacation in Antigua, those
good buddies you made in ceramics class, all
those Saturday night potluck suppers with your
ten incredibly close personal friends. You'll
feel satisfied, filled with the spirit of
camaraderie and the joy of new experience.

In addition to the basic package, which
infuses you with all of the above, Social-
Life-in-a-Can is available in three more
specific models to suit your every mood:

College-Buddies-in-a-Can. Aim, spray, and
relive those carefree days with the best pals
you've ever had! Reminisce about the drugs you

took, the all-nighters you pulled before exams, and all those wacky food fights!

Best-Friend-in-a-Can. With just one spritz, you'll feel what it's like to stay up until three a. m. sharing your deepest, most personal feelings. You'll experience the special joy of "telephone ear." And for an extra $29.95, we'll throw in a special package called "Falling Out and Making Up."

Surrogate-Siblings-in-a-Can. That older brother you've always longed for is just a spray away. Ready! Aim! Idolize!

CyberMom

If you are like most busy professionals, your domestic life has gone to hell in a hack. The dust on your tabletops is a half-inch thick. You haven't changed your sheets for a month. There are living things in your refrigerator, and because you haven't used your oven in months, the utility company periodically calls to see if you still actually live there.

You need CyberMom. For just $169.95, we'll provide you with an exact replica of a human mother, someone who can stay home, wash the clothes, do the dishes, vacuum the rugs, and do your errands while you go off to work. Your CyberMom can be specially programmed to resemble you physically, making for easy, in-person transactions such as banking and clothes shopping. Special Jewish CyberMom models are also available for those with

special needs, such as chicken soup or
matchmaking. Call for details.

Identi-Rent

An innovative service for those inevitable
moments when you just cannot stand who you are,
Identi-Rent allows you to slip into the
persona of somebody completely different at a
moment's notice. Feeling tired of your work
life? Just slip this special Identi-Rent disk
into your computer, type in your dream job,
and—easy as one, two, three—you'll be
transformed, via modem, into Jeff Bridges's
personal assistant.

Sick of your boyfriend? Your apartment? The
way you look? Try "Paul Newman," "Fabulous
Chalet in Vail," or "Elle McPherson."

Identi-Rent is also handy for personal
changes, too. Say you're feeling depressed,
anxious, and conflicted. Simply type in a few
words and phrases (Perky! Really upbeat!
Psychotherapy? Not me!) and feel those inner
struggles melt away.

See, corporate America? If only you'd apply
a bit of imagination, fabulous wealth for you—
and major life changes for us—would only be a
keystroke away.

bad work days: pns

Alice K. sits at her desk, writhing with existential despair.
Alice K. is thinking, *Don't look at me. Please.*

Alice K., you see, is having one of those days. PNS: paranoid-neurosis syndrome.

You know those days? You walk into work and it feels like everyone is looking at you like they hate you? Like they're all in a bad mood and it's *your fault?*

Alice K. loathes this. Her hair looks funny. She's wearing a badly ironed blouse. She ate too much last night and she feels bloated and grotesque, and when she woke up, she couldn't find anything to wear, and then she spent twenty minutes pulling things on and sneering in the mirror and pulling things off and feeling like a loser.

That's how it started, she supposes, squirming there at her desk in discomfort. Then, when she finally got to work an hour late, the first person she saw was a woman she barely knows, and this woman looked at her kind of sideways and said, "Good morning, Alice K.," in this suspicious tone, like she knew something Alice K. didn't. At least it seemed suspicious to Alice K. Who knows, maybe she was having PNS, too.

Alice K. hears little voices on PNS days, mean-spirited little paranoia-inducing voices: *You're a loser,* they say. *You walk around pretending to be a competent, functioning human being, but we know. We know what you really are: a miserable slob, an imposter.*

Logic does not do much to counter this. She can stand in front of the mirror (although this is not recommended during extreme bouts of PNS) and she can remind herself of all her fine qualities and all her blessings, and the only thing that's really likely to happen is that someone will walk in on her mid-speech leaving her feeling like even more of an idiot than she did before. *Oh my God, I've been caught talking to myself in the bathroom.*

One of the main problems with PNS is that it makes you feel like an outcast: Everyone else in the world seems confident and full of vim and vigor and completely unburdened by concerns about being a loser. Alice K. stopped for gas on her way to work and wondered, *Does this gas station attendant have days like this? Days when he thinks his boss is mad at him and his co-workers hate him?* Then she stood in line at a coffee shop behind an attractive, professional-looking woman and wondered, *What about her? Does she have days when she's sure her work is shoddy and lacking in value? When she's convinced that it's just a matter of time before she's exposed as the fraud she really is?*

Her rational mind says, Of course. Her PNS says, Absolutely not. This is only true about *you.*

Of course, as Alice K. knows, this is because PNS has access to certain truths about the self that the rational mind, in its noble effort to protect you, tries to suppress. Truths (in Alice K.'s case) like these:

- You are not Princess Grace.
- You are not Cindy Crawford.
- In fact, you haven't gotten a damn thing done all week. You've spent the last three nights eating Wheaties for dinner on your sofa, and your skin has been looking particularly blotchy for days.

Why such truths tend to bubble up on some days and get blown all out of proportion is a mystery to Alice K. Other days she can be perfectly comfortable with the knowledge that she is not equipped with Princess Grace's social skills or Cindy Crawford's legs. But that is the nature of PNS: When you have it, all your worst suspicions about yourself, all your darkest secrets, come flooding to the forefront of your mind, and they cause you to beat up on yourself relentlessly. *You haven't done your laundry in a month—slap! You didn't call your mother today—SLAP! You didn't exercise, or pay your bills, or even read the newspaper—WHAM! Who the hell do you think you are, out there masquerading as a grown-up?*

For that's what PNS is, isn't it? It's what happens when all your self doubts and all your fears of inadequacy and incompetence come crashing up against a vision of what a "real" adult is supposed to be like. *Real grown-ups are confident and directed and self-sufficient. You, on the other hand, are a fake, and everybody knows it.*

On her worst PNS days, Alice K. has been known to actually sit down at work and make a list of people who know her well and (yes!) still like her.

Other times, she calls up Beth K. and asks her to outline her theory about the difference between one's chronological and internal ages. You can be thirty-five or forty-five or fifty-five, Beth K. says, but inside, most of us really tend to define ourselves by a different (and usually far younger) age. For her part, Beth K. was shocked—shocked!—to discover not long ago that she is actually *four-and-a-half years old.*

That gave her PNS for a long time. (Beth K., after all, has a kid; it's hard to be a mother if you really feel you should be outside playing on the swing), but she got over it.

But this, Alice K. believes, is why companies should offer special programs for their employees: Grown-Up Schools. No one should have to struggle with this alone.

At Grown-Up School, some wise figure of authority would enter the office and, one by one, divest people of the debilitating myth that people in their thirties and forties actually know what they are doing. He would make us feel better about the fact that most of us are really four-and-a-half-year-olds who run around feeling worried to death about what the other kids think. He would make these feelings of self-doubt and paranoia seem normal, legitimate, acceptable.

But alas, there's no such thing. So on days like this, Alice K. does the next best thing.

She hides under her desk.

ALICE K. IN LOVE, PART V: RESOLUTION (MAYBE)

One week later:

Alice K. (not her real initial) lies in bed, writhing with anxiety and confusion.

Mr. Cruel, you see, is not only back. Mr. Cruel is back with a vengeance. Mr. Cruel is hot after Alice K.

Alice K. is having a difficult time processing this information. On the one hand, that was exactly her hope—Mr. Cruel would beg her to come back to him, and she would reject him flat out. *Sorry, Mr. Cruel. I don't need you; I don't want you; I'm flourishing without you.*

On the other hand, of course, Alice K. is having a hard time living up to her part of this scenario. She and Mr. Cruel have seen each other four times since his return. He has wined her and dined her. He has brought flowers. He has organized a champagne picnic on a river bank, left sweet messages on her answering machine, even said things that have indicated apology and regret and change. "God, I was a selfish bastard back then," he said once. And, another time, "I must have been an idiot to let you go."

Alice K. finds this enormously seductive, his attentiveness, his courtship. She is still enormously attracted to Mr. Cruel, too—he's intelligent, witty, just a little overconfident, and (above all) he still has that knack, that way of imparting in Alice K. a rare sense of validation and worthiness.

But has he changed? Is he really the New and Improved Mr. Cruel? Alice K. tosses in her bed.

Earlier that night, she had a long dinner with Beth K., who had seen Alice K. through her initial involvement and breakup with Mr. Cruel and was very, very suspicious about his return.

"I would just be very careful," Beth K. said. "I have a really hard time trusting this guy."

"I *am* being careful," Alice K. protested. "It's not like I'm jumping into bed with him or anything."

Beth K. sighed. "Yes, Alice K. But I know guys like this and I know you. He'll chase you and chase you and he'll be wonderful to you as long as he can't have you. And finally he'll get you hooked and then—wham. He'll be out of it, just like last time."

Alice K. considers this. She knows that Beth K. is right. In the four times she has seen Mr. Cruel, she has been aware of a certain dynamic between them, the same dynamic (she believed) that caused him to pursue her with such vigor in the early stages of their relationship. Cautious, unsure of his motives, a little risk-aversive, Alice K. had forced herself back then to remain just a little aloof in Mr. Cruel's presence, a little detached, a little evasive about the details of her life. She is doing that now, too, and she can't help but wonder: Is that all this is? A chase? A repeat of history?

Alice K. understands that there are many other reasons to be cautious, too, many unanswered questions. Mr. Cruel has been very reticent about his relationships in the years they've been apart: on their third date, Alice K. mustered the courage to ask him about his love life and he turned slightly edgy. "Oh, a couple of people," he said. "Nothing too serious."

Alice K. dropped the subject, but it made her wonder: Was he covering something up? Indicating that he was still incapable of sustaining a long-term relationship? Was his elusiveness evidence of a continued reluctance on his part to deal with matters of the heart?

Meanwhile, Mr. Cruel had not expressed the slightest interest in Alice K.'s past romantic life, and that made her wonder, too: Does he care about my emotional life? Is he interested in whether I've grown, or how much?

At the same time, Alice K. wanted terribly to give Mr. Cruel the benefit of the doubt. *We've only seen each other four times,* she kept telling herself. *Maybe we're just taking things slowly. And maybe that's okay.*

Whatever doubts she had about a future with the (possibly) New and Improved Mr. Cruel seemed more pronounced in her sessions with Dr. Y., where Alice K. found herself squirming with discomfort in the chair.

"He really seems different," she told Dr. Y. after their second encounter. "He really seems to have grown."

Her voice sounded strained and a little false as she said that and Dr. Y. merely nodded, expressionless. Alice K. imagined that Dr. Y. didn't believe her, and she felt as though she were trying to convince him (and, in turn, herself) of a reality that might not be true. She found herself trying *not* to talk about Mr. Cruel, not to give in to her doubts, not to face them.

After all, as Alice K. realized, she did not *want* to face them. Mr. Cruel—tall, with a solid jaw and classic good looks—was as handsome and charming as he always had been, more so in some ways. He looked more distinguished and mature than he had in the past, his features more settled and even, his hair just beginning to gray around the temples. He looked like a *man,* a grown man, and Alice K.

realized that her physical attraction to that was accompanied by an emotional hope: that this time he'd *act* like a man, be there for her, understand her needs, take care of her.

But would he? Could he?

At dinner that night, she'd looked across the table at Beth K. "I wish I wasn't so obsessed with the idea of finding a relationship, you know? I wish I could just enjoy this for what it is and see what happens." Beth K. nodded and Alice K. sighed. Inside, she knew, she was still driven by this hunger, this longing for something permanent and passionate and real, and she still didn't know whether she was looking for something that simply doesn't exist.

For a minute, she flashed back to her relationship with Elliot M., which sometimes seemed to lack passion but nonetheless felt *real*. Elliot M. didn't fit Alice K.'s mental image of a "man"—he was quite youthful-looking, he still wore the kinds of preppy clothes he'd probably worn in high school—but when she really thought hard about him, she realized that, in the important senses, he was very much an adult: responsible, self-aware, both willing and able to understand Alice K. and to do what he could to meet her needs. She felt a small pang of longing for him at that moment, and this caused her to wonder how much of this budding relationship with Mr. Cruel remained based on fantasy and illusion, as it always had been.

"I still have this slight feeling that I'm pretending to be something I'm not when I'm with Mr. Cruel," she said to Beth K. "This feeling that I have to act a little aloof, like I'm not allowed to care too much."

"Well, pay attention to that," Beth K. said.

Alice K. nodded. Inside she thought, *I'll try*, but to Beth K., she said, "I will."

Sometimes, things happen that cause Alice K. to believe in telepathy. Late that night, when she got home, there were two messages on her machine.

The first was from Mr. Cruel, a booming, confident voice: "Hey, Alice K. Just calling to say hi. I'll try you later."

The second voice was more tentative: "Alice K. Hi. I've been thinking about you a lot lately . . . um . . . If you'd like to, give me a call. I'd like to talk."

It was Elliot M.

One day later:

Alice K. is standing in the livingroom of Mr. Cruel.

Alice K. is being kissed—and quite tenderly, she notes—by Mr. Cruel.

And Alice K. is thinking about . . . Elliot M.

Argh! What is wrong with me?! Am I nuts? Should I have myself committed and just get it over with?

Alice K.'s mind races. Almost immediately after she'd come home and found Elliot M.'s sweet-voiced message on her machine, she'd called him back. They talked, tentatively at first, and then fondly, and then (Alice K. thought) hopefully.

"I've really missed you, Alice K.," Elliot M. said.

Alice K. responded: "I've missed you, too." At that moment, sitting on her sofa and basking gently in Elliot M.'s affection, Alice K. meant it. They made a plan to meet for dinner several nights later, and Alice K. had gotten off the phone feeling lighthearted and pleased, possessed with a vague feeling of possibility.

Now, standing there with Mr. Cruel, Alice K. shifts her position in his arms and moves back slightly. She is uncomfortable and she clears her throat. "I need a glass of water," she says, and escapes into Mr. Cruel's kitchen.

Standing there, Alice K. thinks about trust—or, in regard to her relationship with Mr. Cruel, the lack of it. True, he is acting like the New and Improved Mr. Cruel, but some part of Alice K. cannot help but believe that all this might vanish as quickly as it appeared, that at the precise moment she gives in to Mr. Cruel, he'll return to his critical, distant ways and pull away.

Alice K. is also deeply bothered by the fact that she and Mr. Cruel have not *discussed* any of this: their past relationship, their feelings about what went wrong, their current hopes and dreams, what's going on *now*. A part of her (the part, she suspects, that's afraid of confrontation) wants simply to sit back and see what happens, not push it, let Mr. Cruel reveal his true self and motives over time. But another part of her wants to march up to him and demand information: What the hell is going on here? Why have you returned to me? What do you want? Who *are* you?

Alice K. walks back into the livingroom. Mr. Cruel is leaning back on the sofa, and Alice K. sits down a few feet away from him and sips her water. Mr. Cruel moves closer, puts his arm around her, and begins to kiss her again. Alice K. allows this, but she feels passive, detached; her body is not responding to his touch as it once did, and Alice K. wonders fleetingly why this is. Before their relationship soured, she and Mr. Cruel had an intense sex life—the kind of dramatic, passionate, sweaty sex life that makes it very easy to confuse lust with love—but after a while, sex became another stressful event, one more area, in a growing series of areas, where Alice K. felt inadequate and self-conscious and compelled to pretend. Alice K. realizes suddenly that she is afraid of sex with Mr. Cruel, afraid of re-entering all that vulnerable, insecure terrain.

And then, suddenly, Mr. Cruel's hand is on Alice's breast. And next it is on her leg, moving up her thigh. Alice K. feels overwhelmed with discomfort, claustrophobic—*this isn't right*, she thinks—and she squirms away from him, sits up straight on the couch.

Mr. Cruel looks at her. "What's wrong?"

Alice K. fusses at her hair. *I have to deal with this*, she thinks. "I . . . um . . ."

She clears her throat and looks at Mr. Cruel. "Listen," she says, "I just feel a little confused about all of this."

"About all of what?"

Alice K. makes a sweeping gesture with her hand. "This. You and me. What's happening."

Mr. Cruel stares at Alice K. for a minute, then sighs and leans back against the couch. "Well," he says, "I guess it's safe to assume that you haven't gotten any more spontaneous in the last five years."

He sounds annoyed and mildly disgusted, and for a moment, Alice K. feels a flash of an old, familiar panic: *He is judging me; he is criticizing me.*

She feels angry for an instant, then, just as suddenly, filled with self-doubt. Questions leap to mind—*am I being a prude? Is this about not being spontaneous, being afraid of risks?*—and she feels compelled to explain.

"It's not . . . I mean . . ." Alice K. notices that her voice sounds whiney and strained and she hates this. She forces herself to continue. "It's just that—well, I mean here we are as though nothing ever happened, you know? As though we're right back where we started a million years ago. And I guess—well, I guess I'm a little confused about what's going on."

Mr. Cruel sighs again. "Alice K.," he says. "Does everything have to be analyzed? Can't things ever just happen naturally?"

Mr. Cruel's voice is soft and Alice K. can tell that he is trying to be patient, trying to coax her into relaxing, but she feels incapable of letting it drop, as though she's opened a door and can't now shut it. She is reminded of the way she used to feel with Mr. Cruel years ago, when she'd let her anger at him, her questions and confusion about their relationship, simmer inside for weeks at a time, and then sit there feeling helpless and out of control as they exploded into the open. He used to say things like that to her back then, too: "Why can't you just relax?" "Why does everything have to be picked apart?" and that used to infuriate Alice K. even more.

They sit in silence for a moment, and then Mr. Cruel

puts his arm around Alice K.'s shoulder. "Listen," he says. "Can we just take things one day at a time here? I mean, it's been great, being together again, but maybe it's okay not to understand every little detail of every little feeling right now."

Alice K. doesn't respond. It strikes her that Mr. Cruel has just juxtaposed the words "little" and "feeling," but she doesn't know what to say. She wants to *talk*. She wants to understand how he feels about her, and she wants to explain how fearful and vulnerable she feels around him, and she wants to feel open about all this, but she feels mute and weak, sitting there. *A part of me,* she realizes, *is still terrified of making him angry. A part of me still feels that if I talk to him about my true feelings, he'll reject me.*

Mr. Cruel cups Alice K.'s chin in his hand and turns her face toward his, so that she has to meet his eyes. He smiles down at her gently, and Alice K. wishes for an instant that he wasn't so attractive, that he couldn't smile at her that way. She wishes she felt *clear.* In her fantasies about Mr. Cruel, Alice K. would always look at him in a critical, detached way, shake her head, and think, *Jesus! What did I ever see in him?* But that hasn't yet happened, and sitting there beside him on the sofa, Alice K. isn't sure it ever will.

Alice K.'s Wish List, Part 6
The Emotional Breathalyzer

As its name implies, the emotional breathalyzer would assess potential levels of complication and conflict in a relationship just as regular breathalyzers assess levels of drunkenness. This breathalyzer would consist of a mask, a set of headphones, and a small microphone. To use it you would strap the headphones and mask onto your partner and then whisper key words and phrases into the microphone while asking said partner to close his or her eyes and walk a straight line.

For example, if you are a woman who is particularly concerned about monogamy, you would hiss the phrase, "You'll never sleep with another woman again" into the microphone and watch what happens. If he stumbles or veers, chances are he's dangerous for you; if he stays cool and unphased, you have less to worry about.

The emotional breathalyzer could reveal many, many hidden feelings. Sample words and phrases include (for her): "I loathe spectator sports," "Oral sex makes me gag," and "I will never wash your underwear." And for him: "I really believe men have no business in the kitchen," "I dislike your mother intensely," and "I am not the cuddly type."

Two days later:

Alice K. lies in bed, writhing with just about everything: angst, confusion, uncertainty, ambivalence.

Alice K., you see, has just returned from dinner with Elliot M., and lying there now, she cannot tell—she simply *cannot tell*—how the evening made her feel.

Happy? Sort of. Fearful? In a way. Attracted? Yes, but . . . when she got home, Alice K. couldn't even get herself to call Ruth E., she was that confused.

She tosses in her bed.

Alice K. and Elliot M. met at Pete's, the same bar where she'd seen him that night with the reedy blonde. They were a bit tentative at first, catching up on work, on movies and books. But after about half an hour, Alice K. began to melt in Elliot M.'s presence—not in the passionate, swept-off-her-feet way that Mr. Cruel sometimes made her feel, but in a quieter way. There was something so comforting and calming and reassuring about Elliot M.'s manner; it gave Alice K. a feeling of ease and warmth, and she realized how much she missed that.

At one point, Alice K. told a joke about something and then looked up and saw Elliot M. beaming at her, chuckling at the joke, *enjoying her humor and her mind and her presence*.

Here is a key difference, she thought. *Mr. Cruel makes me feel as though I have to* look *beautiful; Elliot M. makes me feel as though I* am *beautiful.* Alice K. meant that in both the internal and external sense. With Mr. Cruel, everything was such a struggle; Alice K. felt she had to strain so hard to look right, and to say the right things, to present herself the right way. The first time they'd had dinner after he returned to town, Alice K. had a characteristic fit of wardrobe panic and went out and spent $225 on a new silk blouse—that's how compulsive he made her, how desperate for approval. On their second date, Alice K. actually spent fifteen minutes—fifteen minutes of her life!—obsessing about whether or not to eat a breath mint before meeting him at a movie. *I shouldn't eat the breath mint because if I do, he'll think I want to kiss him and then I'll appear overeager and he'll be turned off. No, I should eat the breath mint, because if I don't I may have bad breath and then I'll appear disgusting and he'll be really turned off. No, yes, yes, no . . .*

This was crazy, neurotic behavior, but when it came to Mr. Cruel, Alice K. could not help herself.

Of course, she couldn't help herself to some extent with Elliot M., too (in fact, Alice K. wore the same $225 silk blouse when she went to meet him for dinner, and she got to the restaurant fifteen minutes early and parked around the corner and spent twenty minutes checking her makeup and hair and then got to Pete's a very precisely timed five minutes late).

But with Elliot M. the obsessiveness didn't last. Once they actually sat down together, the mental gymnastics *(Am I measuring up? Is he laughing at my jokes? Does he think I'm pretty?)* subsided, and Alice K. felt valued and appreciated on her own terms.

Ruth E. had pointed this out on the phone, the day of their date: "The thing with Elliot M. is that he likes the things about you that *you* like. You don't have to pretend with him." Alice K. had agreed, and added that, by contrast, she was never sure *what* Mr. Cruel liked about her: Did he like her the way she was, or did he like some image of her that he carried around in his head, some version of Alice K. that didn't really have anything to do with her real self?

Now, lying there in bed, Alice K. wonders why a part of her is still so attracted to that, to men who don't appreciate that real self, who make her obsess and wonder and strain for approval. For there is something very seductive about that, about struggling to live up to someone else's fantasies about you instead of living up to your own sense of self.

"If Mr. Cruel accepts me, then I don't have to accept myself. I don't have to take responsibility for accepting my own strengths and limitations." Alice K. said that to Dr. Y. in their last session. He had raised one eyebrow and asked, "But how much do you really need that? To let someone else tell you who you are?"

Alice K. couldn't say: "I don't know," she said. "I'm really not sure."

At one point, sitting in Pete's with Elliot M., she got a flash of the same uncertainty. It came at a pause during the conversation; Alice K. had been talking about looking for a new apartment, and Elliot M.—patient, attentive Elliot M.—had said something supportive and insightful, something about how hard it can be to create the right kind of home for yourself, and all of a sudden, Alice K. had the strangest sensation: It hit her that Elliot M. really was the kind of man who'd support her no matter what she did, who'd accept her shifts in self-definition and her struggles to figure out who and what she wanted. And just then, she felt the most confusing wave of feeling—fear mixed with relief mixed with terrible doubt: *He'd be there for me,* she thought, *but I'd still have to do all the work; I'd still have to figure out the hard stuff.* And although Alice K. realized the inevitability of that prospect, she found herself longing for a moment for Mr. Cruel, for someone to lose herself in, someone who insisted, by his very presence, that she pay more attention to his wishes and needs and expectations than to her own.

And that's how Alice K. feels now, tossing in her bed: *I just don't know what I want,* she thinks. *I can't imagine being with someone like Mr. Cruel all my life, but I'm not sure I can imagine being with someone like Elliot M., either. It's too . . . too . . .*

She can't finish the thought.

But she also can't ignore that something about seeing Elliot M. again had touched her, in ways she can't quite define.

After dinner, Alice K. and Elliot M. took a walk. Then Elliot M. walked Alice K. to her car, and then he told her that it had been wonderful to see her again. He stood and looked down at her and smiled, and then he kissed her on the mouth—a single, simple, gentle kiss—and stood back.

He asked, "Do you think we could try this again?"

Alice K. wasn't sure if he meant try another date or try another relationship, but at the time it didn't seem to matter; when she opened her mouth, she heard herself say, "Yes. I'd love to."

Eight days later:

Alice K. lies in bed, writhing with terror and staring at . . . Mr. Cruel.

Actually, this is not entirely true.

Alice K. is lying *on* her bed, not in it. Earlier in the evening, she and Mr. Cruel had a long dinner with too much wine, and then they rented a movie (Alice K.'s VCR is in her bedroom), and then Mr. Cruel fell asleep on the bed. So now Alice K. lies there writhing with terror and staring at Mr. Cruel because she knows that if she wakes him, he will want to spend the night with her and she simply does not want to deal with that reality.

Sex with Mr. Cruel? I CAN'T!

Alice K. has entered one of those periods in life where she is terrified of sex, terrified of entering that horrible, vague, uncertain territory where there aren't enough rules: *Does this mean we have a RELATIONSHIP? Is that what I want? Is that what he wants?* The very thought makes her shudder.

All of this, of course, has become even more complicated by the return of Elliot M., who also wants to give things with Alice K. another try.

Alice K. has seen Mr. Cruel seven times since he came back. She has seen Elliot M. four times. She feels insecure and uncomfortable with Mr. Cruel, and she feels safe and relaxed with Elliot M. She feels certain (intellectually, at any rate) that Elliot M. is capable of making her happier than Mr. Cruel is. And yet, she cannot get herself to *do* anything about this, she cannot get herself to look Mr. Cruel in the eye and say, *This is not right for me. I'm sorry, but that's how I feel.* Hell, she cannot even get herself to wake him up and ask him to leave so she can try to get some sleep.

All of this makes Alice K. feel appallingly passive. *Sure, let's have dinner Friday night. A movie on Sunday? Sure. That'd be fun.* She hears these words just come out of her mouth when she talks to Mr. Cruel. She hears her voice sound light and casual, she feels herself squelch all her other impulses—the impulse to talk about her ambivalence, the impulse to say no, the impulse to be honest or to get angry—and she simply cannot help it. And so it goes: In the past week alone, she saw Mr. Cruel on Monday, Wednesday, and Thursday, and she saw Elliot M. on Sunday and Tuesday, and she didn't tell either man about the time spent with the other, and after every evening she lay awake writhing with anxiety and confusion and feeling deceptive and trapped.

Alice K. has struggled in vain to discuss this state of affairs with Dr. Y., but it makes her feel like an idiot, exposing all this ambivalence and indecision.

"Why is it so hard to be honest with these men?" Dr. Y. asked her the day before. "What's the fear?"

Alice K. stared down at her shoes. "I don't know," she said. "I guess I worry about hurting someone."

Dr. Y. looked unconvinced. "It's all to protect these two men? Keep them from knowing about each other so they won't get hurt?"

"I guess so. I mean, that's how it feels."

Dr. Y. frowned. "I'm not so sure," he said. "I think there's also something about keeping secrets, about not being too vulnerable."

Alice K. didn't say anything at the time, but she considered that thought carefully. There is something to that, she thought, to being secretive. Earlier in the week, she and Elliot M. had gone to dinner and then taken a long walk by a river near his apartment. They'd had wine with dinner, and the air was soft and warm, and they were in the middle of a long, rambling talk about their families, and it occurred to Alice K. that this would have been the perfect opportunity to sit down with Elliot M. and talk, really *talk*, about what was happening in her life: about Mr. Cruel's return, and about the complex emotions he stirred in her, and about how warm and good and yet still uncertain she felt being with Elliot M. again.

And yet ... something had held her back, some profound instinct had told her not to open her mouth, not to rock the boat, not to risk it. Sitting there with Dr. Y., Alice K. realized that this instinct had less to do with protecting Elliot M. than it did with protecting herself, with shielding herself from responsibility.

Now, lying on the bed next to Mr. Cruel, Alice K. thinks, *If I don't confess to my feelings, I don't have to deal with their consequences.* This is probably why a part of her has been wishing lately that Mr. Cruel would meet someone else, that he'd decide Alice K. wasn't right for him, that he'd just up and dump her. That way, she could cry and wallow and feel sorry for herself and blame Mr. Cruel for being an incurable man-pig with an intimacy problem. But Mr. Cruel is not dumping her, and this has forced Alice K. into a position where she has to take responsibility for her own feelings, her own future, a state of affairs that terrifies her.

"I don't know if I've ever ended a relationship myself." Alice K. said that on the phone earlier in the day to Beth K. "I always—you know, push the other person to make the decision. Act like a bitch until they've had enough, or just hang in there no matter how horrible things are until they end it."

She paused. "Am I passive-aggressive? Is that what that means?"

Beth K. said she didn't know. "Maybe you're just confused," she offered. "Maybe neither one of these guys is right for you, and maybe it's not such a bad thing to see them both for a while until you're more certain."

Alice K. agreed in a lukewarm way, but inside, she didn't

really believe this. Inside, she understood that all this talk about "confusion" was really a mask for a kind of emotional risk-aversion, a wish to keep deeper, more honest involvement at bay, a wish to avoid stirring up the kinds of emotions that get stirred up, inevitably, when you reveal your true self to someone else: anger, attachment, disappointment, vulnerability, fear. To talk to either man about her feelings would mean admitting to her own needs and wishes; it would mean the risk of provoking anger, disappointment, *loss*.

Just then, Mr. Cruel stirs on the bed. He opens one eye, then props himself up on one elbow and smiles at Alice K., lying beside him.

"Guess I took a little nap," he says.

Alice K. nods.

Mr. Cruel reaches out and touches the side of her face. He strokes her cheek. Then he leans toward her and nuzzles the side of her neck.

"It's late," he says. "You're not going to make me go home, are you?"

Alice K.'s heart is pounding. She feels Mr. Cruel slip his leg across hers. A voice inside her is saying, *No! No! Don't do this to Elliot M.! Tell him to leave!* But Alice K. can't, for the life of her, find the words.

Twenty-four hours later:

Alice K. lies in bed, overcome with disbelief.

Alice K., you see, has done it. Alice K. has said goodbye to Mr. Cruel. Alice K. has decided (gasp!) to make a commitment to Elliot M.

This is what happened when Mr. Cruel woke up: He wanted to sleep with Alice K.; that was clear. He began to stroke Alice K.'s hair and neck. He slid his leg over hers. He began to kiss her, to slide his hand along her waist and hips.

Inside, Alice K.'s whole body felt twisted into a scream: *No!* Her mind was racing. *Sex. I can't. No. I can't let myself get that re-involved with him. It's wrong. No!*

Mr. Cruel moved his hand toward the button of Alice K.'s jeans.

Mr. Cruel began to unbutton Alice K.'s jeans.

And something in Alice K. snapped. A fully formed sentence sprung into her mind: *This is for him, not for me—this has nothing to do with me.*

And then another: *This man doesn't even know who I am.*

And then, suddenly, Alice K. took Mr. Cruel's hand and pushed it off, wriggled away from Mr. Cruel, sat up and said, simply, "I can't."

Mr. Cruel just looked at her. "What do you mean, 'you can't'?"

Alice K. said it again. "I can't. I just can't."

They sat there for a minute in an awkward silence. Mr. Cruel sighed once or twice, as though Alice K. were being ridiculous and immature. And then he flopped down on the bed and said, "Alice K., what is your problem?"

Lying there now, recalling this, Alice K. hears that phrase again in her mind: *Your problem. Not my problem. Not our problem.* YOUR *problem.*

At the time, Alice K. was aware of a very familiar, fleeting sense of shame, as though she'd done something wrong, exposed some horrible flaw, but it turned just as quickly to fury. She sat there on the bed and thought, *This is always how it was with Mr. Cruel and this is always how it will be: Whatever goes wrong is my fault, my neurosis, my inadequacy.*

She thought, *Elliot M. would never frame an issue like that. Elliot M. would never make me feel like this.*

She continued to sit in silence. Mr. Cruel lay on his back, staring at the ceiling, his expression pulled into a pout. Alice K. felt as though she were watching herself from a distance, waiting to see what she'd do next. Inside, she realized, she was engaged in a fierce battle, different emotions surfacing, conflicting with others, disappearing, then surfacing again.

Scream at him! No! Make him feel guilty! No! Protect the rela-tionship!

That last impulse—to protect the relationship—astonished Alice K. with its potency. *Protect it! Don't do any-thing to alienate him! Don't risk rejection!* Sitting there on the bed, Alice K. realized what an utterly familiar line of thought that was, how utterly driven she felt—now and throughout her romantic life—to repair relationships, to avoid confron-tation, to hold on and hold on and hold on no matter what the cost, no matter how much it conflicted with her true self, her true needs.

And then, suddenly, Alice K. felt a wave of emotion so unfamiliar she could barely name it. Freedom? Strength? Clarity? She didn't know. But she looked over at Mr. Cruel, pouting on the bed, and all of a sudden she thought, *I have options here. Choices. I do not have to sleep with this man, and I do not have to feel guilty about it.*

She said to him, "I do not have a 'problem.' " Four or five minutes had elapsed since he'd uttered that word and Mr. Cruel looked at her in surprise, as though he'd forgot-ten what she was responding to.

Alice K. continued. "It just doesn't feel right to me right now, the idea of sex." She was surprised at how even her voice sounded. "It's just not something I want to do, and I don't think there's anything 'problematic' about it."

Mr. Cruel stared at her. He opened his mouth. "Fine." He snapped the word, defensively, sarcastically. He looked away.

More silence. Alice K. considered the concept of op-tions again. She thought, *I could make this sound like a tempo-rary thing—like, this doesn't seem right at this very instant but it might feel right next week. Or I could be honest.*

She cleared her throat, feeling as though she were brac-ing herself for something critical. "Listen," she said.

She paused. "I haven't mentioned this before because it

never seemed like the right time, but I've been seeing some-one else. Someone besides you."

Mr. Cruel just looked at her. Alice K. forced herself to continue. "His name is Elliot. I met him about six months ago. We . . . um, we were involved for a while and then we stopped seeing each other around the time you came back, but I saw him again a few weeks ago, and . . ."

Mr. Cruel watched her for a moment and Alice K. felt her heart racing. "What are you telling me?" he asked.

Again: options. Inside, Alice K. heard snatches of sam-ple responses: *I'm telling you I'm confused and need time. . . . I'm telling you I'm dating someone else in addition to you. . . . I'm tell-ing you I'm in love with someone else. . . .*

She looked at Mr. Cruel. "I think I'm telling you that I really need to give this other relationship a chance."

Lying there in bed now, Alice K. can't quite remember what happened next, except that on some level, she was aware that she'd said something rather definitive, decisive. It wasn't so much her choice of words as her tone: Somehow she'd closed the door on the discussion, fended off one of those long, late-night, I'm-so-confused dialogues that never do anything but keep both parties entrenched. She remem-bers feeling a little panicky—*What's going to happen next? Will he scream at me? Will I regret this?* She remembers feeling an utterly predictable pang of ambivalence about Elliot M.—*Oh, shit, what am I getting myself into?* She remembers feeling a mix of guilt and relief, looking at Mr. Cruel. And then she remembers what he said.

His voice was snippy and clipped. "Well. I hope he has better luck with you than *I* did."

The undercurrent of insult in that statement was so thick Alice K. could feel it in the room like a third person.

Better luck in making him happy.

Better luck in bed.

Better luck in dealing with a crazed neurotic woman like *you.*

Alice K. repeated the word out loud. "Luck," she said. "Luck." She felt herself clenching her fists so tightly that the nails on either hand dug into her palms. "You think this is all about luck?"

As she said that, Alice K. realized how provocative his statement was intended to be. She also realized she could take the bait, hurl an insult back, and then stay up until five a.m. rehashing their whole relationship. She steadied herself and took a deep breath. "This is not about luck," she said. "It's about life."

Alice K. had absolutely no idea what she meant by that—in fact, she and Ruth E. would scream laughing about it later—but it didn't seem to matter at the time. Something in her voice was clear and strong; something in her voice said, *No, I am not going to play this game with you.*

A full minute passed. Alice K. said nothing. Finally, Mr. Cruel stood up and said, "Well, I have nothing more to say."

Alice K. looked up at him and said, "I guess I don't, either."

And then he left.

Alice K. sat there for a long time after he left. Would that be the end of it? Would she and Mr. Cruel talk again? Would that insult-hurling dialogue have to take place at some point? She didn't have a clear sense one way or another. She didn't know how she'd feel in a day, a week, a month. But the next day, she phoned Elliot M. and he invited her over for dinner. "I'll make lasagne," he said. "How's that sound? Lasagne and salad and a nice bottle of wine." He sounded pleased and enthusiastic, and driving toward his apartment that evening, Alice K. felt lighthearted, as though she were heading toward some new beginning.

She turned down the main street that led toward Elliot M.'s apartment. Then, looking at the road ahead, Alice K. suddenly laughed out loud: There, alone in her car, Alice K. realized, she was headed west, into the sunset.

EPILOGUE

Twenty-four hours later:

Alice K. (not her real initial) lies in bed, writhing with anxiety and distress.

Alice K., you see, is in the hospital, her left leg in a cast.

I cannot believe this, Alice K. thinks. *There I am one minute, heading west into the sunset, and—Boom! Crash! My car ends up wrapped around a telephone pole on South Main Street and I end up in the hospital.*

Alice K. moans softly. *Why me? Why me?* For isn't this just typical of Alice K.? For that one fleeting moment, heading toward Elliot M.'s house for dinner, she felt so sure of herself, so competent and focused and in charge of her life. And then, wham! The cruel hand of fate had to come down and slam home the same old lessons: That life is hard and unpredictable. That feelings of control and competence are almost always illusory. And that it's never—*never*—wise to apply lipstick in the rearview mirror during rush-hour traffic.

Alice K. struggles (in vain) to shift her position in the bed. She can feel herself regressing by the moment. *I want Wheaties,* she thinks. *I want to be sitting at home on my sofa, wearing my bathrobe and eating Wheaties and watching reruns of Mary Tyler Moore.*

But alas. There she is, bedbound.

She tries to solace herself with a thought: *Oh, well, at least I got to meet the handsome Dr. T.* The internist overseeing her case, Dr. T., is young, tall, and Nordic-looking, with large, kind, blue eyes and soft hands. Alice K. developed a crush on him immediately. She has also (typically, she notes) begun to develop elaborate rescue fantasies about him: *Dr. T., emerging as the perfect male specimen, combining Elliot M.'s gentle manner, Mr. Cruel's intellect, and Mr. Danger's cheekbones . . . Dr. T., confessing his love . . . Dr. T., examining the cast on Alice K.'s leg, leaning in closely, whispering, "Alice K. . . . Alice K. . . . has anyone ever told you that you have a lovely tibia?"*

At that, Alice K. gives herself a mental slap and tries to bring herself back down to earth. *What is wrong with me?* she thinks. *Have I learned nothing over this past year? Don't I know by now that a man—even a handsome, blue-eyed, Nordic-looking man with an advanced degree—is not going to be the answer to life's problems?*

Alice K. contemplates these questions and begins to despair. All that effort—saying goodbye to Mr. Danger, leaving Mr. Cruel, deciding to make this commitment to Elliot M. Was it worth it? Deep inside, has she really changed? Has she really become any clearer about who she is, what she wants, what it means to be a woman? Or was the car accident a sign, a metaphor, a signal that every high she experiences is destined to be followed by a crash?

Alice K. sighs, then reaches for a stack of magazines from the table beside her bed. Ruth E. and Elliot M. brought them over earlier in the day—*Cosmo, Glamour, Self,* the most recent J. Crew catalog.

She starts with this month's *Cosmo* quiz ("Test Your

Clitoral IQ!"), then moves on to an article in *Glamour* ("Kitchen Appliances Saved My Sex Life: One Woman's True Story"), and a story in *Self* ("Pedicure Nightmares: How to Keep This from Happening to *You!*").

Alice K. sighs again. *Here I am,* she thinks, *back where I started. Searching for solutions in romantic fantasies and glossy magazines.*

But then, suddenly, Alice K. sees something so astonishing—so life-affirming, so thrilling—it causes her heart to skip a beat.

There it is, right there in *Glamour*'s "Coming Next Month" section, right below the promise of "Hair Tips from Heather Locklear" and an article called *(yes!)* "Jeff Bridges Bares All." There it is, in capital letters, the ultimate reason to go on: "At Last," the copy reads, "Free Shoes."

Alice K. smiles broadly. *I'm going to make it after all,* she thinks. *I'm going to make it after all.*